BOOKS BY PETER HANNAFORD

Presidential Retreats

Reagan's Roots

Ronald Reagan and His Ranch: The Western White House, 1981–1989

The Quotable Calvin Coolidge

The Essential George Washington

The Quotable Ronald Reagan

My Heart Goes Home: A Hudson Valley Memoir (editor)

Recollections of Reagan

Remembering Reagan (co-author)

Talking Back to the Media

The Reagans: A Political Portrait

PRESIDENTIAL RETREATS

Where They Went and

Why They Went There

PETER HANNAFORD

THRESHOLD EDITIONS

NEW YORK   LONDON   TORONTO   SYDNEY   NEW DELHI

Threshold Editions
A Division of Simon & Schuster, Inc.
1230 Avenue of the Americas
New York, NY 10020

First Threshold Editions trade paperback edition October 2012

THRESHOLD EDITIONS and colophon are trademarks of Simon & Schuster, Inc.

For information about special discounts for bulk purchases, please contact Simon & Schuster Special Sales at 1-866-506-1949 or business@simonandschuster.com.

The Simon & Schuster Speakers Bureau can bring authors to your live event. For more information or to book an event, contact the Simon & Schuster Speakers Bureau at 1-866-248-3049 or visit our website at www.simonspeakers.com.

Designed by Ruth Lee-Mui
Map by Paul J. Pugliese

Manufactured in the United States of America

1   3   5   7   9   10   8   6   4   2

Library of Congress Cataloging-in-Publication Data

Hannaford, Peter.
Presidential retreats : where they went and why they went there / Peter Hannaford. — 1st Threshold Editions trade pbk. ed.
p. cm.
Includes bibliographical references.
1. Presidents—Homes and haunts—United States. 2. Presidents—Travel—United States. 3. Presidents—United States—Biography. 4. Dwellings—United States—History. 5. Vacation homes—United States—History. 6. Historic sites—United States. 7. United States—History, Local. 8. Presidents—Homes and haunts—United States—Guidebooks. 9. Dwellings—United States—Guidebooks. 10. Historic sites—United States—Guidebooks. I. Title.
E176.1.H28 2012
973.09'9—dc23
[B]
2012014646

ISBN 978-1-4516-2714-5
ISBN 978-1-4516-2715-2 (ebook)

For Irene,
who puts the sunshine in my days

Presidental Retreats

WASHINGTON

MONTANA

NORTH
DAKOTA

OREGON

IDAHO

MINNE

SOUTH
DAKOTA

■ Clinton

WYOMING

■ Coolidge

NEBRASKA

NEVADA

UTAH

Ford ■

■ Eisenhower

CALIFORNIA

COLORADO

KANSAS

■ Reagan

■ Nixon ■ Ford

ARIZONA

NEW MEXICO

OKLAHOMA

Pacific
Ocean

TEXAS

G.W. Bush ■

L. Johnson ■

■ Obama

HAWAII

MEXICO

0   100   200   300 miles

0   200   400 kilometers

CANADA

MAINE

Pierce

G.H.W. Bush

Coolidge

Coolidge

VT.

Taft

NEW YORK

N.H.

J. Adams & J.Q. Adams

Van Buren

MASS.

WISCONSIN

MICHIGAN

R.I.

Kennedy

Arthur

CONN.

Garfield

PENN.

Grant

Clinton & Obama

Buchanan

Wilson

T. Roosevelt

Hayes

Eisenhower

F. Roosevelt

McKinley

Polk

N.J.

ILLINOIS

INDIANA

OHIO

MD.

CAMP DAVID

DEL.

B. Harrison

Kennedy

W. VA.

Lincoln

Madison

Washington

Jefferson

Hoover

Monroe

VIRGINIA

W.H. Harrison

KENTUCKY

Tyler

OURI

NORTH CAROLINA

Polk

Jackson

A. Johnson

TENNESSEE

NSAS

SOUTH CAROLINA

Eisenhower

GEORGIA

MISSISSIPPI

ALABAMA

F. Roosevelt

Atlantic

Carter

Ocean

Taylor

Wilson

SIANA

Arthur

FLORIDA

Gulf

of

Mexico

Harding

Nixon

Truman

CUBA

CONTENTS

INTRODUCTION

Forty-three men have held forty-four presidencies (one had two terms not in succession). Some were tall; some were short. Some were thin; some were fat. Most were in between. Some were intense; some were gregarious. Some brought to office clear objectives of what they wanted to accomplish; some brought none. Some got on well with Congress; some did not. Some led; some followed. They all had one thing in common, however: the need, now and then, to get away from the nearly constant pressures of the job.

For most of the early presidents, "home" was a substantial farm, a plantation. It represented peace, quiet, and reassuring normalcy away from contentious Congressional factions, office-seekers, and unsolved policy problems. Thus it was their "retreat." One, Thomas Jefferson, decided to go one step further to get away from the many friends and relatives who descended on his home, Monticello, and the money troubles he usually faced there. So he created the first dedicated presidential retreat, Poplar Forest, about sixty miles away. Although he oversaw its construction throughout his presidency, the new building was not ready for his first overnight stay until a few months after he had left the White House.

There might have been more such "hideaways," but the exigencies of early-nineteenth-century travel made it difficult to get away for a weekend or a few days. Some went to popular spas not far away from Washington, or took speaking tours as a means of changing pace and temporarily putting the problems in Washington behind them. Lincoln was the next to have a dedicated retreat. He lived there for three summers and he never had to leave the District of Columbia to do so. It was a large guesthouse on the grounds of the Soldiers' Home.

Several presidents chose beach cottages so they could enjoy cooler air than the capital would give them in summer. The supporters of one, Benjamin Harrison, wanted to make a gift to his wife of such a cottage. Worried that this might appear improper, he insisted on buying it.

Theodore Roosevelt was the first to move the White House staff and business for the summer, to his home, Sagamore Hill, overlooking Oyster Bay on the north shore of Long Island.

William McKinley had a small farm not far from his hometown, Canton, Ohio, where he and his wife spent weekends and vacations. More than a century after Jefferson built Poplar Forest, Herbert Hoover built the next dedicated retreat, in the Shenandoah Valley, Camp Rapidan. It was a relatively short drive from Washington and could be enjoyed on many weekends and for longer periods when Congress had left town for its summer recess. Having a special retreat has become the dominant—but not exclusive—presidential pattern since.

When the demands of World War II made it necessary for the president to rarely be far from the capital, Franklin Roosevelt discovered what would become Camp David. Every president since has used it for weekend "getaways." Some have used it a great deal. Harry Truman, however, visited it only nine times in his nearly eight years in office.

FOREIGN TRAVEL AS A RETREAT

Although several presidents took overseas trips after they left office, Theodore Roosevelt was the first to take one as presidential business.

In 1906 he went to Panama to inspect the land that would become the Panama Canal. This helped generate public enthusiasm for the project. Presidents have been going overseas ever since. Franklin Roosevelt was the first to use airplanes.

There is a Washington adage to the effect that when the president faces trouble or knotty problems at home, he travels in order to change the subject. That has been true in a number of cases; however, the international nature of many issues today is such that multinational conferences in various places and the need for frequent conferences with allies have led to many bilateral meetings. The bilaterals are often exchanges, one in the United States, the other in the partner's capital city. Today's presidents, traveling on Air Force One, take with them family, staff, news media, and all the trappings of communication they have at the White House. For most on board there is a festive air about going to faraway places and experiencing new sights.

FIRST LADIES

Nearly all presidents who came to the capital were accompanied by wives who had been their partners through many career phases. There were exceptions. James Buchanan was a bachelor and Andrew Jackson was a widower. Some First Ladies thrived in the social atmosphere of Washington; others shied from it. A few were in more or less perpetual ill health and stayed out of public sight. Some were great assets to their husbands. Indeed, some were very outgoing and charming, making up for their husbands' reserved nature.

PRESIDENCIES IN CONTEXT

Retreats, vacations, and travels all existed within the context of each presidency. To understand their significance, one needs to know the president's background, career development, and method of operation in office. All of this has to be set against the background of the issues of the day and the forces that were shaping those issues. Therefore, each of the chapters attempts to provide you with a short summary of each presidency.

We have had Federalists, Democratic-Republicans, Democrats,

Whigs, and Republicans as presidents. In studying all forty-four of them it is hard to escape the conclusion that every one did the best he could to advance the interests of the nation. Many succeeded; some did not, but all tried.

If, on reading about these presidential retreats and other places associated with them, you become interested in visiting them, you will find information at the end of each chapter. Descriptions, who operates them, operating days and hours, and contact information are all included.

Peter Hannaford
Eureka, California
July 2011

—◆—

Chapter One

GEORGE WASHINGTON

THE 1ST PRESIDENT

April 30, 1789—March 4, 1797

In his personal life George Washington cared most about two things, his beloved wife, Martha (whom he called "Patsy"), and his estate, Mount Vernon. From the time he left for the Second Continental Congress in Philadelphia, in spring 1775, until just before the final battle of the Revolutionary War, in October 1781, he saw Mount Vernon only once. When he left in 1775 he left behind a 6,500-acre farm and a prosperous enterprise that he had built through years of determined work and experimentation. He referred to it as his "peaceful abode."

AMBITION AND DETERMINATION

George Washington was born February 22, 1732, on the Pope Creek estate of Augustine and Mary Ball Washington in Westmoreland County, Virginia. He was the first of five children born to the couple. Mary was Augustine's second wife. His father had two sons, Lawrence and Augustine, Jr., by his first wife. George's father died when he was eleven. His older half brother Lawrence became a substitute father in his formative years. Lawrence's father-in-law, William Fairfax, a cousin of Thomas, Lord Fairfax, Virginia's largest landowner, was also influential.

Many of George's boyhood years were spent at Ferry Farm, which he inherited from his father. Lawrence had inherited a farm on the Potomac River that he named Mount Vernon in honor of his British commander in a Caribbean expedition. After Lawrence's death, George ultimately acquired Mount Vernon.

In 1749, Lawrence helped seventeen-year-old George get appointed as the official surveyor for Culpeper County. He earned enough money to make his first of many land purchases, this one in the Shenandoah Valley. At six foot two, George towered over most of his contemporaries. His red hair and fair complexion also made him stand out. In 1751 he accompanied Lawrence to Barbados (his only overseas trip) in the hope the climate would help alleviate his half brother's tuberculosis. On that trip, George contracted smallpox. It left him only lightly scarred, but immune to what was a widespread disease at the time. Lawrence's health did not improve and he died at Mount Vernon the following year. Upon his death, his duties as adjutant general of the Virginia militia were divided into four district positions. In 1753, George was appointed to one of them with the rank of major. He also became a Freemason.

That year saw the beginning of the French and Indian War. The British wanted to expand settlements and trade westward. The French were establishing outposts in the Ohio Valley. Washington was dispatched by the Virginia governor to ask the French to withdraw; they declined. The governor then ordered Washington to protect a British group building a fort there at what is Pittsburgh today. The French were constructing their own fort, Fort Duquesne. Along with Indian allies, Washington's troops ambushed the French, who then attacked Washington at Fort Necessity, capturing him in July 1754. He was subsequently released and took his troops home.

By 1756 the British and French were formally at war. By 1758, as commander in chief of all the Virginia militia, Washington captured Fort Duquesne and forced the French to leave the Ohio Valley. Disappointed that he was not offered a commission in the regular British Army, Washington resigned his commission, but the military experience he had gained was to prove invaluable in the Revolutionary War.

He understood the strengths and weaknesses of the British Army, the tactics used by the Indians, and the importance of good organization and logistical support.

BACK AT MOUNT VERNON

Although some surviving letters suggest he may have been in love with Sally Fairfax, the wife of a friend, George began courting Martha Dandridge Custis, a wealthy widow. They were married on January 6, 1759. Martha's land holdings were added to his, and her social standing enhanced his. By all accounts theirs was a happy marriage. Martha was a gracious hostess and wise in the ways of managing a plantation. They raised her two children from her first marriage, John Parke Custis and Martha Parke Custis. (George was apparently sterile from smallpox, so they could have no offspring of their own.)

Washington's political career began in 1758 with election to Virginia's House of Burgesses. In the years 1759–74, he led a life typical of the Virginia planter aristocracy. He enjoyed music and dancing, horse races, card games, and the theater. He imported his clothes and many other items from England. Tobacco was his main cash crop, sold through agents in London. In 1766 he began the switch to wheat, milled locally and sold within the colonies. This opened him up to talk of independence. He further diversified Mount Vernon to include commercial fishing in the Potomac, horse breeding, and making textiles. During this time, the Virginia governor made good on an earlier promise and gave Washington twenty-three thousand acres in what is today West Virginia.

HEADING TOWARD INDEPENDENCE

Beginning with the Stamp Tax of 1765, the first direct tax on the colonies, Washington became interested in the independence movement. In May 1769, with the help of his neighbor George Mason, he put forth a proposal for Virginia to boycott British goods until the Townshend Acts were repealed. Parliament did so in 1770. In July 1774, he was chairman of a meeting that called for a Continental Congress to be convened; he was then elected as a delegate to attend.

The Battles of Concord and Lexington in spring 1775 led to the creation of the Continental Army. Nominated to be commander in chief, Washington accepted and set out to command the troops withstanding a British siege of Boston and environs. He reorganized his army and made the British forces vulnerable. They withdrew from Boston in March 1776. Washington then moved his men to New York City, where he lost the Battle of Long Island in August and had to retreat with his men first to Manhattan, then across New Jersey and the Delaware River to regroup on the Pennsylvania side. Morale was low. Then, in the dead of Christmas night, he and his men crossed back over the Delaware and made a surprise attack at Trenton and captured a thousand Hessians. The next month they defeated British troops at Princeton. By summer 1777, Washington began to shift his strategy to fixed battles. The British strategy was to have General Burgoyne move south from Quebec to isolate New England. His counterpart General Howe, instead of moving north to join him at Albany, New York, went south, where he defeated Washington's forces at Brandywine, in Pennsylvania, and repulsed them again at Germantown. The then–American capital, Philadelphia, fell to British forces. But balancing that loss was a major American victory at Saratoga, New York, where Howe surrendered his entire army. The news of this brought France openly into the war on the American side.

Washington and his troops wintered at Valley Forge, Pennsylvania. Despite the cold and outbreak of disease, the army was a better fighting force by early 1778. That year, the British left Philadelphia for New York, with Washington shadowing them. Then, in 1779, Washington had his troops attack Iroquois villages in central New York. In 1780, a five-thousand-man French force landed at Newport, Rhode Island. By the following summer twenty-eight French ships, abetted by French infantry and artillery, had the British cornered at Yorktown and Hampton Roads in Virginia.

On his way south to Yorktown, Washington made his first stop at Mount Vernon since spring 1775, although Martha had managed to spend nearly half of the 105 months of actual war with her husband, wherever the fighting took him. He arrived home on September 9. Soon to join him there were his aides and two French generals. One aide, Jonathan Trumbull, wrote later that he found Mount Vernon to be an "elegant seat and situation, great appearance of opulence and real exhibitions of hospitality and princely entertaining." This was a testimony to Mrs. Washington's skills as a hostess and manager. A few days later Washington continued southward. The British Army surrendered on October 19, effectively ending the military phase of the war.

WAR'S AFTERMATH

The American victory at Yorktown marked the end of hostilities, but Washington and his men did not know this at the time. The British still had more than twenty-five thousand occupation troops present, backed by their naval fleet's power. In 1782 and 1783, the French sailed away. Negotiations for a peace treaty dragged on, but one was finally signed in September 1783. In it the British recognized the independence of the United States. At Fraunces Tavern in lower Manhattan on December 4, Washington said farewell to his officers and on the twenty-third resigned as commander in chief. In an age where, in Europe, winners of wars did not give up office, Washington's act was historic.

Washington longed to return to Mount Vernon and Martha, and did so. However, when a Constitutional Convention was called for the summer of 1787 in Philadelphia, he was persuaded to attend. Once the Constitution was agreed upon, Washington's active support helped ensure its ratification by all thirteen states.

THE PRESIDENCY

Washington was elected president unanimously in February 1789. He left Mount Vernon for New York, the nation's temporary capital, on April 16. Martha was unhappy about it. She wrote to a nephew, "I am truly sorry to tell that the General is gone to New York. . . . I think it was much too late for him to go into publick life again, but was not to be avoided."

Washington took the oath of office on April 30, 1789, on the balcony of Federal Hall.

Martha and her two youngest grandchildren joined him in May. They made their home at 3 Cherry Street, which had been rented for them by Congress. The next year the Residence Act was passed.

It authorized the president to select the location—on the Potomac River—for the permanent seat of government.

TRAVELS AND RETREATS

In late August 1790 the Washingtons, the two grandchildren, two aides, two maids, eight other servants, and sixteen horses left New York for a vacation at Mount Vernon. After a two-month respite there, the Washingtons and the two youngest grandchildren moved into their new Philadelphia home, rented from financier Robert Morris. In mid-September the family left the capital for another monthlong retreat at Mount Vernon. Thomas Jefferson visited them there, along with the French foreign minister.

In 1792, the Washingtons, the grandchildren, and all of the president's secretaries except Lear left Philadelphia for a nearly three-month vacation at Mount Vernon. On October 1 Jefferson again called at Mount Vernon, this time to persuade Washington to stand for a second term. The family returned to the Executive Mansion in Philadelphia on October 13. In 1793, the family left Philadelphia again for Mount Vernon on September 10. While home, Washington laid the cornerstone of the new U.S. Capitol building in what was to become the city of Washington, D.C. It was an elaborate Masonic ceremony. While the president headed north again on November 1, it was to Germantown, outside Philadelphia, as there was danger of yellow fever in the city. Mrs. Washington and the grandchildren stayed at Mount Vernon until he sent for them. The entire family returned to Philadelphia on December 9.

In mid-June of the next year, 1794, President Washington left for what was to be a quick visit to Mount Vernon. Martha and the family stayed in Philadelphia. At Mount Vernon he had a riding accident and suffered a severe back injury requiring almost a month to heal. By late July, he had returned to Philadelphia and moved the family out to Germantown for nearly two months until fear of a recurrent yellow fever epidemic had passed. In 1795, after a retreat at Mount Vernon in late summer and early fall, the Washingtons returned to Philadelphia. In summer 1796, they had nearly seven weeks at Mount Vernon. The president returned to Philadelphia in mid-August for a month, then came home for a month. When he was at Mount Vernon, Washington still entertained officially, from Cherokee chiefs to the architect Benjamin Latrobe, who did a number of sketches at Mount Vernon.

RETIREMENT AT LAST

On March 4, 1797, Washington retired from the presidency upon the inauguration of John Adams. He had insisted that two terms was all that he would serve. In retirement he turned his attention once again to agricultural pursuits. He had a sixteen-sided barn constructed, and milled wheat there. He added a distillery, which began turning out rye whiskey. Some of Washington's other farms were barely profitable. Then, in 1798, with reluctance, he agreed to head an enlarged army to be raised in case of war. He participated in planning but left operational details to Alexander Hamilton. The war scare lasted from July 13, 1798, to December 14, 1799. Two days before that last date, Washington rode on horseback to inspect his farms. He spent hours in the saddle in freezing rain, hail, and snow, then sat down to dinner in his wet clothes. The next day he awoke with a very sore throat and was hoarse. On Saturday, the fourteenth, his condition became worse and he died at 10 p.m. He was about two months shy of his sixty-eighth birthday.

Washington's will specified that, upon the death of Martha, all of his slaves were to be freed. It also specified training in useful skills for the younger slaves and established a pension fund for older ones who were also allowed to live in retirement at Mount Vernon. Both George and Martha Washington are buried in a tomb on the grounds of Mount Vernon.

Mount Vernon, George Washington's estate, is owned and operated by the Mount Vernon Ladies' Association, the oldest national preservation organization in the United States. It is open every day of the year. Approximately one million visitors come to Mount Vernon every year.

Ann Pamela Cunningham, a young woman of Charleston, South Carolina, began what was then the nation's first historic preservation campaign in 1853, for the purpose of raising funds to purchase Mount

Vernon. The association did so in 1858 and has welcomed more than 80 million visitors since its doors opened in 1860.

While Washington ultimately expanded the plantation to eight thousand acres, today the property encompasses five hundred acres, which includes twenty structures and fifty acres of gardens. Visitors arrive at the Ford Orientation Center, then may explore the mansion, kitchen, stables, slave quarters, and greenhouse. There are four distinct gardens, all restored to their 1799 appearance. There are representative animals of the breeds found at Mount Vernon in Washington's time. There is also the Pioneer Farmer site, a four-acre working farm with Washington's re-created sixteen-sided treading barn.

One can visit also the Washingtons' tombs, where a daily wreath-laying ceremony is held. Nearby is the Slave Memorial and Burial Ground. There is also a forest trail nearby.

The Donald W. Reynolds Museum, which opened in 2006, is entirely underground and contains twenty-five galleries and theaters that tell the story of George Washington's life. It contains some five hundred original Washington artifacts and many interactive video presentations.

The Mount Vernon Inn, adjacent to the main entrance, serves lunch daily and dinners by candlelight Tuesday through Saturday in six intimate dining rooms. For diners on the go, there is the Food Court Pavilion. A gift shop has gifts, jewelry, books, and reproductions of Mount Vernon furniture.

The Mount Vernon Ladies' Association is governed by a board of regents, made up entirely of women. In addition there is an advisory board of men and women in various fields from around the United States to provide advice and counsel. Mount Vernon has a staff of 450 as well as four hundred volunteers.

The next major addition at Mount Vernon will be the George Washington National Library, to be built within a wooded area on the property. Just down the road from the main entrance to Mount Vernon are the restored and operational Grist Mill and Distillery.

Location: on the George Washington Parkway, south of Alexandria, Virginia, and sixteen miles south of Washington, D.C. Telephone 703-780-2000. Website: www.mountvernon.org.

The George Washington Masonic National Memorial is a tall structure located in Alexandria. It was built between 1922 and 1932 from voluntary contributions from all fifty-two local governing bodies of the Freemasons in the United States. Their website (www.gwmemorial.org) provides an online tour. For in-person tours, contact the facility via the website or telephone 703-683-2007. Address: 1010 Callahan Drive, Alexandria, VA 22301.

———◆———

Chapter Two

JOHN ADAMS

THE 2ND PRESIDENT

March 4, 1797 — March 4, 1801

*P*eacefield. The very word paints a picture of serenity: summer breezes under shady trees, apples ripening in the orchard, vegetable gardens nearly ready for picking. That was the picture John Adams could easily conjure for himself, for Peacefield was his home. Visualizing that picture was a way to escape the contentious arguments of members of Congress and the insults hurled by Thomas Jefferson's allies in the press, until Adams could go on retreat to the real Peacefield.

DESTINY'S PATH

The eldest of the three sons of John Adams, Sr., and Susanna Boylston Adams, John, Jr., was born in Quincy, Massachusetts, just south of Boston, on October 30, 1735. He was a sixth-generation descendant of Henry Adams, a Puritan who emigrated from England around 1638. A serious boy, young John took to heart the Puritan values of his ancestors and prized the concept of individual freedom. At age sixteen he entered Harvard College. He graduated four years later and began teaching. In time he decided to study law and did so under John Putnam, a prominent Worcester lawyer. He also sharpened his writing skills, which he came to use to great effect. He married Abigail Smith, the daughter of a Congregational minister, on October 25, 1764. They were distant cousins. They had six children, one of whom, John Quincy Adams, ultimately became the sixth president of the United States.

When Parliament passed the Stamp Act in 1765, Adams argued in a series of articles that it denied two rights: to be taxed only by consent and to be tried by a jury of one's peers. In 1774 and again in 1775–77, Massachusetts sent Adams to the Continental Congress. During his times in Philadelphia for the Congress, he and his independent-minded and highly articulate wife maintained a frequent, and subsequently famous, correspondence.

THE DECLARATION OF INDEPENDENCE

Adams was one of a five-man committee appointed to draft a declaration of independence. Thomas Jefferson was the principal writer, but gave much credit to Adams's floor leadership in the debate over it. After the Declaration on July 4, the war went forward in earnest. On August 27, British General Howe defeated the Continental Army on Long Island. He invited the Continental Congress to send a delegation to discuss peace. Adams, Benjamin Franklin, and others were in the delegation. Howe insisted that the Congress rescind the Declaration of Independence before any other terms would be discussed. The delegation refused, and the war continued. General Washington took his troops across New Jersey to fight another day.

TO EUROPE

Twice Congress sent Adams to Europe, first in 1777 and again in 1779. Accompanying him was his young son, nicknamed Quincy. The first trip was largely unproductive. The mission for the second was to negotiate a trade treaty with Britain, using France as an intermediary. This did not work, so Adams, Franklin, and John Jay met directly with the British delegation. The treaty was signed on November 30, 1782.

It recognized American ownership of the lands east of the Mississippi River, except for Florida. Afterward, Adams became ambassador to the Dutch Republic. The house he bought during his stay there was the first American embassy anywhere. He negotiated recognition of the new nation by the Dutch and secured substantial loans for the American government. He then negotiated a successful trade treaty with Prussia.

In 1785 Adams was appointed minister to the Court of St. James's, a position he held for three years. In 1787 he and Abigail purchased the forty-acre property in Quincy, Massachusetts, that he ultimately named "Peacefield." They went home to it in 1788. He was familiar with the main house, for it had been built in 1731 and was about seventy-five feet from the New England "saltbox" house in which he had been born. Called the Old House, the main building then consisted of two rooms on the ground floor, two bedrooms above, and an attic, rustic in comparison to their London home off Grosvenor Square.

ELECTIVE POLITICS

Adams became the first vice president in 1788 and actively presided over the Senate. Abigail wrote to him in 1789 that she had been unable to find someone to lease their farm and she was short of funds. He urged her to borrow money or sell some livestock so she could join him soon. Washington and he were reelected four years later, in 1792. During their second term political parties were beginning to form (though Washington disapproved of the idea). Adams joined the Federalist Party and was nominated for president by his party in 1796, although he stayed home at Peacefield and did not personally campaign. His party's followers did so for him. On election day 1796, Adams prevailed closely with 71 electoral votes to 68 for Jefferson, the candidate of the Democratic-Republican Party, who became the vice president.

During Adams's years as vice president and then president, when he was first in New York City, then Philadelphia, it fell to Abigail to turn Peacefield into the stately Georgian home it was to become. She oversaw a major addition to the house and managed the farm. Abigail had to miss John's presidential inauguration in Philadelphia, for she stayed at Peacefield tending his sick mother. She wrote to him that she would come as soon as she could, and she did, in May.

MOVING INTO THE WHITE HOUSE

Adams wanted to be reelected in 1800, but Hamilton, who did not like him, successfully tried to undermine his campaign. As a result, Jefferson won. On November 1, 1800, John moved into the unfinished President's House (not called the White House until much later) for the remaining months of his term. Abigail followed shortly after. Some of the rooms were not yet plastered and Abigail complained about the lack of urgency in completing the building. She wrote that Washington "is (a city) only . . . in name." Nevertheless, she knew that in public she should replace her frankness with diplomacy. She wrote to her daughter, "When asked how I like it, say that I wrote you the situation is beautiful." The first couple lived in the new building for a little over four months altogether. Meanwhile, the Congress had moved from Philadelphia to hold its first session in the new Capitol building on November 17. (Only the Senate wing was completed.)

THE ULTIMATE RETREAT

Although he was a learned man, steeped in the history of constitutions and the law, Adams was at heart a farmer. Just as his father did, he loved the land and what it produced. In his time, Congress adjourned as early as late April or early May and did not reconvene until autumn. The stifling heat and humidity of the summers, first in Philadelphia, then even worse in Washington, were a major cause. Outbreaks of yellow fever were another. There were especially bad epidemics in the government's Philadelphia years. Beyond that, government lacked today's complexity, and the nation's population was small. In short, the business of the nation did not require, as it does today, only short breaks in the schedule.

In 1796, his last year as vice president, Adams left Philadelphia for the farm on May 6. After seemingly endless days of sitting in the Senate, he relished getting out of doors. He doffed his wig, put on farming clothes, and worked in the beds and field along with as many as ten hired men. He wrote in his diary of felling cedars, harvesting hay, admiring the cornstalks, threshing, and watching his men mix the compost pile. He and Abigail spent quiet summer evenings reading and writing. Of this particular season, he wrote, "Of all the summers of my life, this has been the freest from care, anxiety and vexation for me."

In 1797, the year Adams was inaugurated as president, Congress did not adjourn until July 10. The Adamses left for Peacefield on July 19 and spent a little over two months there, leaving in early October for Philadelphia. They delayed their arrival with a stay in East Chester, Pennsylvania, while the yellow fever outbreak of that year passed. By June 1798, war talk filled the air as the temperature climbed into the 90s. On the sixteenth, Congress adjourned and fled as a new yellow fever epidemic took hold. The Adamses left once more for Peacefield on the twenty-fifth.

Unbeknownst to John, Abigail had arranged to add a new wing to the house, with a large parlor and a library above it. In effect, she had doubled the size of their house. He was delighted with the news, but it was overshadowed by the illness that had overtaken his wife by the time they arrived home on August 8. Their daughter Abigail ("Nabby") and granddaughter Caroline were there to help, but the First Lady's condition did not improve. Adams spent little time outdoors that summer. He kept up a steady flow of official correspondence and responses to dispatches from Philadelphia. It was not until early November that Abigail felt well enough to leave her bed. She had been bedridden for eleven weeks. On the twelfth, John left for Philadelphia, which again had just been declared clear of yellow fever.

The following summer Adams was criticized by many for leaving to go to his farm, but he was convinced that he could attend to all his official business just as effectively from Peacefield as in Philadelphia. Nevertheless, news from France indicated conditions had become chaotic there. Secretary of the Navy Benjamin Stoddert twice wrote to Adams urging him to return, lest his political enemies take advantage of his absence. He said the government had set up temporary headquarters in Trenton, New Jersey, until the yellow fever epidemic was over.

Adams wrote that he would be in Trenton by October 15. With the beginnings of a cold, he stopped on the way in East Chester to see his daughter Nabby. Sally, the wife of his second son, Charles, was there with their children. He learned from her that Charles had disappeared, bankrupt and an alcoholic. With this devastating news and in poor health, John pressed on to Trenton.

On December 3, with Abigail once more with him in Philadelphia, he addressed a joint session of Congress, explaining that the nation must now turn its energies to "prospects of abundance."

Eleven days later, George Washington died. On May 19, Abigail left the President's Philadelphia Mansion on Market Street for the last time, bound for Quincy. Eight days later, John left for Washington, where he addressed friendly crowds. There wasn't much to Washington: cleared land, a few shops and boardinghouses, a partially completed Capitol, a Treasury building, and the unfinished "President's House." Yet, by all accounts, he enjoyed his visit. He made a side trip to Mount Vernon to call on Martha Washington and to Alexandria, Virginia, where he was feted at a dinner at the home of the attorney general.

Early on June 14 he left for Quincy. He drew great pleasure from being at his farm once again. As an official of the Adams National Historical Park said recently, "At Peacefield, his soul was regenerated." On October 13 he began the coach trip back to Washington. At the end of October, Hamilton published a scathing essay attacking Adams's character and his "ungovernable temper." Though he cited no corruption or misconduct by Adams, the very strong essay, coming from a leading Federalist, had the effect of undercutting support for Adams's reelection.

On November 1, Adams arrived at the President's House. Abigail arrived on November 16 for their short sojourn together there.

AFTER THE PRESIDENCY

Abigail left Washington on Friday, February 13, 1801. Adams did not attend Jefferson's inauguration. He left the city at 4 a.m. that day, March 4, by public stage. Once back at Peacefield, he settled comfortably into quiet routines and, as the spring came, into farm life. He began work on his autobiography, but never finished it. Adams and Jefferson revived their on-again, off-again friendship in 1812. This led to a spirited and friendly correspondence for fourteen years. Adams, at age ninety, died on July 4, 1826. Jefferson died on the same day. Abigail Adams had preceded her husband in death in 1818 (of typhoid fever). Sixteen months before John Adams's death, his son John Quincy Adams became the sixth president of the United States.

Both John and Abigail Adams are buried at the United First Parish Church in Quincy.

———•◦•———

The Adams National Historical Park, operated by the National Park Service, comprises the birthplaces of John and John Quincy Adams, the Stone Library, and "Peacefield" (earlier known as the Old House), in which four generations of Adamses resided from 1788 to 1927.

The park is open for two-hour guided tours from 9 a.m. to 5 p.m., seven days a week from April 19 through November 10. Tours begin frequently, but advanced reservations are not available.

The last tour departs at 3:15. Tickets are available at the Visitor Center, 1250 Hancock Street, Quincy.

Peacefield was built in 1731 and purchased by John and Abigail Adams in 1787 for occupation the next year when they returned from his diplomatic assignment in London. The Stone Library, built in 1873, contains over fourteen thousand volumes. It fulfilled an inspiration of John Quincy Adams to have a separate fireproof structure for his books and papers.

Address: 135 Adams Street, Quincy, MA 02169–1749. Telephone: 617-770-1175.

Website: www.nps.gov/adam.

———•◦•———

Chapter Three

THOMAS JEFFERSON

THE 3RD PRESIDENT

March 4, 1801 — March 4, 1809

Thomas Jefferson couldn't get away from his home Monticello fast enough. It was, June 1806, and after thirty years of planning, designing, and building, the place was nearly complete, but that was no cause for celebration by the president. Dozens of details still needed supervision. The place was overrun with family, friends, and friends of friends. His daughter, Martha, her husband, and her six children had moved in. He loved them all, but their presence, along with overnight guests who might stay for weeks, left him little time for thinking, writing, and reading. Added to this were his debts, pressing as always. He would have to raise more tobacco to get the cash to pay them. He hated the weed. It wore out the soil faster than other crops, required intensive labor, and the fields in which it grew needed to lie fallow longer than did others. Nevertheless, tobacco brought him more money than other crops did and money was what he needed.

POPLAR FOREST

That's where Poplar Forest came in. This 4,819-acre plantation had been inherited by his wife, Martha, from her father in 1773. Over the years it had become an important source of income for Jefferson and his family. More recently, he had been thinking about it as a place to get away from the hubbub of Monticello. The major events of his presidency—the Louisiana Purchase and the Lewis & Clark expedition—were behind him. He was thinking about his retirement and designing a retreat for himself at Poplar Forest. Now, on this sixteenth day of June, he was going there to lay the foundation of the house that would be his very own retreat. On his way from the capital city he would stop at Monticello only long enough to pick up his thirteen-year-old grandson, Thomas Jefferson Randolph ("Jeff"), to accompany him on the three-day, ninety-mile carriage journey to Bedford County, southwest of Monticello and near the Blue Ridge Mountains.

Poplar Forest, named for a cluster of handsome large poplar trees (some still stand in front of the house), consisted of many large fields, some forest, kitchen gardens, the overseer's small house, and log cabins for the slaves who were resident at the time. (There were eleven slaves there in 1774, but by 1806 the number had grown to sixty and later to as many as one hundred, with most of the newcomers having moved over from Monticello.)

Jefferson and his grandson stayed for several days, with Jeff exploring the sprawling farm while his grandfather worked with his Monticello carpenter-bricklayer, Hugh Chisolm, overseeing the laying of the foundation for the house.

The previous September, Jefferson had sent Chisolm to Poplar Forest to supervise the clearing and grading of ground for the house. There Chisolm also dug clay for the bricks that would be made for building, and he obtained supplies of stone and sand for mortar.

The house at Monticello reflected Jefferson's wide-ranging mind and his enthusiasm for new gadgets and architectural design ideas. It was a work in progress for several years. By the time he designed his retreat at Poplar Forest, he had spent five years in Europe. He absorbed many design ideas while there. He was especially influenced by the work of Andrea Palladio, the great sixteenth-century Italian architect who revived the concept of the Roman country villa. He studied closely Palladio's seminal work, *Four Books on Architecture.* Between 1789 and 1794, Jefferson worked on a variety of drawings for his retreat. By the time he completed them, his Palladio-inspired house reflected Jefferson's architectural sensibility at its most sophisticated and mature level.

Jefferson envisioned an intimate home, filled with light and air. He designed it as an octagon—the first octagonal residence in the nation. Just inside the entrance, on either side, would be two small rooms for various purposes. Behind them would be two bedchambers, his on the right (west) side of the house; guests (later and often, two of his grandchildren) on the left. The center of the house would be a twenty-foot cube, the dining room. It would be topped by a sixteen-foot-long skylight, filling the room with light, even on dark days. Beyond that would be Jefferson's parlor, where he would one day spend hours at a time, reading, writing, and thinking. A small portico would open to views of a large sunken garden south of the house. All of the exterior rooms were designed with large windows. It would appear to be a one-story house, but because of the way he designed the roof line and the "mounds" (berms) on each side of it, the dining room was two stories high and the basement below, for utilitarian activities, would actually be at ground level at the back of the house.

INFREQUENT EARLY VISITS

Jefferson visited the Poplar Forest plantation infrequently between the time he and his wife acquired it and his formulation of plans to make it his retirement retreat. Although it became the first true presidential retreat in the nation's brief history, it was more than a gleam in Jefferson's eye well before he became the third president. His interest in making Poplar Forest a get-away-from-it-all home may have had its beginning with an enforced visit in June 1781, when he was alerted that British troops were on their way to Monticello to capture him (he had just completed his term as governor of Virginia and a successor had not yet been appointed, but the British apparently did not know this). The family fled to Poplar Forest. On the way, Jefferson was injured in a fall from his horse. Once at the plantation, they stayed in the overseer's tiny house about five weeks. If he did have an idea for a retreat at Pop-lar Forest at that time, it was years before he could expand on it. In the intervening time there was tragedy. His wife died in 1782. Three children had died in childbirth or infancy. From 1784 to 1789 he served abroad. On his return, President Washington asked him to become secretary of state. By the end of 1793, weary of a political tug-of-war with Secretary of the Treasury Alexander Hamilton and suffering from headaches, he resigned and returned to Monticello to retire.

He threw himself into remodeling and rebuilding parts of Monticello and added innovations including alcove beds, a feature he was later to in-corporate into the Poplar Forest floor plan. He also put to use a plow he had designed several years before. It could be pulled with less resistance and reduce plowing time. A planned visit to Poplar Forest was canceled because of the demands at Monticello. During this period his political allies kept him informed by letter of the goings-on in government. As President Washington's second term was coming to an end, Jefferson's friends pressed him to run against Vice President John Adams. Adams prevailed with 71 electoral votes to his 68. Jefferson automatically be-came vice president. They were inaugurated on March 4, 1797.

Not long after Congress adjourned in May 1800, Jefferson visited Poplar Forest. Soon after he arrived, a thunderstorm and steady rain drenched the countryside. For three days he was cooped up again in the overseer's small house. His granddaughter years later wrote that this visit might have been the catalyst for Jefferson to begin seriously planning a comfortable retreat.

When Jefferson left Virginia that November 1800 he first went to inspect the new federal city, Washington, then continued to the capital, Philadelphia. He and Aaron Burr ended up tied in electoral votes for the presidency, so the decision fell to the House of Representatives, where Hamilton was instrumental in persuading members to vote for Jefferson. Burr became his vice president. They were inaugurated on March 4, 1801. Jefferson soon moved into the tan, sandstone Presi-dent's House (the name "White House" was to come later). To relieve the tension of the job he would sometimes step outside and clear brush from around the building. The Louisiana Purchase, of land from Na-poleon, which doubled the size of the United States, and the Lewis & Clark expedition were the major achievements of his first term.

Jefferson was reelected president in November 1804, with former New York governor George Clinton as his vice president. He now began to think more actively of his ultimate retirement and brought to completion his plans for Poplar Forest.

LAYING THE FOUNDATION

Once the foundation was laid in 1806, Jefferson corresponded regularly with Hugh Chisolm and other workers about the construction. He would have a sunken garden stretching out about one hundred yards from below the parlor's portico. The soil taken up in the process would be worked into two mounds, one on each side of the house, to be planted with a variety of trees. Windows and doors were made on the property from lumber felled there and at Monticello. All the bricks were made there, too. Jefferson himself designed molds for two special types: five-sided and curved. A steady stream of workers and materials flowed from the one plantation to the other.

In September 1807, Jefferson returned to Poplar Forest to check on the progress. He was pleased. Had it not been for the demands of his office, it is likely that Poplar Forest would have been completed several years sooner. As it turned out, he spent his first night in the house in November 1809, eight months after he had left office. Even then, the interior walls had not yet been plastered. He made up for lost time, however, in subsequent years, visiting three and four times a year, often for up to a month at a time. On August 17, 1811, he wrote to his friend Dr. Benjamin Rush, a cosigner of the Declaration of Independence, "I have fixed myself comfortably, keep some books here, bring others occasionally, am in the solitude of a hermit, and quite at leisure to attend to my absent friends."

The more time he spent at Poplar Forest, the greater his enthusiasm became. In September 1812 he wrote to his son-in-law, John Wayles Eppes, "When finished, it will be the best dwelling house in the state, except that of Monticello; perhaps preferable to that, as more proportioned to the faculties of a private citizen."

In 1814 Jefferson made the only alteration to the house by adding a low, 110-foot-long wing he called "offices." The rooms of this wing were actually used for various household functions such as laundry, kitchen, smokehouse, and storage. The wing had a flat roof on which Jefferson liked to stroll in the evening. By 1816 all of the interior plastering was finished.

Jefferson hoped that his descendants would settle at Poplar Forest. His grandson, Francis Eppes, and wife, Mary Elizabeth Cleland Randolph, went to live there in March 1823. Jefferson left approximately a thousand acres and his house to young Francis. Accompanied by his daughter Martha and granddaughters Ellen and Cornelia, Jefferson returned to Poplar Forest for a visit on May 14, 1823. This was to be his last visit to his beloved retreat. Still deeply in debt, Jefferson hit upon the idea of selling portions of his Monticello property and some of the Poplar Forest land in a public lottery. The lottery tickets were printed, but not sold before his death. He died on July 4, 1826, the fiftieth anniversary of the Declaration of Independence. He was eighty-three. Coincidentally, his old colleague (onetime ally, later adversary) John Adams died on the same day. In their later years they had maintained a cordial correspondence.

Discouraged by poor tobacco crops, bad weather, and a house in need of repair, Francis Eppes sold Poplar Forest two years after Jefferson's death and moved his family to Florida. Although the property was appraised at twenty thousand dollars, he sold it for five thousand to a neighbor whose daughter married Sixtus Hutter in 1840. Their descendants owned it for over a century, until 1946. After that, there were two more owners, until 1984, when the nonprofit Corporation for Jefferson's Poplar Forest was created, bought the property (and some adjacent land), began restoration, and opened it to the public on July 4, 1986. Restoration continues at this writing.

Poplar Forest is owned and operated by the Corporation for Jefferson's Poplar Forest, a nonprofit organization. Located in Bedford County, Virginia, approximately eight miles west of Lynchburg and 190 miles southwest of Washington, D.C., it is open to the public and tours are provided. For information see the website, www.poplarforest.org, or telephone 434-525-1806.

—•—

Chapter Four

JAMES MADISON

THE 4TH PRESIDENT

March 4, 1809 — March 4, 1817

In physical stature he was small—just five feet, four inches tall—but he was a giant politically in the early days of the republic. His singular reputation rests on his contributions to the United States Constitution, the Bill of Rights, and the Federalist Papers.

James Madison was born March 16, 1751, at his grandfather's Belle Grove Plantation near Port Conway, Virginia. He was the eldest of twelve children born to James, Sr., and Nelly Conway Madison (six others lived to maturity). His youth was spent at Montpelier estate, near Orange, Virginia, and about sixty miles south of Washington, D.C. His paternal grandfather, Ambrose Madison, and brother-in-law Thomas Chew acquired its 4,675 acres in 1723 as the Piedmont area of Virginia began to open up. In exchange for title to the land, they were required to clear it and build a house within three years. Montpelier became primarily a tobacco-growing estate. It was essentially James Madison's lifetime home and the place to which he always repaired for respite whenever he badly needed a break from weighty issues or troubles.

Known as "Jemmy," young Madison was tutored by Donald

Robertson, a Scot who taught him geography, languages, and mathematics. Latin became his specialty. From the ages of sixteen to eighteen, he studied under the Reverend Thomas Martin in preparation for college. His parents worried that because he was delicate, the climate of Williamsburg, the colonial capital in the Tidewater region of Virginia, where the College of William & Mary is located, might strain his health. Instead, he went in 1769 to the College of New Jersey (today's Princeton University). He graduated in 1771 but stayed on for another year to study political philosophy and Hebrew. He also studied law. He believed a good knowledge of legal procedure would be valuable for public policy. He returned to Montpelier in 1772.

INTO POLITICS

Four years later, in 1776, Madison was elected to the Virginia legislature, where he served for four years. Elected to the Continental Congress in 1783, he led successful efforts to get Virginia and other states to forgo claims to western lands so that they could be under Congressional jurisdiction. He was elected again to the Virginia House of Delegates in 1784. Largely at Madison's urging, a national convention of the states was called in 1787 in Philadelphia to seek ways to solve the problems created by the Articles of Confederation. He was the only delegate to come with a plan, known afterward as the Virginia Plan, the foundation for what was ultimately the U.S. Constitution. Madison believed that it was essential to divide government power between state and federal governments and, within the federal government, among its three branches. Madison was the leading speaker at the Constitutional Convention. On September 28, the convention voted to send the new constitution to the states for ratification.

Madison, along with Alexander Hamilton and John Jay, wrote the Federalist Papers in 1788. Initially, these appeared as eighty-five newspaper articles, later published in book form. They were widely distributed in all thirteen states. They explained how the Constitution would work. Madison drafted the Bill of Rights. On December 15, 1791, the necessary number of states had ratified the first ten amendments of the Constitution, the Bill of Rights. He served in the House of Representatives from 1789 to 1797.

THE REMARKABLE DOLLEY

On September 15, 1794, Madison, then forty-three, married Dorothea (Dolley) Payne Todd, a widow with a young son. She was twenty-six. Their mutual friend Aaron Burr arranged for them to meet in May that year in Philadelphia, the capital. It was a "whirlwind" courtship. He proposed marriage in August and they were married a month later.

Dolley grew up in a Society of Friends (Quaker) community, which emphasized simplicity.

Young women were expected to be demure. Yet she turned out to be an eminent hostess who charmed almost everyone she met. She liked to dress well and ordered her shawls and what became her "signature" turbans from Paris. While James was awkward and diffident in large groups, he could be relaxed and comfortable in private settings. Dolley's warmth and affability took the edge off his public reserve. When he was elected president in 1808, she opened her Georgetown house for a reception for several hundred guests.

Early in his first term, Madison let the First Bank of the United States' charter expire. Without it, financing the War of 1812 proved difficult. In 1815, Madison changed his mind and asked Congress to found a Second Bank of the United States. It did, in 1816.

For years the United States endured British impressment of American merchant sailors—among other violations of neutrality. Although the nation was not prepared to fight a war, "hawks" were creating ever more pressure. Madison asked Congress for a declaration of war and got it in 1812. Some "war hawks" said it would be easy to invade British Canada. It was not. The army was short on troops and ammunition. The British blockaded U.S. ports, cutting off imports, which led to economic hardships. Congress turned down Madison's request to enlarge the navy.

While Madison was away from Washington rallying troops, the British marched on the capital and burned the White House down to its sandstone walls. This was not before Dolley rescued the Gilbert Stuart portrait of George Washington by cutting it out of its frame, rolling it up, and taking it with her, along with a few other artifacts she could carry. James was finally reunited with her nearly a week after the sacking of Washington.

The British also sought to create troubles for the United States among Indian tribes. Generals Andrew Jackson and William Henry Harrison won significant victories that ended these threats. Naval ships on Lake Erie destroyed or captured the larger British fleet there. Meanwhile, U.S. merchant ships had been armed as privateers and captured nearly two thousand British ships. Fort McHenry, which guarded the entrance to Baltimore Harbor, sustained a twenty-four-hour bombardment by the British and remained in U.S. hands. It inspired a witness, Francis Scott Key, to write the words to what was to become (many years later) the national anthem, "The Star-Spangled Banner."

Peace was ratified with the Treaty of Ghent in 1815. Neither side gained territory. But the nation breathed a collective sigh of relief that the war was over. Some called the ensuing months an "Era of Good Feeling." The Federalist Party disappeared, leaving only the Democratic-Republicans. Madison agreed by now that the nation needed a steady source of tax funds derived from tariffs. He knew also the importance of a strong army and navy. During his first term the Barbary War was brought to a successful conclusion, when U.S. marines stormed ashore at Tripoli to end the years of extortion and tribute by pirates based on the shores of the Mediterranean.

TIME OFF AT MONTPELIER

At least nine times during his presidency—including all of their summers—Madison and Dolley took the two- or three-day carriage trips to Montpelier. Like other early presidents, their summer trips usually coincided with the adjournment of Congress and ended when it reconvened in the fall. Sometimes Dolley and her sisters would return earlier than James if the capital city's social season began earlier.

Montpelier plantation was tended by an average of one hundred slaves. Earlier, Madison oversaw additions to the main house. He built a single-story, flat-roofed extension at both ends, a Tuscan portico, and a Greek-style temple rather like a very formal gazebo. He also created a spacious drawing room by combining two smaller rooms. When his presidency was over, the Madisons retired to Montpelier. Dolley hoped that their newfound freedom would lead to a trip to Europe, but this was not to be. Madison, now sixty-five, had left the presidency a poorer man than when he began it. The plantation was yielding less, was expensive to maintain, and was adding to his debts. He became eccentric about his legacy and papers. He refused to let the official records of the Constitutional Convention or his own notes about it be published in his lifetime. Some thought he believed they would bring a large sum after his death, thus providing enough for Dolley to live on.

Over several years he altered many of those documents. It was as if he were editing his own legacy for the history books.

In 1826, Madison became rector (in effect, president) of the University of Virginia, in Charlottesville, a position he held until his death in 1836. He was seventy-eight in 1829 when he was selected to be a representative to the convention in Richmond to revise the state's constitution. Western members wanted more representation (their numbers were growing) and universal suffrage for white men. Easterners wanted to keep the status quo, including property ownership as a criterion for voting. Madison sought to make a compromise, but failed. He died at Montpelier, July 26, 1836, his beloved Dolley at his side. At age eighty-five he was the last of the founding fathers to die. He is buried in the family cemetery at Montpelier. Dolley, who moved to Washington after his death, died on July 12, 1849, and is also buried there.

———•◦•———

Montpelier, the Madison estate, is located four miles south of Orange, Virginia. Today it consists of approximately 2,700 acres. In addition to the mansion, it includes a Greek temple built by Madison, farm buildings, a formal garden, a forest of first-growth hardwoods, the Madison Family cemetery, the Slave Cemetery, Civil War trails, and an archeological site.

It was owned by the family from 1723 to 1884. In 1901 it was acquired by William and Annie Rogers duPont. They built stables and a racing track for equestrian activities. In 1928, their daughter Marion duPont inherited the property and enlarged the main house to fifty-five rooms. It was declared a National Historic Landmark in 1960. When Marion died in 1983 her wish was for the property to go to the National Trust for Historic Preservation, along with funds to maintain it. She had no children, however, and her father's will specified that under those circumstances it would go to her brother, William. He died in 1985, so it passed to his five children. Three of them sold their interest to the National Trust; two did so only after extensive legal proceedings.

The National Trust began a restoration program in 2003. When it was completed in 2008, the mansion looked as it did when it was the home and retreat of James and Dolley Madison, The Visitors' Center has a room dedicated to the duPonts and is in art and decor just as they had it in the main house. Operated as well as owned by the National Trust for Historic Preservation, Montpelier is open from November to March, 9 a.m.–4 p.m. (when the last tour of the day begins) and from April to October, 9 a.m.–5 p.m. (when the last tour begins). Closed Thanksgiving and Christmas Day.

Contact information: James Madison's Montpelier, 11407 Constitution Highway, Montpelier, VA 22957 (P.O. Box 911, Zip 22960). Telephone: 540-672-2728. Website: www.montpelier.org.

Chapter Five

JAMES MONROE

THE 5TH PRESIDENT

March 4, 1817—March 4, 1825

*L*and developed as plantations formed the basis of the prosperity of most early presidents, including James Monroe. At age sixteen he inherited his father's farm. He dreamt of one day owning a large plantation. He sold that farm in 1783 to have enough money to open a law practice and go into politics. Over the next several years, he bought and sold plantations, but these barely supported the expensive lifestyle he had adopted. In 1793 he was able to buy a 535-acre farm about two miles down the road from Thomas Jefferson's Monticello. He called it "Highland." (Today it is known as Ash Lawn–Highland.) He and his wife owned it until 1826. It was their official residence from 1799 to 1823, and his regular retreat when Congress wasn't in session. The Monroes entertained there lavishly—friends, neighbors, political figures, foreign dignitaries. Monroe called it his "place of comfort and hospitality."

A YOUNG REVOLUTIONARY

James Monroe was born April 28, 1758, in Albemarle County, Virginia, the youngest of three sons of Spence Monroe, a descendant of Scots, and his wife, Elizabeth. From age eleven until sixteen, James was educated at Campbelltown Academy, a school run by a clergyman. He excelled and entered the College of William & Mary at sixteen. There he found most students filled with patriotic rebellion against King George III. In June 1775, after the battles of Lexington and Concord, he and two dozen other young men raided the arsenal of the Governor's Palace in Williamsburg. They made off with enough muskets and swords to arm what became the local militia. The next year, Monroe left college to enlist in the 3rd Virginia Regiment of the Continental Army. He was wounded in the Battle of Trenton. After the war he returned to Virginia to study law under Jefferson.

INTO POLITICS

Monroe was elected to the Virginia House of Delegates in 1782 and served in the Continental Congress from 1783 to 1786. In Virginia, ratification of the new Constitution did not come easily.

Washington and Madison were for it; George Mason and Patrick Henry opposed it. Monroe was a key figure in the middle between the two sides. He objected to the absence of a bill of rights and believed the Constitution would give too much power to the central government. Ultimately, these "centrists" lifted their reservations and the Constitution was ratified.

On February 15, 1786, James married Elizabeth Kortright, a woman of great beauty and the daughter of a wealthy New York family. After honeymooning on Long Island, they temporarily moved into her father's home in New York City. In 1788, Monroe stood for a House seat in the U.S. Congress but lost to Madison. Two years later, in 1790, he was elected a U.S. senator. He joined the Democratic-Republican Party (precursor to the modern Democratic Party), led by Jefferson and Madison. The next year, he became party leader. In 1794, President Washington appointed Monroe as minister to France. There he arranged for the release of Thomas Paine, who had been jailed by the

Jacobins. Back home, Monroe returned to his law practice in Virginia and was elected governor of Virginia, serving from 1799 to 1802. President Jefferson then sent him to help negotiate the Louisiana Purchase. After that, he was sent to London as minister to the Court of St. James's, where he served until 1807. After returning to the Virginia House of Delegates and a portion of another term as governor, Monroe became secretary of state under President Madison in April 1811 and secretary of war as well in 1814. He held both jobs until 1815, when he resigned as secretary of war. Monroe remained secretary of state until his own presidential term began.

THE PRESIDENCY

In 1816, Monroe was elected president; four years later, he was re-elected, completely unopposed. The first two years of Monroe's presidency came to be called the "Era of Good Feeling." He took two extensive tours of the young nation to build national unity. He was welcomed everywhere. Then the Panic of 1819 caused an economic depression. The same year, Missouri sought unsuccessfully to be admitted to the union as a slave state. Instead, the Missouri Compromise was passed, with Maine as a free state and Missouri a slave state, but forever barring slavery north of latitude 36'30". In 1857 the Supreme Court declared this act unconstitutional.

THE MONROE DOCTRINE

In 1819, Spain ceded Florida in exchange for U.S. assumption of $5 million in debts and the relinquishing of any U.S. claim to Texas. A few years later, in Monroe's December 1823 message to Congress, he defined what came to be known as the Monroe Doctrine. It stated that the Americas would be free of European colonization, that it would be neutral in any European wars, and it would consider interference with any of the independent countries of the Americas as a hostile act.

Monroe later added that Russia must not continue moving southward on the Pacific Coast.

In 1824, the West African country of Liberia, settled by freed American slaves, renamed its capital Monrovia, in honor James Monroe.

RETREATS

When Congress was out of session, the Monroes had long retreats at Highland, where they entertained a great deal. During his White House years, Elizabeth absented herself frequently from Washington, not liking the social life. She contented herself at Highland or made long visits to their two married daughters. Upon the completion of his second term in March 1825, the Monroes moved briefly to a house at Monroe Hill, on the campus of the University of Virginia. They sold Highland a year later in order to retire debts he had acquired during his terms in office. For twenty-two years, from 1808 until 1830, they also owned property farther north near Leesburg, called Oak Lawn. It was but one of their homes during those years. Initially, their residence on the estate was the Monroe Cottage, a small wooden building. In 1820 James engaged James Hoban, the architect of the White House, to design for them a Federal-style mansion. Thomas Jefferson was offered (and accepted) an invitation by Monroe to make design suggestions, too. The Oak Lawn mansion was completed in 1822. From 1827 to 1830 it was their only residence. In August 1825 the Monroes entertained the Marquis de Lafayette and the new president, John Quincy Adams, at Oak Lawn. Elizabeth Monroe died there on September 23, 1830, whereupon James moved to New York City to live with their youngest daughter and her family. He died there on July 4, 1831, at age seventy-three. After his death, Oak Lawn passed out of the family.

The Monroe estate, Ash Lawn–Highland, is an historic house museum, working farm, and performing arts site. It is owned and operated by the College of William & Mary. It is at 1000 James Monroe Parkway, Charlottesville, VA 22902. Tel.: 434-293-8000. Email: info@al-h.us. Website: www.ashlawnhighland.org.

Oak Lawn is privately owned and not open to the public.

The James Monroe Museum and Memorial Library, site of Monroe's law office, is located at 908 Charles Street, Fredericksburg, VA 22401–5801. Tel.: 540-654-1043. Website: http://jamesmonroemuseum .umw.edu/. It is the largest repository of artifacts and documents related to *James Monroe. It is owned by the Commonwealth of Virginia and administered by the University of Mary Washington.*

The James Monroe Memorial Foundation makes grants to the Museum and Memorial Library for the expansion of its collections. It also has as a major project the restoration of the James Monroe Birthplace Farm at Colonial Beach, Virginia (not far from George Washington's birthplace). Its offices are at 113 North Foushee Street, Richmond, VA 23220. Tel. 804-231-1827. Email: pres@monroefoundation.org.

Chapter Six

JOHN QUINCY ADAMS

THE 6TH PRESIDENT

March 4, 1825 — March 4, 1829

Like his father, John Quincy Adams was intelligent, but short on charm. And like his father, he called Peacefield, the family's forty-acre Massachusetts farm, home. Being the son of a leading diplomat and a bright mother, John Quincy (born July 11, 1767) was destined to get an international education. He accompanied his parents on his father John's diplomatic mission to France in 1778–79 and to the Netherlands in 1780–82. In 1779, at age thirteen, he began a diary that he kept to within a few days of his death. He studied at Leiden University in the Netherlands and also in Paris. In 1779 he accompanied Francis Dana on a mission to Russia to seek diplomatic recognition of the United States. He became fluent in French and Dutch. Once back home, John Quincy entered Harvard College. He graduated in 1787, then he studied law.

President Washington appointed him at the age of twenty-six as minister to the Netherlands. Two years later he was made minister to Portugal. Then he was posted to Berlin. In 1797 his father, now president, appointed John Quincy to Prussia, where he served into 1801.

During this mission he married Louisa Catherine Johnson, born in London to an American merchant father. They were married in London, July 26, 1797, and had four children.

Arriving home to Peacefield in 1801, he was briefly appointed commissioner of bankruptcy in Boston. Afterward he practiced law. In April he was elected to the Massachusetts Senate. His fellow Federalists saw promise in him and he was then elected to the U.S. Senate, serving from 1803 to 1808. During this time he was also a professor of rhetoric at Harvard. In the Senate he supported Jefferson's Louisiana Purchase, a very unpopular position with his state's Federalists. They voted to replace him. He resigned instead from both the Senate and the party and became a member of the Democrat-Republican Party. The following year, 1809, the new president, James Madison, chose Adams to be the nation's first minister to Russia. Louisa accompanied him, providing the charm he lacked when it came to court social events. They were in St. Petersburg during Napoleon's disastrous attempt to invade Russia.

In 1814, they returned to Washington. Madison had a new assignment for him. He was to head the U.S. delegation for the Treaty of Ghent, ending the War of 1812 with Britain. Then he served as minister to the Court of St. James's (a post his father had held) from 1815 to 1817. James Monroe, now president, called him back to Washington to become secretary of state for eight years. Adams authored the Monroe Doctrine, which warned the world that the United States would tolerate no outside meddling in the Western Hemisphere. Most of Spain's possessions in the hemisphere were in revolt. In an address on July 4, 1821, Adams said that U.S. policy was to offer independence movements moral support, but not military intervention. Most declared their independence and were diplomatically recognized by the United States.

Florida was an ambiguity. Runaway slaves and Indian raiders were numerous. Monroe sent in General Andrew Jackson to straighten things out. Adams then negotiated the Florida Treaty with Spain, which turned Florida over to the United States, while we recognized Spanish control over Texas as part of Mexico (for the time being, as it turned out).

ELECTED PRESIDENT

Adams saw the secretary of state's position in 1824 as the logical step toward the presidency. Andrew Jackson won the popular vote, but the electoral vote was widely split. Jackson received 99, Adams 44, Crawford 41, and Clay 37. With no one getting a majority, the decision went to the House. Adams eventually won.

A strong believer in regular exercise, as president John Quincy frequently went swimming nude in the Potomac early in the morning.

In 1826, he and Clay formed a new political party, the National Republican Party, but they lost control of Congress to the Democrats in 1826. The charismatic Andrew Jackson swept him away in a landslide in Adams's bid for reelection. The electoral vote was 219–49, with 18 for candidates of two other small parties.

HOME TO PEACEFIELD

Throughout his presidency, Adams did as his father had done: returned to Peacefield for the summer as soon as Congress adjourned. He took to calling it the Summer White House. He and Louisa would return to Washington shortly before Congress reconvened. His special interest at the farm was trees—arboriculture. In Washington he regularly asked visiting dignitaries from other countries to send him seeds to plant at Peacefield. When his parents were still living, he visited Peacefield as often as his duties would allow. He was unable to be there when his father died, and afterward he considered selling it because of the cost. But he wrote later that the thought of selling "struck me as an arrow to the heart." He kept it, and so did his heirs.

A FULL LIFE AFTER THE WHITE HOUSE

Adams skipped Jackson's inauguration and went directly home to Peacefield. Two years later, he was elected to the House—the only former president to have done so—for a little over eight terms. During all those years, he and Louisa continued to spend contented summers at Peacefield.

He was an outspoken opponent of slavery. His moves to bring

antislavery petitions before the House so infuriated some of his southern colleagues that they began a campaign to have him censured. Finally, on February 7, 1842, the House voted to table the motion of censure. In 1841, he defended several African slaves in the case of *United States v. The Amistad Africans,* and charged them nothing for his services. He not only succeeded in winning their freedom, but also sent a message nationally against the institution of slavery.

On February 21, 1848, in the midst of a floor debate, Adams collapsed, the result of a cerebral hemorrhage. He was taken to the Speaker's Room in the Capitol. He died there two days later, with Louisa and their son Charles Francis by his bedside. He was a few months short of eighty-one years of age. Louisa died in 1852. They are both buried in the United First Parish Church in Quincy, Massachusetts.

———•◦•———

The Adams National Historical Park is covered in detail under chapter 2 (John Adams, p. 16).

John Quincy's son, Charles Francis, built the nation's first memorial presidential library in 1870 when he commissioned the construction of the Stone Library on the grounds of Peacefield.

It contains more than fourteen thousand books.

Chapter Seven

ANDREW JACKSON

THE 7TH PRESIDENT

March 4, 1829—March 4, 1837

For forty-one years, through wars, duels, political battles, scandals, and retirement, the Hermitage was his refuge and retreat—a place of calm, peace, and family for Andrew Jackson.

At six foot one, Jackson was taller then nearly all of his contemporaries. At 140 pounds, he was lean, but tough. He was courageous, determined, and often impulsive. He was also a shrewd politician. Andrew Jackson was born of Irish-Scotch immigrant parents, Andrew and Elizabeth, on March 15, 1767, probably in the Waxhaws, an area in South Carolina. He was an orphan by the time he was fourteen. His father had died in an accident three weeks before Andrew was born. His mother died of cholera while nursing prisoners of war aboard a ship in Charleston Harbor. His eldest brother, Hugh, died in a Revolutionary War battle.

At age thirteen, young Andrew joined the war effort as a courier for a local militia unit. He and his brother Robert were captured by the British and imprisoned under harsh conditions. When he refused to clean the boots of British Major Coffin, the man slashed his hand and head with his sword, leaving Andrew with permanent scars and a lifelong hatred of the British. Both brothers contracted smallpox in prison and Robert died of it in 1781.

After his release, Andrew worked for a time for a saddle maker. His schooling had been occasional. He went to Salisbury, North Carolina, to study law and was admitted to the bar in 1787. He then moved to the Jonesborough area in the Western District of North Carolina. The district's name changed to the Southwest Territory a few years later and ultimately became Tennessee. Jackson proved to be a good country lawyer. In 1788 he became solicitor for the Western District and then for the Territory South of the Ohio River. In 1796 he was a delegate to the Tennessee constitutional convention and, as it became a state, was elected U.S. representative. The following year he was elected U.S. senator, but he resigned several months later to be appointed to the state supreme court, where he served until 1804.

Jackson prospered. He opened a general store in the town of Gallatin and built a home there. In 1804 he bought the Hermitage, a 640-acre cotton plantation. He was a slave owner (nine at first; ultimately as many as 150 at any one time). He added acreage, to a total of 1,050 acres. He also engaged (profitably) in land speculation in West Tennessee and was one of the founders of Memphis.

JACKSON THE WARRIOR

In 1801, he became a colonel and commander in the Tennessee militia. He showed his aptitude for battle in the War of 1812. His first assignment was to quell the attacks of "Red Stick" Creek Indians from Alabama and Georgia, who were attacking settlers, four hundred of whom were killed in one skirmish alone. Jackson led Tennessee militiamen, U.S. Army troops, and members of the Cherokee, Choctaw, and Southern Creek tribes into the Battle of Horseshoe Bend in 1814. Eight hundred "Red Sticks" were killed. Both Sam Houston and David Crockett served under Jackson. He dictated the terms of the Treaty of Fort Jackson, by which the defeated Indians ceded 20 million acres for white settlement. For his work, Jackson was promoted to the rank of major general.

The Battle of New Orleans made him a national hero. British forces were advancing against the city. Jackson was asked to pull together troops from several states and territories to defend it. He did, and earned a reputation for being fearless and strict—"tough as old hickory," his troops said of him (hence his nickname, Old Hickory). Outnumbered, the American troops decisively won the battle on January 8, 1815. The British had 2,037 casualties (including three generals killed) and the Americans only 71. Two years later, President Monroe ordered him to pacify the Seminole and Creek tribes in Georgia and to prevent Spanish Florida from becoming a refuge for runaway slaves. Jackson decided the best way was to seize Florida, so he did. He easily captured Pensacola, sent the Spanish governor packing, and executed two Britons who had been advising the Indians. The Spanish wanted him punished, but Secretary of State John Quincy Adams told the Spanish minister that they should either put enough troops in Florida to keep the peace or else give it to the United States. The latter was the ultimate outcome. Jackson became military governor of Florida throughout much of 1820 and 1821.

SEEKING THE PRESIDENCY

In 1822 the Tennessee legislature elected him to another U.S. Senate term. It also nominated him to run for president in 1824. Jackson won the popular vote but not a majority of electoral votes. Nursing his disappointment, he resigned his Senate seat in 1825 to prepare for another try at the presidency. In 1828, running for what would become the modern Democratic Party, Jackson handily beat Adams in his effort to be reelected.

During the campaign, partisan newspapers accused Jackson's wife, Rachel, of being a bigamist. He had first met Rachel Donelson Robards in Nashville in 1788. She was in a very unhappy marriage and subject to jealous rages. She separated from her husband in 1790 and believed they had been divorced. She and Jackson married in August 1791. She later discovered that, although Robards had received permission from the Virginia legislature to obtain a divorce, he had not followed through. This made Rachel's marriage to Jackson technically invalid. She took immediate steps to complete the divorce process and, once that was done, remarried Jackson in 1794. Jackson resented these attacks on his wife's honor and fought thirteen duels about it over time. He shot and killed one duelist, but not before the man could shoot him. The bullet lodged so close to Jackson's heart that the doctors dared not try to remove it. This and other wounds caused him much pain as the years wore on.

Rachel was not relishing the move to Washington from the Hermitage. She had been to the capital city when Andrew was a senator and found the rigid social customs stifling. She was high-spirited, a woman of the frontier, happier riding a horse than in a carriage. Two weeks after her husband's election, on December 22, 1828, she died of a heart attack. She was sixty-one. The Jacksons had two adopted sons, Andrew Jackson, Jr., the son of Rachel's late brother, and Lyncoya, an orphaned Creek Indian boy who died of tuberculosis at age sixteen.

INTO THE WHITE HOUSE

Andrew Jackson's inaugural party was like nothing ever seen. He invited the public to come to the White House. Hundreds did, filling the building, breaking dishes, spreading mud everywhere, and making a general mess of the place. It is said that staff members filled tubs on the lawn with punch to lure the celebrants outside the building. Now a widower, Jackson asked Rachel's niece, Emily Donelson, to take on the duties of First Lady. Her husband, Andrew Jackson Donelson, became the new president's private secretary. In 1834, Sarah Yorke Jackson, the wife of Andrew Jackson, Jr., became co-hostess, the only time the White House had two women in that role. Emily died from tuberculosis in 1836 and Sarah continued as the sole hostess.

For years before he became president, Jackson had been involved in the issue of removing Indian tribes west of the Mississippi to Arkansas and some as far west as Oklahoma—to make more room for white settlers. In 1830 he signed the Indian Removal Act, which authorized him to negotiate the purchase of tribal lands in exchange for western ones. During his eight years in office, some forty-five thousand Indians were moved west.

The Democratic Party ticket of Andrew Jackson and Martin Van Buren in 1832 won handily. Set for a second term, Jackson swung into action. By January 1835 he had paid off the entire national debt—the only time in U.S. history this has happened.

On January 30, 1835, as Jackson was leaving the Capitol after a funeral, a deranged man aimed a pistol at him and misfired twice. The two pistols he used were tested afterward and found to be in good working condition. The fact they had misfired added to Jackson's popularity and the belief that he was under God's special protection.

Jackson thought that rotation in federal offices was a good thing, To implement this, he set out to give jobs to loyal members of his party. Thus the "spoils system" was born and it took more than half a century before it was eliminated.

GETTING AWAY FROM IT ALL

Throughout his presidency, Jackson took time off at Rip Raps, an artificial island of fifteen acres at the mouth of Hampton Roads harbor, Virginia. It was built by the U.S. Navy beginning in 1817 as part of the harbor defenses. It is southeast of the other harbor guardian, Fort Monroe. Jackson stayed at Fort Calhoun, the fortification built on the island (it was renamed Fort Wool during the Civil War). Jackson took an entourage with him, usually including family members. Because it was easily accessible by sea from Washington, he stayed at Rip Raps far more often during his presidency than he did at the Hermitage. His retreats were usually made when Congress had left town for the summer. In alternate years, he would go to the Hermitage.

The Hermitage was where he most wanted to be, but its distance from Washington (about seven hundred miles) made journeys there possible only if he could stay for several weeks. He made four trips during his eight years as president: June until October, 1830; July through September, 1832; July 8 through September 30, in 1834; and in August and September, 1836. A good-sized entourage accompanied him with several family members. There might be his two acting First Ladies, Emily Donelson and Sarah Yorke Jackson; Emily's husband, Andrew Jackson Donelson, who was Jackson's private secretary; and Jackson's adopted son, Andrew Jackson, Jr. Indeed, when President Jackson retired to the Hermitage in 1837, Andrew, Jr., and Sarah and their family moved in with him, as did Sarah's widowed sister and her children.

Although the plantation was prosperous, Jackson had to deal with his son's considerable debts.

He did so and otherwise enjoyed his retirement, surrounded by his family. He kept up a steady correspondence with leading figures in Washington and offered advice as they sought it. Among his famous visitors at the Hermitage were Martin Van Buren, Sam Houston (by then president of the Republic of Texas), and James Polk.

By the time he became president, Jackson's red hair had turned gray, but his eyes were still a strong blue. In retirement, his health began to ebb as old wounds caused him much discomfort. He died in his bedroom on June 8, 1845, aged seventy-eight. He left his estate to Andrew, Jr. He is buried next to his wife, Rachel, under a cupola tomb at the Hermitage.

———◆———

Jackson's first Hermitage was an 1804 log farmhouse. The family moved into the present and splendid brick Hermitage in 1821. Visitors see furniture and furnishings from all the Jackson years. As Curator Marsha Mullin has put it, "The history of The Hermitage mirrors American history—Indians, westward expansion, slavery, freedom, women's roles, cotton, and industrialization."

Owned an operated by the Ladies' Hermitage Association, the estate is open from April 1 to October 15 from 8:30 a.m. to 5:00 p.m. and from October 16 through March 21, from 9 a.m. to 4:30 p.m.

It is closed Thanksgiving and Christmas Day and the third week of January.

It is located at 4580 Rachel's Lane, Nashville, TN 37076. Telephone: 615-889-2941.

Website: www.thehermitage.com.

Rip Raps (Fort Wool) is accessible by boat on regular Hampton, Virginia, harbor cruises. Contact: Three Hour Harbor Cruises, 888-757-2628. Email: info@misshamptoncruises.com. Website: www.miss hamptoncruises.com. Originally called Fort Calhoun, Fort Wool was decommissioned and became a Hampton City park in 1970.

Chapter Eight

MARTIN VAN BUREN

THE 8TH PRESIDENT

March 4, 1837—March 4, 1841

*M*artin Van Buren hadn't been in the New York state legislature long before he established the first political "machine" in the country—the Albany Regency—and was dubbed "the Little Magician" for his adept use of the "spoils system"—the doling out of political patronage jobs.

("Little" came from the fact he was short, as well as plump and bald.)

By 1821, at age thirty-nine, he was elected U.S. senator from New York and was a key figure in organizing the Jacksonian Democrats.

Born in Kinderhook, New York, into a Dutch family that ran a tavern, Van Buren ultimately had several presidential "firsts" to his credit: the first president not of British decent; the first to be born an American citizen; the first from New York; the first not to have spoken English as his first language (at home, Dutch was the first language). He was also the first president to grant an exclusive interview to a reporter.

Bright and ambitious, Van Buren had only a basic education, augmented by Latin. At age fourteen he began to study law at the offices of a well-known Kinderhook attorney. Six years later he was apprenticed to a New York City lawyer who was active in politics. Van Buren was admitted to the bar in 1803. He became a county judicial officer at age twenty-six, then was elected to the state senate and the office of attorney general. In 1828 he was elected governor, but he spent only seventy-one days in office, before the newly inaugurated President Andrew Jackson recruited him as secretary of state (he had managed Jackson's 1828 campaign). He became Jackson's running mate in his 1832 bid for reelection and they won in a landslide.

Four years later Jackson was determined that Van Buren would succeed him. Largely because of Jackson's enthusiastic support, Van Buren won the election.

Economic depression plagued Van Buren for all of his term. Nevertheless, he was renominated unanimously in 1840 by his party, against William Henry Harrison. the hero of Tippecanoe. The latter waged a log-cabin-themed campaign to contrast him to the elegant Van Buren.

Harrison and his running mate, John Tyler, won. Van Buren was the first of eight consecutive presidents—between March 4, 1837, and March 4, 1861—to hold the office for a single term or less.

WHITE HOUSE LIFE AND GETTING AWAY FROM IT

Van Buren and his wife, Hannah, were married in 1807, when he was twenty-five and she twenty-four. She died of tuberculosis twelve years later, so she never witnessed her husband's rise in politics. They had four sons: Abraham, John, Martin, and Smith. Van Buren entered the presidency as a widower and remained so. In November 1838, his second year in office, his son Abraham married Angelica Singleton, a niece of Dolley Madison. After their honeymoon, she and Abraham moved into the White House, where she became the official hostess.

Van Buren kept a small house in the Georgetown section of Washington as a short-term retreat from time to time. He took his first real—and short—vacation as president after Congress adjourned in October 1837. He went to Berkeley Springs, Virginia.

The next year, 1838, he decided to take a six- to eight-week vacation to restore his health, for he was exhausted. Arrangements were made for Van Buren, his sons Abraham and Smith, and Secretary of War Joel Poinsett and his wife to go to White Sulphur Springs in what is now West Virginia. Son Martin, Jr., would stay behind as the president's acting secretary and had a copy of the party's itinerary. Van Buren's travels the next year, 1839, amounted to a real retreat. Once Congress had left in late spring, he planned a trip home to New York . He had not been there since 1836. Traveling by railroad and coach he arrived in New York City on July 2. His reception was even greater than the one accorded Jackson in 1833. He reviewed troops and led a parade up Broadway. For the next week he met with political allies and appeared at several events.

He left for Kinderhook, up the Hudson River, on July 9 and took a relaxed eleven days to arrive there. He was greeted by a friendly crowd at the local hotel, where former governor William Marcy extolled Van Buren's support for the Erie Canal, among other things. On the hotel's balcony Van Buren's response was mostly a reminiscence about his boyhood days in Kinderhook.

He had recently purchased the Van Ness estate, two miles south of Kinderhook, for fourteen thousand dollars. He envisioned it as first a retreat if he were to have a second term, and, after that, his home in retirement. During the week he and son Smith were in Kinderhook, they spent time at the estate. The house was much in need of repair, so they made plans to immediately begin renovating it.

Over a celebratory meal of ham with champagne, they decided to name the place The Locusts. Later, Van Buren recalled that this place-name had been used by James Fenimore Cooper in his popular novel *The Spy,* and so he decided to change the name of his place to Lindenwald (which it remains to this day).

He went on from Kinderhook to spend the first three weeks in August at Saratoga Springs, then toured western New York state, returned to Kinderhook for another visit, went on to Albany, and finally went back to Washington to begin preparations for his reelection campaign.

When he lost that bid, he decided to actually retire to Lindenwald. He purchased adjacent land so that it grew to 220 acres. He intended it be a working farm. His sons either lived with him or stayed for long periods of time. In 1849, he invited Smith and his wife to join him there. Smith initiated, with his father's approval, modernization and expansion of the house. The number of rooms doubled, from eighteen to thirty-six. They added a coal-burning furnace, running water, tub, and toilet.

The latter was not only a luxury, but a curiosity in the mid-nineteenth century. An Italianate four-story brick tower was added, as were window dormers. The 1792-vintage house was transformed into a nineteenth-century one in the popular Italian style.

Martin, Jr., was often ill. He lived at Lindenwald after his father left the White House. In 1853, Martin, Sr., took him to Europe to seek medical help; however, it was unavailing, as the younger Van Buren died of tuberculosis at age forty-two, in 1855. Abraham, a West Point graduate, and his wife, the beautiful Angelica, moved in after the White House years. John was the only son who followed his father into politics. And, like his father, he lost his wife after only a few years of marriage. John had his own room at Lindenwald. He was attorney general of New York from 1845 to 1847.

Van Buren settled into the life of a country gentleman. He died at his home on July 24, 1862, of bronchial asthma and heart failure. He was seventy-nine.

Lindenwald and its remaining twenty-two acres are owned and maintained by the U.S. National Park Service.

The home has been fully restored to look as it did during the years Martin Van Buren owned it.

Hourly tours are available daily from late May until late October. Tour sign-ups take place at the Visitor Center. For further information visit the website, http://www.nps.gov/mava/index.htm, or telephone 518-758-9689.

Chapter Nine

WILLIAM HENRY HARRISON

THE 9TH PRESIDENT

March 4, 1841 — April 4, 1841

*U*ntil Ronald Reagan came along, William Henry Harrison had been the oldest person ever elected and inaugurated as president. Unlike Reagan, however, he did not live long enough to enjoy relaxation from the rigors of office at a country retreat. He died thirty-one days after his inauguration.

It was a cold March day when the sixty-eight-year-old Harrison, "Old Tippecanoe," took the oath of office on the East Steps of the Capitol. He gave a one-hour, forty-minute inaugural address (still a record) and refused to wear an overcoat. In his platitude-filled speech he promised to be a one-term president and said he would use the veto sparingly. After the festivities, he named his cabinet, with Daniel Webster as secretary of state. Weary from the rivalry of his colleagues and pestered by office-seekers, Harrison came down with a fever, which became pneumonia. He took to his bed and died on April 4.

THE WOULD-HAVE-BEEN RETREAT

We can infer from his pre-inaugural schedule that, had Harrison lived to complete his term, he would have made the family plantation (and his birthplace), Berkeley, his country retreat. Located on the James River in the Tidewater region of Virginia, Berkeley was where Harrison repaired in late February 1841 to find the peace and quiet he wanted for writing his inaugural address.

His wife, Anna Symmes, did not accompany him to Berkeley and never saw the White House. Berkeley had been in the Harrison family since 1691. Benjamin Harrison IV in 1726 built the stately home that stands on the 1,400-acre estate. It is the birthplace not only of a president, but also of a signer of the Declaration of Independence and two governors of Virginia. The Harrison family lost Berkeley in the mid-nineteenth century as a result of financial setbacks.

Born in 1773, William Henry Harrison became a medical student in his late teens. When his father died in 1791, he left school to join the army. He was commissioned and served in the west, becoming governor of the Indiana Territory in 1800. In 1811, he led his troops to repulse an attack by the Shawnee, led by the vaunted Tecumseh, on the banks of the Tippecanoe River in what is today Ohio.

He went on to lead victories in the War of 1812. After that, he concluded two Indian peace treaties, served in the U.S. House of Representatives and U.S. Senate, and, briefly, served as minister to Colombia.

In 1836, the young Whig Party picked him as its candidate. Chosen because of his image as a hero of the War of 1812, he had, in the intervening years, sustained financial reverses and was, at the time of his nomination, employed as clerk of the courts in Cincinnati. He lost to Van Buren, Andrew Jackson's favorite. But by 1840, the country's poor economy, which had plagued Van Buren's presidency, made him a weak candidate.

In 1840, after several ballots, Harrison again became the Whig presidential candidate.

As the campaign began a newspaper opined that Harrison should be given "a barrel of hard cider and a pension of two thousand a year and . . . he will sit the remainder of his days in a log cabin . . . and study moral philosophy." Instantly, Harrison was the "log cabin, hard cider" candidate. Thus Harrison became the man of the people who would give them back their government. No one bothered to note that his "log cabin" was a splendid Virginia plantation.

William Henry Harrison's presidency was echoed forty-eight years later, when his grandson, Benjamin Harrison, was inaugurated as the twenty-third president.

———•◦•———

Berkeley Plantation is located at 12602 Harrison Landing Road, Charles City, VA 23030, between Richmond and Williamsburg, and approximately 120 miles southeast of Washington, D.C. It is open to the public. For information see the website, www.berkeleyplantation.com, or telephone 804-829-6018.

Chapter Ten

JOHN TYLER

1 OTH PRESIDENT

April 4, 1841 — March 4, 1845

W ith President William Henry Harrison dead just a month after his inauguration, Vice President John Tyler was sworn in as the tenth president on April 6.

Fifty-one years old at his inauguration, Tyler was the youngest person to hold the office up to that time.

He was tall and slender, clean-shaven, with a Roman nose and receding light hair, brushed back. He favored black broadcloth coats, standing collars, open at the throat, with a soft neck cloth.

On April 13, Tyler issued a proclamation making the next day one of fasting and prayer in memory of the dead Harrison. On that memorial day, Tyler, his long-ailing invalid wife, Letitia, and those of their seven children not away at school moved into the White House. Tyler was no stranger to politics and public office. A lawyer by education, he had been a member of the Virginia House of Delegates, a U.S representative, governor of Virginia, then U.S. senator before his 1840 election as vice president.

First Lady Letitia Tyler was a mystery to Washington. She stayed in her room upstairs and was seen on the main floor only once, on

January 31, 1842, at the marriage of their daughter Elizabeth, then
eighteen. It is unlikely that Tyler returned to his Williamsburg home
more than once or twice in the first eighteen months of his presidency,
as he did not wish to leave his wife for very long. The visits would have
been brief, hardly a retreat in the sense of getting away from the cares
of office.

Letitia died in September 1842.

In 1844, when Captain Robert "Fighting Bob" Stockton, commander of the new sloop-of-war *Princeton*, told Tyler he was planning
a gala first cruise down the Potomac, the president was delighted. February 22 was set as the date. This cruise was to be a great social occasion as well as a successful demonstration of the latest technology with
which to impress Congressional appropriators. Nearly four hundred
people attended, including Dolley Madison; the influential Missouri
senator Thomas Hart Benton; Abel Upshur, new secretary of state;
Thomas Gilmer, secretary of the navy; and Captain Beverley Kennon,
head of the Navy Bureau of Construction. A little before noon, the
Princeton cast off, stopping in Alexandria for a brass band to board.

The crowd was in high spirits the day the *Princeton*—the first war-
ship with screw propellers below the waterline that could not be hit
by enemy cannonades—sailed. The navy had shifted from wooden to
iron ships and sail to steam, but the broadside cannonade was still the
preferred method of attacking enemy ships. The *Princeton* was also
armed with forty-two carronades and two long guns, christened the
"Peacemaker" and the "Oregon." Stockton had the crew fire the two
giant guns at ice floes two and three miles downriver in demonstration. Then the guests went below for champagne and food. After a time
some of the guests asked the captain to fire one more round from the
ten-ton Peacemaker. The women stayed below, as did some of the men,
including Tyler. Just as he raised his glass in toast, a deafening explosion
rolled the ship sharply.

The president and others ran up to a scene of carnage on deck. The
Peacemaker had exploded, killing the secretaries of state and navy, New
York state senator David Gardiner, and five others. Captain Stockton
and Senator Benton survived.

Tyler decided soon after to take a retreat of a special kind. He went
to New York to court and marry Julia, one of Gardiner's daughters,

who had been on board when her father died. He had first met her the previous autumn, when Senator Gardiner had brought them to Washington for the social season. For John Tyler, it seems to have been love at first sight with Julia. They were married on June 26; no reporters covered the event. On their return to the White House, the Tylers entertained almost daily. In time this tapered off to evening parties on Thursdays and Saturdays, plus special occasions. The biggest party was their last, on February 18, 1845. Two thousand guests were invited; three thousand came. The Marine Band played and the punch bowls were refilled many times.

Tyler's four years as president were marked by much political turmoil. Understanding reelection would be difficult, he instead chose to throw his support behind Democrat James Polk as his successor. Polk won.

In his final annual message to Congress, Tyler declared that the majority of people and states supported the annexation of Texas, a controversial proposition because of the fear of spread of slavery. In February 1845, both houses approved a joint resolution and Tyler signed the bill into law annexing Texas just three days before his term expired.

SHERWOOD FOREST

After his first wife died, Tyler purchased Sherwood Forest near Charles City, Virginia, on the north bank of the James River, some twenty miles southeast of Richmond. He paid $1,200 for the home and its 1,600 acres. It has been in the Tyler family ever since. It was to become a post-honeymoon retreat. The main house, built in 1720, was of typical Virginia Tidewater design but given Greek Revival enhancements by the president and his bride: columns, lattice, pilasters on porches, carved medallions. It is said to be the longest wood-frame residence in the nation. They created twenty-five acres of gardens and lawns, with a woodland that includes more than eighty specimen trees, including a gingko given to Tyler by Captain Matthew Perry on his return voyage from Asia in 1850.

Tyler had named the property "Sherwood Forest." When asked why, he said, "Because it's a good place for an outlaw."

The Tylers had an elegant barge, *Pocahontas*, for comfortable cruises on the river or to go to the south shore for a picnic. The First Lady decorated the barge with blue damask cushions. The four oarsmen, all slaves, wore white trousers and blue-checked shirts. The brims of their white hats had the name *Pocahontas* on them.

When his presidential term was completed, they retired to Sherwood Forest in 1845 and lived peacefully there. A believer in states' rights, Tyler thought each state should decide the slavery question for itself. He came back to public life in early 1861 to chair the Virginia Peace Convention in Washington to find a way to prevent civil war. The convention did not find one.

When civil war broke out, Tyler was elected to the Confederacy's House of Representatives, but he died on January 18, 1862, before he could take office. He was seventy-one. He is buried in Richmond. His horse, "The General," is buried on the grounds of Sherwood Forest, with this inscription on the gravestone: "Here lies the body of my good horse 'The General.' For twenty years he bore me around the circuit of my practice and all that time he never made a blunder. Would that his master could say the same."

———•·•———

Sherwood Forest is privately owned. Groups of ten or more may request a guided tour of the grounds. Tours of the house are available by appointment (a fee is charged). Call 804-829-5377, leaving details of your request. Your call will be returned. Website: www.sherwoodforest.org.

Chapter Eleven

JAMES K. POLK

THE 11TH PRESIDENT

March 4, 1845 — March 4, 1849

*I*f presidential success was measured by how many of a president's stated objectives had been met, James Polk would be in the top rank of all of them. He set out four objectives: Obtain California and the interior west; settle with Britain the international border of the Oregon Territory; lower tariffs; and reestablish the independence of the U.S. Treasury. He achieved them all in a single four-year term.

An intense man, hardworking, methodical, and mindful of details, Polk would have been called a "workaholic" today. He did not make friends easily, and by the end of his term he had few allies within his party. He had been a dark-horse candidate. An Andrew Jackson protégé, Polk had been Speaker of the House, governor of Tennessee, and, before that, a Tennessee legislator.

Running on a ticket that favored the acquisition of Texas, he ran against Henry Clay. Most of Clay's followers opposed Texas expansion, fearing it would expand slavery. Polk won with 170 electoral votes to 105.

Tending to keep his own counsel, Polk appeared colorless, self-contained (and self-righteous), and not given to political camaraderie.

The first of his goals—reductions in tariffs and restoration of an independent Treasury department—were soon achieved. He then turned his attention to Texas.

Tyler had obtained Congress's consent to annex it just before leaving office; Polk had only to complete the negotiations.

Settling the Texas boundary, coupled with his desire to acquire California and the interior West, quickly led to the Mexican War, which was fought and won within two years. Polk was able to negotiate the Oregon boundary with Britain, however, without the prospect of conflict ever entering the discussions.

During the Mexican War, Polk decided upon a sixteen-day trip. As it had a serious "business" purpose, he did not think of it as a vacation, but in one sense it was. Traveling by train, steamship, and carriage, he stopped in Baltimore; Philadelphia; South Amboy, New Jersey; New York City; New Haven and Hartford, Connecticut; Springfield, Boston, Concord, and Lowell, Massachusetts; Portland, Hallowell, and Gardiner, Maine; Portsmouth, New Hampshire; and Princeton and Trenton, New Jersey. He and his party traveled nearly every day, leaving almost no time for leisure.

Local leaders were proud to show off local achievements, such as the aqueduct in New York, or the public schools in Boston. In his correspondence and diary, Polk noted the divisiveness of the war effort and his determination to counter the growing antiwar sentiment in the North.

On September 14, 1847, Mexico City fell to U.S. forces. On February 2, 1848, the Treaty of Guadalupe Hidalgo was signed, ceding California and the interior West that was not part of the Oregon Territory to the United States. "Manifest Destiny"—an ocean-to-ocean nation—was fulfilled.

Five days before the treaty was signed, landholder August Sutter discovered gold in northern California. It soon became clear that California contained a large amount it. The beginnings of what would be the Gold Rush of '49 was on.

ENDURING HIS VACATIONS

Because he was fixated on achieving his four goals, Polk did not look forward to vacations. But his wife, Sarah, liked the idea of a change of scene. The Polks took three trips that could be called retreats or vacations during his term in office. From August 19 to 25, 1846, the Polks (who had no children) and friends went on an excursion to Fortress Monroe, Virginia. Beset by throngs anxious to meet him, he fell ill, exhausted from the activity. In 1847, the Polks and friends traveled to Chapel Hill, North Carolina, for eight days to attend the commencement events at the University of North Carolina, Polk's alma mater. The following year, his last in office, he took a vacation at Bedford Springs in Pennsylvania's Pocono Mountains. Polk was exhausted before the trip began. He was accompanied this time by his nephew, Samuel Polk Walker; Dr. Jonathan Foltz, a Navy surgeon; and a manservant, a free black man, William Day. On the way home, he stopped at Berkeley Springs, Virginia, to bathe in its springs. Altogether the trip consumed twelve days, August 18–29. In his first year, 1845, the new president took one day off to visit Mount Vernon, George Washington's home, then still in the hands of the first president's descendants.

STANDING ASIDE IN 1848

Polk did not wish to run for a second term.

On March 5, 1849, the outgoing president Polk rode with incoming president Zachary Taylor in an open carriage from the White House to the Capitol. Polk, the ardent expansionist who spoke of the United States as "the empire of liberty," was taken aback when Taylor remarked to him that California and Oregon were too remote to become states; they should be left to become independent. Of the short trip, Polk later confided to his diary that Taylor was "a well-meaning old man. He is, however, uneducated, exceedingly ignorant of public affairs, and, I should judge, of very ordinary capacity."

POLK PLACE

The day after his term ended, Polk and his wife took a twenty-seven-day trip. At last, finished with his work, Polk enjoyed traveling. They then moved into Polk Place, a large home they had purchased in downtown Nashville, Tennessee. His enjoyment of retirement was to be very short. Never robust, he succumbed to diarrhea a few months later, on June 15, 1849. Sarah Polk lived on until 1891.

———•◦•———

The Polk Home in Columbia, Tennessee, is the only James Polk home (except for the White House) still standing. It was built in 1816 by his father, when James was a student at the University of North Carolina. James lived there until 1824, when he married Sarah Childress. During the years there he practiced law and first ran for and was elected to the state legislature.

The home includes more than one thousand objects that belonged to President and Mrs. Polk, including furniture, paintings, silver, and memorabilia. It is open for visitors year-round.

For hours, days, and fees, visit the website, http://www.jameskpolk .com/new/polkhome.asp, or telephone 931-388-2354, or email jamesk polk@bellsouth.net. The address is 301 West 7th Street, Columbia, TN 38402.

President and Mrs. Polk are buried on the grounds of the State Capitol in Nashville.

Chapter Twelve

ZACHARY TAYLOR

THE 12TH PRESIDENT

March 4, 1849—July 9, 1850

eneral Zachary Taylor, "Old Rough and Ready," won major victories in the Mexican War and was considered a national hero. Taylor's ancestors had settled in Virginia in the 1640s. His grandmother was a Lee, of the aristocratic Virginia family. Taylor himself looked like anything but an aristocrat. He was heavy, short, usually ruffled, with a large head and nose, thinning hair, and the complexion of one who has spent much of his life outdoors.

Zachary was one of nine children of Richard Taylor, an officer in the Revolutionary War, and his wife, Sarah. Zachary was born in 1784 in Virginia, but when he was eight months old, the family moved to the four-hundred-acre plantation his father had purchased near Louisville, Kentucky. They lived in a log cabin there for a time, until Richard Taylor built a house on the property's highest point. He called it "Springfield." In 1800 he added three hundred more acres to the plantation.

Zachary grew up at Springfield, living there for twenty years. In 1810 he returned there to be married to Margaret Mackall Smith, the daughter of a prosperous planter. Five of their six children were born at

Springfield and over the years he returned often to visit his father, who died there in 1829, after which it was sold to pay debts. Over the years he continued to visit Springfield periodically even after it was acquired by new owners. Zachary would later be buried there at what was to become the Zachary Taylor National Cemetery.

A SOLDIER'S LIFE

Schooled by tutors, Zachary was an indifferent student (though he wrote clearly). He joined the army in 1808, receiving a lieutenant's commission, thanks to his cousin James Madison. He distinguished himself in the War of 1812, established an important "listening post" fort between Louisiana and Texas, and led a regiment in the Black Hawk War. By 1841 he was commander of the army's Southern Division. In 1845, as Texas became a state, President Polk ordered Taylor to its border with Mexico.

He was ordered to defend the spot against any armed effort by Mexico to retake it, which he did successfully.

A POLITICAL CIPHER

Even though he was a slave owner, he was against extending slavery west because he thought the new economies could not sustain it.

IN OFFICE

The Taylors were a close family. Margaret Taylor was in frail health and asked their daughter Elizabeth to take her place as hostess of the many official functions that took place, especially in the first months. Mrs. Taylor presided over the private household, spending much time with their grown children and their grandchildren.

In July that year a cholera epidemic was plaguing parts of the country. Taylor proclaimed a national day or fasting and prayer. On August 9, he began a tour that included many stops in Maryland, Pennsylvania, and New York. He was buoyed by large, enthusiastic crowds. In Meadville, Pennsylvania, he fell ill. After three days of rest he was well enough to visit Niagara Falls, New York; however, his doctors urged him to cancel further appearances and he returned to Washington after first visiting Albany and New York City.

In February 1850 he accepted an invitation to dedicate the cornerstone of a new monument to George Washington in Richmond. A large crowd greeted him. In Fredericksburg, on the way back to Washington, he remarked, "As to the Constitution and the Union, I have taken an oath to support the one and I cannot do so without preserving the other, unless I commit perjury, which I certainly don't intend to do. We must cherish the Constitution to the last . . . we must fall back on Washington's farewell advice and . . . preserve the Union at all hazards." Thick-skinned, Taylor was not surprised when supporters and adversaries spoke out sharply for or against this declaration, for it dealt with the divisive issue of slavery.

AN UNUSUAL OWNER OF SLAVES

When Zachary was a young man, his father gave him a small plantation. He sold it for a profit. Despite his modest soldier's salary, over the years he bought plantations, usually with slaves on them. When he died, his estate was worth $140,000 (approximately $2 million today).

He was always a slave owner, with 145 of them by 1848, the year he was elected. Unlike the stereotype of the cruel or indifferent slave owner, he considered them "servants." He made sure his plantation managers fed and housed them well. He never sold a slave.

An English visitor to a plantation that Taylor owned by the Mississippi River in Louisiana wrote enthusiastically about Taylor's arrival one time by boat. She said that his slaves all gathered to greet him and shake his hand. The informality of the occasion and the slaves' lack of servility surprised her.

Typically, Taylor made special provision for his slaves at Christmastime. One note from him instructed his plantation overseer to "distribute . . . five hundred dollars . . . among the servants . . . in such a way as you think they deserve by their good conduct."

He never denounced antislavery champions, and he did not bristle when they criticized the practice. He neither defended it nor sought its expansion.

In spring 1850, he authorized his son Richard, who had been

managing his Louisiana plantation, to replace it with another one, less susceptible to flooding. Richard found one with "a number of servants (slaves)" for $115,000. President Taylor, always the astute business-man, calculated that the new plantation could turn an annual profit of $20,000.

UNTIMELY DEATH

On July 4, 1850, President Taylor attended a groundbreaking ceremony for the Washington Monument. The heat in the city was stifling. After-ward, back at the White House, he drank a pitcher of iced milk and ate a bowl of cherries and raw vegetables. He became ill and his doctors administered ipecac, calomel, opium, and quinine. They also bled him, still a common practice at the time. Two days later he felt well enough to sign a treaty and write one letter. However, he declined in health and died on July 9.

Springfield, the Taylor home in Louisville, Kentucky, is privately owned and not open for tours.

It has been designated a National Historic Landmark. The large original acreage was subdivided in the 1850s and the two-and-a-half-story, L-shaped Georgia Colonial house sits on the remaining three-quarters of an acre.

Nearby and originally part of the property is the Zachary Taylor National Cemetery, 4701 Brownsboro Road, Louisville. Taylor and his wife, Margaret, are entombed in the mausoleum on the site. In 1883, the commonwealth of Kentucky erected a fifty-foot granite monument and the federal government built a memorial building in 1926. The cemetery is open to the public from sunrise to sunset, year-round.

Chapter Thirteen

MILLARD FILLMORE

THE 13TH PRESIDENT

July 9, 1850—March 4, 1853

Zachary Taylor came from an aristocratic family but didn't look it. His successor, Millard Fillmore, came from a very poor one but looked every inch the aristocrat.

Fillmore's childhood was a hard one. His parents, Nathaniel and Phoebe, moved from Vermont the year before Millard was born (in a log cabin in 1800), buying a small farm in Locke, Cayuga County, New York. The poor soil was unproductive and Nathaniel lost it, moving the family to Sempronius, where he became a tenant farmer.

Millard had little early schooling, but was strong and became used to hard labor on the farm.

Most of all he wanted to escape the fate of his father. When he was fourteen, he was apprenticed first to a wool carder, then to a textile mill. His reading skill was rudimentary, but he was determined to improve it. He carried a dictionary with him to expand his vocabulary and read constantly from books in the local library. During winter when the mill was closed, Fillmore enrolled in the Academy of Good Hope. There he met Abigail Powers, a minister's daughter, who was smitten with him and encouraged him.

When he was eighteen he began to teach in a country school during winter. Walking forty miles a day was not unusual for him. Nathaniel had moved again, becoming the tenant of a Quaker judge, Walter Wood. Nathaniel had arranged with the judge to take young Millard into his office as a student and to study law. Later Millard moved to East Aurora, near Buffalo, to teach school and practice law. In 1822 he became a clerk in a Buffalo law office. He was admitted to the bar the next year. He and Abigail were married in 1826.

Tall and handsome, Fillmore always dressed in fine clothes and represented his clients in court with strong arguments. In time, the Fillmores became leading citizens of Buffalo, supporting many "good works," such as the YMCA and the University of Buffalo, which he cofounded. He was also a founder of the Buffalo Historical Society and the Buffalo General Hospital.

INTO POLITICS

Fillmore was elected to the New York State Assembly for a two-year term in 1828, then elected to the U.S. House of Representatives, where he served from 1832 to 1834, and again from 1836 to 1842.

In 1848 he became Zachary Taylor's running mate.

In office, Fillmore and Taylor disagreed on slavery. To the surprise of some, Taylor wanted the new states to be free ones, while Vice President Fillmore, the northerner, wanted to appease the South and supported the extension of slavery into the new states.

On the sudden death of Taylor in 1850, Fillmore became president. He requested and received the resignation of every cabinet member. His own appointees, with one exception, favored the Compromise of 1850, as he did. The compromise called for the admission of California as a free state and left unresolved the question of slavery in the newly organized territories of New Mexico and Utah, to be decided by "popular sovereignty."

In 1850, Fillmore appointed Brigham Young as governor of the new territory of Utah. In gratitude, Young named the capital "Fillmore" and its county "Millard."

In 1852, Fillmore and his secretary of state, Daniel Webster, were at odds and would not combine forces to create a ticket, which might have won. Instead the nomination went to General Winfield Scott, another Mexican War hero. Scott lost to Franklin Pierce.

At White House social occasions, the Fillmores' vivacious daughter Mary Abigail usually substituted for her mother, who was ill much of the time. While the Fillmores always had a home in Buffalo, they did not have a country "getaway" for vacations or sojourns. They returned to Buffalo during his term, as time permitted. After Pierce's inauguration, they planned to settle into retirement in Buffalo; however, wife Abigail's health—long tenuous—failed and she died on March 30 that year, 1853. Daughter Mary Abigail, twenty-two, died of cholera the following year.

In 1855, Fillmore toured Europe. The itch for public office was still with him in 1856 when he ran for the presidency as a third-party presidential candidate and lost.

In 1858 he married Caroline McIntosh, a rich widow. They bought a large home in Buffalo (a residence soon widely known as the Fillmore Mansion) and for a time entertained extensively. They entertained President Lincoln when he visited Buffalo in 1861. In 1865, Fillmore was chairman of the citizens' committee that met the Lincoln funeral train as it came through the city.

On February 13, 1874, Fillmore suffered a stroke. He died on March 8 and is buried in Forest Lawn Cemetery, Buffalo. There is a statue of Fillmore outside Buffalo City Hall.

The Fillmore Mansion in Buffalo was sold and converted to a hotel in 1881. It, in turn, was razed in 1919 for a new Statler hotel. The small house in East Aurora that he built in 1826 for his first bride and himself still stands. They lived there until 1830.

Chapter Fourteen

FRANKLIN PIERCE

I 4TH PRESIDENT

March 4, 1853—March 4, 1857

*B*orn in a log cabin near Hillsborough, New Hampshire (a site now covered, ironically, by the Franklin Pierce reservoir), Franklin Pierce studied law after graduating from Bowdoin College in Maine (where Nathaniel Hawthorne became a good friend). He later volunteered for service in the Mexican War and rose to the rank of brigadier general, in command of a brigade of reinforcements for the march on Mexico City.

Pierce was elected to the state House of Representatives in 1828 and served as Speaker when his father was governor. In 1832 he was elected to the U.S. House of Representatives. At age twenty-seven, he was its youngest member up to that time. He advanced to the U.S. Senate in 1837. His wife, Jane Appleton Pierce, disliked Washington, D.C., and her husband's involvement in politics so much that she persuaded him to resign his Senate seat in 1842 and return to New Hampshire. Franklin Pierce resumed his successful career in law there, but found he could not stay away from politics. By the time the 1852 Democratic convention was held in Baltimore in June, Pierce had not held office for a decade. Nonetheless he was nominated as the presidential candidate. He defeated Whig candidate General Winfield Scott in November.

AN OMEN

Two months before his inauguration in 1853, Pierce, his wife, and their eleven-year-old son, Benjamin, after attending a funeral in Boston, left for Andover and then Concord. On the Concord-bound train husband and wife sat together in front with their son behind them. Barely a mile out of the station, the back wheels of the one passenger car gave way. The car lurched sharply, tore away from the locomotive, and plunged down an embankment. It came to rest on its roof. Pierce and his wife were uninjured, but young Benny was crushed in the wreckage.

The horror of the accident gave Pierce feelings of guilt that hung over his four presidential years.

Worse, the shy, tubercular, and deeply religious Jane saw the tragedy as an example of God's wrath brought on by Franklin's political career. There was no joy during his White House years. Franklin hired a couple to look after Jane. She was widely known as "the shadow of the White House."

Pierce's campaign had been fought on support for the Compromise of 1850, that delicately created a group of bills that had kept the great regional differences over slavery from boiling over.

He saw the compromise as reflecting the mood of the entire country, so he assembled a cabinet that included both northern Free Soilers and southern states' rights advocates. He included all regions and a number of friends. That his cabinet stuck with him for all four years is remarkable considering that they were a group with deep divisions.

In July 1853, Pierce decided that a patriotic tour to the nation's first world's fair—at New York's Crystal Palace—would be a good way to unite the divided elements of his party and the government. He and his party, which included Secretary of War Jefferson Davis, made stops in Baltimore, Wilmington, Philadelphia, and New Jersey, with speeches at each. In one, Davis described Pierce as a "glorious patriot" who knew "no North, no South, no East, no West."

In Philadelphia, Davis introduced a daring idea: a network of railroads to connect all parts of the nation. Although the trip was popular, Pierce showed signs of a fondness for drinking. This problem was to grow over time.

UNRAVELING THE COMPROMISE

While Pierce and his cabinet talked over such ideas as splitting Cuba from Spain and opening trade with Japan, it was the slavery issue that most occupied the president.

Pierce harbored the hope that northerners could be persuaded to allow some expansion of slavery. At the same time he hoped that the South, with political power disproportionate to its population, might give up some of that power. A man of limited political skills, he was overwhelmed by the job as the North and the South became more polarized and the old political system cracked at the seams.

At their convention in 1856, the Democrats turned away from Pierce and nominated James Buchanan for president.

ONE RETREAT

After he lost the nomination, Pierce traveled to New Hampshire (without his wife) in October 1856 to locate a place to live when his term expired the next March. The only vacation retreat they took during his four years in the White House was in August 1855, when he and Jane spent several days at Old Point Comfort, Warm Springs, and White Sulphur Springs, West Virginia. After he left the presidency, Pierce and Jane traveled to Europe once, returning in 1859.

During the Civil War, in 1863, Union troops captured Jefferson Davis's Fleetwood Plantation after the Battle of Vicksburg. They found correspondence between Davis and Pierce, who were close friends as well as colleagues. In one 1860 letter, Pierce referred to "the madness of northern abolitionism." After this, author Harriet Beecher Stowe referred to Pierce as an "archtraitor." The consensus of historians is that Pierce was a well-meaning man in well over his head as president. For the most part, his efforts to ease the growing passions over the slavery issue inflamed them instead.

Jane Pierce died on December 2, 1863. After that, Pierce built a cottage at Little Boar's Head, on the New Hampshire coast. The location brought fond memories of fall visits he and Jane had taken at a hotel at nearby Rye Beach both before and after his presidency.

Franklin Pierce died of cirrhosis in Concord, New Hampshire, on October 8, 1869.

The Pierce Manse, in Concord, was owned by Franklin and Jane Pierce from 1842 to 1848. In 1971, the Manse was scheduled for demolition as part of an urban renewal project. Concerned citizens banded together as the "Pierce Brigade" to raise funds to buy the house and move it to its present location. This volunteer group now owns and operates the property.

———•·•———

The Pierce Manse is available for tours by appointment, year-round. Call 603-225-4555. For more information visit the website, www.pierce manse.org.

The Franklin Pierce Homestead in Hillsborough was Pierce's boyhood home. It is on a thirteen-acre site. Built in 1804 by Pierce's father, the homestead remained in the family until 1925, when it was purchased by the state of New Hampshire, to be operated by the state park service. For tour information, including times, dates, and fees, call 603-478-3165. Website: www.nhstateparks.com/franklin.html.

Chapter Fifteen

JAMES BUCHANAN

THE 15TH PRESIDENT

March 4, 1857—March 4, 1861

When he learned that Wheatland was for sale in 1848, James Buchanan thought of it as the perfect retreat from the cares accumulated in thirty-four years of public service. Built in 1828, in Federal America's first truly "native" architectural style, Wheatland had ten rooms, set in twenty-two acres of garden and pasture lands. Buchanan paid $6,750 for it.

Buchanan, who had been born in a log cabin near Harrisburg, Pennsylvania, longed for the bucolic life of Lancaster. Wheatland would be a comfortable home for himself and his family. Although he was a lifelong bachelor, in the late 1830s he took in a niece, Harriet Lane, and nephew, James Buchanan Henry, both orphaned, and raised them. To complete the household was Esther "Miss Hetty" Parker, the housekeeper. Some years later, nephew James wrote, "No father could have bestowed a more faithful and judicious care upon his own children than this somewhat stern but devoted bachelor uncle of ours bestowed upon us."

For years, the trajectory of Buchanan's career seemed to be leading to the presidency. After graduating from Dickinson College, he served as a volunteer in the defense of Baltimore in the War of 1812, then was elected to the Pennsylvania House of Representatives, serving from 1814 to 1816. He was elected to the U.S. House in 1821 and served until 1831. President Andrew Jackson then appointed him minister to Russia, where he served until 1833. In December 1834, the state legislature elected him to fill a vacant U.S. Senate seat. He was reelected in 1837 and 1843, resigning in 1845 to accept President James Polk's appointment as secretary of state.

In 1819 Buchanan was engaged to marry Anne Caroline Coleman, daughter of a wealthy family. At the time, Buchanan's political activities and law practice often kept him away from her, leading to rumors that he was carrying on with other women. Shortly after he visited a friend's wife and Anne found out about it, she called off the engagement. She died a few weeks later. Buchanan was devastated. When friends urged him to seek another mate he said, "Marry I could not, for my affections were buried in the grave." His family instincts were later lavished on his niece and nephew.

During each year from 1817 on, Buchanan always set aside two weeks for a vacation at Bedford Springs, Pennsylvania, where he enjoyed the cool mountain air and the mineral waters. A group of friends and neighbors often accompanied him to the sprawling hotel there. He continued this tradition in the 1860s, after he retired from the White House.

Buchanan eventually purchased Wheatland. Visions of occasional peaceful weekends there competed with his duties.

The presidential "bug" first hit Buchanan when he was a U.S. senator. In 1844, 1848, and 1852, he made his interest known to all, but the nomination eluded him.

When Zachary Taylor was elected president in 1848 (succeeded, after his death in 1850, by Millard Fillmore), Buchanan "retired" to Wheatland, enjoying the warmth of his family and good relations with his neighbors, with whom he was popular.

Buchanan was nominated for president in 1856 and won the election. He saw the major issues as preservation of the Union, slavery, and abolitionism. He believed that conciliation between the increasingly intransigent forces in the North and South was possible.

On election day, after he learned he had carried Pennsylvania and Indiana, he made his only speech of the campaign, a flowery piece of oratory ending with the statement that "all we of the North have to do is to permit our Southern neighbors to manage their own domestic affairs, as they permit us to manage ours."

IN THE WHITE HOUSE

This theme carried through into his presidency. He believed that the Constitution provided the framework for compromise between the slave states and the forces of abolition.

Two days after Buchanan's inauguration, the Supreme Court delivered its decision in the Dred Scott case, ruling that Congress had no constitutional power to exclude slavery from the territories. Southerners were pleased, the abolitionists inflamed. Abraham Lincoln saw it as a conspiracy to attempt to make slavery legal nationally.

During his White House years, Buchanan asked his niece to be First Lady.

He continued to be challenged on the policy front. He was ambivalent about territorial expansion. He believed in Manifest Destiny, and though he did not like slavery, he felt that, under the Constitution, states that wanted to have it should be able to.

When he was inaugurated, Buchanan had promised to serve only one term.

RETREATS NEAR AND FAR

During his term, Buchanan availed himself of an offer from the directors of the Soldiers' Home (originally called the Military Asylum), a cluster of buildings in the northeast corner of the District of Columbia. At an elevation of about five hundred feet, it was a place where breezes played and mitigated the humid heat of summer. The original "cottage" was built by banker George W. Riggs as a summer place for his family. When the society was formed to create a home for indigent veterans, four other buildings were added. Buchanan stayed at the one called Quarters 1 and found it much to his liking. In 1858 he wrote to niece Harriet that he "slept much better at the Asylum than at the White House."

It is almost certainly Buchanan who recommended the Soldiers' Home as an in-city retreat to Abraham Lincoln, probably sometime between Lincoln's 1860 election and his inauguration the following March.

During his White House years, Buchanan and his niece returned for several short retreats to Wheatland. There, away from the daily pressures of office, he welcomed visits from friends and neighbors. He also continued his tradition of taking a two-week summer vacation at Bedford Springs, thus avoiding the cloying humidity of the capital city.

Wheatland was very much on Buchanan's mind in his final presidential year, when he wrote to William Carpenter on September 13, "If my successor is as happy on entering this house [the White House] as I am, in leaving it and returning home, he will be the happiest man in the country." He later explained, "I was then thinking of the comforts and tranquility of home, as contrasted with the troubles, perplexities and difficulties inseparable from the Presidential office."

He had eight years of a largely tranquil and happy retirement before his death at age seventy-seven. During that time he wrote the first presidential memoir to be published, Mr. Buchanan's *Administration on the Eve of the Rebellion* (1866).

Wheatland is on the National Register of Historic Places and is owned and maintained by LancasterHistory.org, the result of a 2009 merger of the James Buchanan Foundation and the Lancaster County Historical Society. The property comprises ten of the original twenty-two acres. In addition to the main house there is a carriage house that serves as a visitor center.

Wheatland is open to the public for tours April–October, Mondays through Saturdays; November–December, Fridays and Saturdays; January–March, by appointment. Call 717-392-8721 or visit the website, www.lancasterhistory.org, for specific times and admission charges.

The home is located at 230 North President Avenue, Lancaster, PA 17603.

— • —

Chapter Sixteen

ABRAHAM LINCOLN

THE 16TH PRESIDENT

March 4, 1861 — April 15, 1865

*W*alt Whitman wrote in August 1863, "I SEE the President almost every day, as I happen to live where he passes to or from his lodgings out of town. He never sleeps at the White House during the hot season, but has quarters at a healthy location about three miles north of the city, the Soldiers' Home. . . . I saw him this morning about 8 1/2 coming in to business. . . . He always has a company of twenty-five or thirty cavalry. . . . Mr. Lincoln on the saddle rides a good-sized, easy-going gray horse, is dress'd in plain black, wears a stiff black hat, and looks about as ordinary attire, &c., as the commonest man."

Originally called the Military Asylum, the Soldiers' Home had become a haven for disabled and indigent veterans of the nation's earlier wars. Most of them were immigrants without families. The Home provided them with a restful place to live in what was then open countryside but still within the boundaries of the District of Columbia. One of its great advantages was that it was several hundred feet above the city of Washington and enjoyed cooling breezes in the summer. It also had a guest "cottage," which became a place of peace and quiet for President Lincoln in three of the tumultuous Civil War years.

The "cottage" had been built in 1842 as a summer home for banker George W. Riggs. Its architecture could be described as English Gothic Revival. It had a stucco-covered brick facade and a spacious porch. Inside were thirty-one rooms.

Late that decade, in the wake of the Mexican War, the federal government purchased the land to create a sanctuary for servicemen. It built two other buildings, Quarters 1 and Quarters 2, for guests, and Scott Hall, the main building for the veterans. Another, Corlisle Cottage, was built to accommodate officers and others working at the Home.

The military commissioners in charge of the project judiciously concluded that if they invited presidents and other senior government officials to enjoy summer retreats in the cottages, continued funding by Congress would follow. They were correct.

THE LINCOLNS' FIRST VISITS

Shortly after Lincoln's inauguration on March 4, 1861, he and First Lady Mary Todd Lincoln made separate visits to the Soldiers' Home with an eye toward living there during the summer.

North-South tensions were very high by then. The month before his inauguration, seven cotton-growing states announced they had seceded from the United States to form the Confederate States of America. Lincoln considered this illegal and a rebellion. Lincoln, in his inaugural address, said that the Constitution had made "a more perfect union." He said the secession was void and appealed for a restoration of the bonds of union. Saving the Union was clearly his priority. He said he did not intend to invade any southern state, nor to end slavery; however, he would use force in order to maintain possession of federal property. In April he announced a naval blockade of secessionist states' ports.

All this soon came true. On April 12, when Confederate forces fired on Fort Sumter, in the harbor of Charleston, South Carolina, the tension turned to war. Lincoln soon decided that he could not leave the White House that summer, even for overnight sojourns on a hilltop just three miles away.

THE SUMMER SOJOURN IN 1862

In February 1862, twelve-year-old Willie Lincoln died (probably of typhoid fever). The loss was hard on both parents, but especially on Mary, who had lost another son, Eddie. Despite the president's heavy workload, he agreed that they would move to the Soldiers' Home that June, and they did, without ceremony, during the second week of the month. There were no official records of their move or who accompanied them, although it must have been only a few servants, for there was no military guard present for the move.

On arriving, Lincoln decided to take the former Riggs home, then occupied by the Soldiers' Home's commandant. He could not escape the fortunes of war even there, for just opposite the residence was a recently opened military cemetery with dead from the Union's July 1861 defeat at Manassas, Virginia (the First Battle of Bull Run).

Nevertheless, the place had a relaxing effect on the president. He enjoyed evenings with his wife and their lively young son, Tad. "Aunt Mary," an escaped slave hired by the Lincolns to be their cook at the Soldiers' Home, became like one of the family. When the president went out for walks in the evening, he had relaxed conversations with the soldiers on guard detail at the residence. Son Robert, a student at Harvard, joined them when the semester ended.

Privacy was less than complete. It soon became widely known that the Lincolns were summering there. Both invited and uninvited guests showed up, some to plead for this or that cause. The total number of the guests of the three summers they spent there was not recorded, but it probably numbered in the hundreds.

That first summer, the family stayed at the Soldiers' Home from mid-June until early November—nearly five months. Even there, Lincoln was an early riser—up, dressed, breakfasted, and riding into the city before 8 a.m.

During the early days of that first summer's retreat, Lincoln often rode to the White House without an escort, military or civilian. In time, the concerns of colleagues and friends prevailed and the army ordered a Pennsylvania infantry unit to guard the residence and a New York cavalry unit came to accompany the president to and from the

White House. This was no ceremonial escort. They were trained and ready to repulse any attack on their leader. Once the Lincolns settled in, the First Lady began to visit wounded soldiers in hospitals, usually without any notice to the press. Hers was a mission of charity, unlike her misplaced priority of spending on White House renovations in wartime.

RELAXED EVENINGS

Lincoln was a good storyteller, especially if only a few friends were on hand. He also liked to read aloud from his favorite poets. John Hay, his secretary (and a future secretary of state), said that Lincoln would read such dramas as *Richard III* "for hours with a single secretary for [an] audience." He also enjoyed reading from humorists of the day, and is said to have been a talented mimic.

By 1864, for their third summer at the cottage, Mrs. Lincoln set out to spruce up the decor. She had wallpaper added in some rooms and grass matting laid on the floors of what most described as lightly furnished rooms. Underscoring the relaxed atmosphere at the cottage, in contrast to the White House, when Lincoln returned home at the end of the day he removed his boots and went about in carpet slippers. On hot days he carried a fan with him to stir the air.

AT WORK

As relaxing as the days at the Soldiers' Home could be, the time there was not spent only on reading, oral recitations, and conversation with family and friends. Because it took Lincoln away from the steady, rhythmic ebb and flow of White House work—meetings scheduled and unscheduled, dispatches from the war front, interviews, pleadings by various people, dealing with Congress—it provided him with the quietude in which to do some of his most important thinking and writing. For example, he thought through and then wrote the Emancipation Proclamation there in the summer of 1862. His first vice president, Hannibal Hamlin, later recalled that on June 18, the president asked him to come to the cottage for the evening. After dinner they went upstairs to Lincoln's library, where the president showed Hamlin a draft of the proclamation. This would be a signal that the abolition of slavery would be a war goal equal to preservation of the Union.

September 17, 1862, at Antietam, Maryland, proved to be the bloodiest day in the war. The timing was serendipitous for Lincoln to announce the Emancipation Proclamation. He released the Second Draft of the document (which he had shared in confidence with the cabinet in July) on September 22.

Edwin Stanton, who once said he thought Lincoln was incompetent, had become the president's secretary of war and soon began spending his summers at a Soldiers' Home cottage. Their many times together on the hilltop led to Stanton becoming Lincoln's closest cabinet confidant.

MRS. LINCOLN'S MEDIUM

During those days, Lincoln's spirituality seemed to be deepening and he made increasing references to the divinity. Meanwhile, Mary was turning to spiritualism and apparently had a séance at the cottage with a bogus English aristocrat, Charles J. Colchester. He purported to communicate with the dead through tapping tables. Mary, longing for her dead son Willie, hoped this would work. Lincoln suspected a fraud and asked the head of the Smithsonian Institution to check out the man. He did and unmasked him, but not before Colchester attempted to blackmail the First Lady.

THE COMPASSIONATE PRESIDENT

That Lincoln cared deeply for the welfare of the men under arms was underscored by an article that appeared in the *New York Tribune* on July 8, 1862: "The President . . . while on his way to his Summer Residence at Soldiers' Home, meeting a train of ambulances conveying wounded men from the late battles to hospitals . . . rode beside them for a considerable distance, conversing freely with the men and seeming anxious to secure all the information possible with regard to the real condition of affairs on the Peninsula and the feeling among the troops from those who had borne the brunt of the fight."

AUTUMN ARRIVES

By October cooler weather arrived. Young Tad was having the time of his life, riding his pony and visiting with the soldiers on guard. They made him a "third lieutenant." Some days he even joined them in their mess line.

But Mary was restless for a change of scene and on October 20 left for a shopping trip in New York City, taking Tad with her. She was away for a month, leaving the president alone except for the household staff.

Lincoln often visited with the infantry and cavalry soldiers camped on the grounds. Captains David Derickson and Henry Krotzer became favorite dinner companions when Lincoln was by himself at the cottage.

This was a time when problems with the military were vexing Lincoln. After much contemplation and consultation with others, he relieved General George B. McClellan of his command and put General Ambrose Burnside over the Army of the Potomac.

Lincoln wired his wife that day in New York, asking whether he should stay at the Soldiers' Home, now that the weather was getting chilly, or move back to the White House. She replied that he should move and, over the next several days, he and the staff made the move—after nearly five months living at the cottage.

A FATEFUL SUMMER—1863

On June 22, as the Lincolns prepared to go by carriage to the Soldiers' Home for the summer, Confederate General Robert E. Lee's army was again crossing the Potomac and heading north to points unknown, although capital city scuttlebutt imagined a direct attack on the seat of government.

This time the Lincolns were accompanied by a large contingent of infantry and cavalry as they headed toward their hilltop cottage. This time the infantry's camp was relocated down the hill, for the cemetery had been enlarged and now had the remains of some eight thousand soldiers interred in it. Lee's army of seventy-five thousand troops was moving north with occasional skirmishes with federal forces in

Maryland and Pennsylvania. From their hilltop retreat the Lincolns could hear artillery exchanges in the far distance.

Lincoln was worried about the state of the leadership of the federal forces. He then appointed General George Meade as commander of the Army of the Potomac as that army moved toward Pennsylvania. Visitors to the cottage noticed that Lincoln appeared exhausted from the weight of the decisions he had to make. He is described as being disheveled, wearing slippers and without a tie at meetings at the cottage.

The Battle of Gettysburg took place July 1–3, 1863, and was the turning point in the war. With nearly a third of his army lost, Lee was forced to withdraw. Vicksburg, Mississippi, the last Confederate stronghold on the Mississippi River, fell the next day, July 4.

On July 2, Mary Lincoln was injured in a freak carriage accident. Lincoln was worried about her condition, but was also urging General Meade to pursue and destroy Lee's army. Meade's idea was simply to stop once he had forced Lee's troops south across the Potomac.

The First Lady's condition worsened. In that era before antibiotics, the infection she suffered as the result of her accident could be fatal. The family nurse kept an around-the-clock vigil. The president wired son Robert to return from Harvard. It look him several days to make the journey from Cambridge, Massachusetts.

Gradually, Mary's health improved, but she wanted to get away from Washington. On July 20 she left for New York and Vermont, taking Tad with her. She did not return to the cottage until late September. On July 29, Robert also left the cottage and joined his mother and Tad.

By August even the Soldiers' Home was not escaping the heat.

On August 9, President Lincoln wrote to General Ulysses S. Grant to recommend that he increase the number of black troops in his command.

As August wore on, Lincoln talked of going to New England to join his family, or to take a few days at Cape May, New Jersey, with a good friend, but nothing came of these ideas. He felt he could not leave the capital.

Mary and Tad returned to the cottage in late September. He was glad to have the family back.

The family stayed at the Soldiers' Home until October 29, then returned to the White House.

FATEFUL AUTUMN DAYS

With some good news coming from the front, the First Couple decided to have a night out on November 9. They went to Ford's Theatre, where, in an irony of history, they saw John Wilkes Booth star in *The Marble Heart*. Lincoln apparently liked the play, for he sent a note backstage offering to meet with the star. The latter sidestepped the request—not surprisingly, as things turned out.

Lincoln began work on the remarks he had been asked to make on November 19 at the dedication of the new Soldiers' National Cemetery at Gettysburg, Pennsylvania.

His remarks ended up only ten sentences long, but they were powerful. On November 18 he arrived in Gettysburg by train. The next morning, riding a chestnut bay horse, he joined the procession to the cemetery. Today, Lincoln's succinct but deeply moving speech is considered to be one of the finest pieces of public speaking in American history.

SUMMER 1864

In late June 1864, Mary Lincoln went to New York to meet Robert upon the completion of his spring semester at Harvard. They went to Washington on July 2 and within a day or two the entire family went to the Soldiers' Home—but not for long. The Confederate forces were not yet through trying to invade the north. That month, General Jubal Early led a rebel force to within one mile of the Soldiers' Home. Several battles elsewhere had not been going well for the Union forces and thus tension in the capital was high.

The capital city was ringed by a series of small forts. But by summer 1864 they were staffed largely by green soldiers, partially disabled ones, and short-term militiamen. Early's forces moved south from Frederick, Maryland. A Confederate cavalry colonel, Bradley T. Johnson, had prepared a plan to kidnap Lincoln when he moved to the Soldiers' Home for the summer. This plan was never put into effect, but Early's troops nevertheless moved closer. They were close to the northwest boundary of the District of Columbia by Sunday night, July 10, when Secretary of War Stanton, in a message, urged the president to get back to the

White House without delay. The family left at once, though the president expressed some irritation at having to go.

The Signal Corps had established a post atop the largest building at the Soldiers' Home. It was in constant communication by flags and lights with the forts around the district's perimeter. This, along with regular army reinforcements now on their way, threw Early's plans off schedule.

The next afternoon, Lincoln decided to visit the defensive forts himself. He was at Fort Stevens when it was attacked. He was thus the first (and still the only) president to come directly under enemy fire.

The signal corpsmen did an effective job of spotting Early's men everywhere they went, eliminating their efforts to make surprise attacks. Although what came to be called the Battle of Seventh Street seemed to be over, fighting continued sporadically the next day. That day, the twelfth, the president took the First Lady and several members of the cabinet back to Fort Stevens. There they first visited the fort's hospital to console wounded soldiers, then mounted the parapet, which was still under occasional fire. By Wednesday the thirteenth, the rebels were gone. On Thursday, the president returned to the Soldiers' Home to find that his infantry guard unit had gone to one of the local forts to help fight off Early's raid.

Lincoln knew the war had a ways to go when, four days later, he issued two public papers. One called for another half-million men to be called up for army service. The other stated that any peace negotiations would have as a precondition the "abandonment of slavery" in the Confederate states.

On July 25, taking Mrs. Lincoln and a few others with him, Lincoln went to Fort Monroe, Virginia, to confer with General Grant. Over the next days Grant reorganized his command structure on several fronts.

Son Robert joined the Lincolns at the cottage after his Harvard graduation ceremonies on July 20. Mary had objected to any effort on his part to serve in the war. Finally, in spring 1865, Lincoln persuaded her to let him serve on General Grant's staff.

Despite shows of affection, there was distance between the first couple. By mid-August, Mary, with Tad in tow, left for Vermont, and she did not return until September 18. Once again the president was alone during a crucial time in the war.

Soon there was Lincoln's reelection campaign to occupy his time. Nevertheless, nervousness had been growing about his safety, what with threats and attempts to harm him. Now his guard detail went with him wherever he went. Late in October, the Lincolns moved back to the White House. Their interrupted retreat had lasted a little less than four months.

On election day, November 8, Lincoln and his running mate, Andrew Johnson of Tennessee, won.

A FINAL VISIT TO THE SOLDIERS' HOME

By the spring of 1865 the war was swiftly moving to a conclusion. Grant took Richmond on April 2. On the ninth, General Lee surrendered to Grant in the McLean home in the hamlet of Appomattox Court House, Virginia. Scattered fighting continued, since it took several days for the news to travel to all outposts, but the war was effectively over.

On the thirteenth, Lincoln, by himself except for a cavalry escort, took a horseback ride to the Soldiers' Home for a customary look around the grounds and perhaps to think of how much the place had meant to him as a retreat and private place to think. He may also have been thinking of happy times ahead at the cottage in the coming summer.

The next evening, the Lincolns returned to Ford's Theatre for a performance of *Our American Cousin*. Between acts, John Wilkes Booth stole his way to Lincoln's box and shot the president. The wounded president was taken to a house across the street. He died the next morning.

Lincoln had saved the Union and ended slavery. Despite his own enlightenment, however, it would be many decades before prejudice itself would decline, let alone disappear from the nation.

———•◦•———

President Lincoln's Cottage at the Soldiers' Home. In 2000, Lincoln's Cottage was designated a national monument. After extensive restoration by the National Trust for Historic Preservation, the cottage opened to the public in 2008. Guided tours, approximately one hour long, are conducted beginning at 11 a.m. daily, with the last tour beginning at 3 p.m. (The site is closed on Thanksgiving, Christmas, and New Year's Day.) Visitors will find that the rooms of the cottage are lightly furnished so that, as the guide describes the events of Lincoln's time there, they can better imagine the scene. Lincoln spent one-quarter of his presidency living at the cottage. There he held important meetings, impromptu meetings, relaxed with his family, and had time for contemplation of the momentous events in which he was involved.

Tickets for tours must be purchased at the Visitors' Center, across the lane from the cottage.

It also contains a museum, which tells the story of the Soldiers' Home and of Washington in Lincoln's time.

The cottage is located on the campus of what is now called the Armed Forces Retirement Home, at the intersection of Rock Creek Church Road N.W. and Upshur Street N.W., Washington, DC 20011.

Entrance is through the Eagle Gate, the only open gate on the premises. Website: www.lincolncottage.org. Operated by the National Trust for Historic Preservation, a private, nonprofit organization.

The Abraham Lincoln Presidential Library and Museum is in Springfield, Illinois. The museum has many interactive exhibits depicting the life of the sixteenth president. It is open from 9 a.m. to 5 p.m. daily. Advance tickets may be purchased online. For information, call 217-782-5764 or 800-610-2094. Location: 212 North Sixth Street, Springfield, IL 62701. In addition to the Lincoln Collection of letters, manuscripts, published materials, and artifacts, the library contains material on all aspects of Illinois history. It is operated by the Illinois Historic Preservation Agency. It is open Monday–Friday, 9 a.m. to 5 p.m. On Saturday and Sunday it is open for exhibit viewing only. Location: 212 North Sixth Street, Springfield, IL 62701. Telephone: 217-558-8844. The website for both the library and museum is www.alplm.org.

Chapter Seventeen

ANDREW JOHNSON

THE 17TH PRESIDENT

April 15, 1865—March 4, 1869

*N*ot quite six weeks after his second presidential inauguration, Abraham Lincoln was fatally shot. His vice president, Andrew Johnson, was sworn in at about 10 a.m. on April 15 at Johnson's lodgings at Kirkwood House.

A strongly pro-Union Democrat from East Tennessee, Johnson, who favored emancipation, was also a white supremacist. This created ambivalence in his policies as president that was very nearly his undoing. Johnson presided over his first cabinet meeting at noon that day. With the war nearly over, his thoughts were focused on the aftermath.

HUMBLE BEGINNINGS

Johnson was born in Raleigh, North Carolina, in 1808. When he was a little over three years old his father died. His mother took in spinning and weaving to support his brother and him.

He had no formal schooling and was apprenticed to a tailor when he was about ten years old. When he was sixteen he and his brother took flight to Greeneville, Tennessee, where he worked at the tailoring trade. He began to teach himself to read and write. His ability to write, along with learning mathematics, was greatly aided by a friendly young woman, Eliza McCardle, seventeen. They married. He was nineteen. They had five children, three boys and two girls. He ultimately owned his own tailor business and prospered. He became an alderman, then mayor, then member of the state legislature, then a member of the U.S. House of Representatives, governor of Tennessee, and finally, a member of the U.S. Senate, which position he held when war broke out.

After Lincoln's death, some six weeks passed before Mrs. Lincoln moved out of the White House. Johnson meanwhile accepted the hospitality of a Boston merchant who offered use of his house in downtown Washington. During that period, Johnson conducted his business in the Treasury Department.

It was not until June that Johnson's family joined him. Because Eliza's health was frail, daughter Martha became the official hostess for most White House events during her father's years there.

The high point of his first few months was a large victory parade on May 22. He received many laudatory press reviews for his beginnings as chief executive. They were not to last.

Gradually, Johnson's views on "reconstruction" of the South became clear. He took the position that those states never left the union; they hadn't seceded but rather had been "in rebellion." If so, this meant their civil governments could be restored and, as soon as they were ready, elections could be held and members of Congress returned to Washington. As to black suffrage, he asserted that the Constitution left voting requirements entirely to the states. While he was popular in the southern states for his restoration policies, his National Union strategy got no real traction.

He created the first "Presidential Reconstruction" with a proclamation on May 9, 1865, authorizing a provisional government in Virginia. Similar proclamations followed for North Carolina, South Carolina, Georgia, Alabama, Mississippi, Florida, and Texas. The Radicals were furious.

He sent a telegram to a Mississippi state convention when it assembled, recommending the voting franchise for some blacks—with restrictions. A prospective voter would have to be able to read the

Constitution, write his name, own real estate valued at not less than $250, and pay taxes on that property. Johnson knew, of course, that few freedmen would qualify.

He then began to issue pardons to former Confederate generals, diplomats, cabinet members, and other prominent people.

By July 1865, he fell ill from exhaustion. Secretary of the Navy Gideon Welles, a staunch ally, took him on a short cruise down the Potomac and around Chesapeake Bay. This improved his health, but August brought two blows. His thirty-one-year-old son, Robert, joined his staff as private secretary but soon began to drink heavily, a problem that became progressively worse. Also in August, Johnson's brother, William, died from an accidental gunshot while hunting in Texas.

His annual message to Congress for 1865 reiterated his position that "all pretended acts of secession were, from the beginning, null and void." With the holidays came a Congressional recess and relaxation for the embattled president.

His grandchildren were there for him to play with, and daughter Martha had taken charge of sprucing up the White House from its poorly maintained wartime days.

A gala reception on New Year's Day of 1866 was the first real social event of the Johnson White House.

Things went from bad to worse between Johnson and Congress. In late March he vetoed a civil rights bill.

PERSONAL TRIPS

On June 1, 1867, Johnson left for Raleigh to attend the unveiling of a monument to his late father, followed by commencement activities at the University of North Carolina.

An active Mason, Johnson left again on June 21, 1867, for Boston to dedicate a new Masonic temple. On the way, he stopped in New York, then New Haven, Connecticut, to address the students at Yale. He arrived back at the White House on the thirtieth, looking robust and in good spirits.

FOURTEENTH AMENDMENT

Moderates put forth the Fourteenth Amendment to the Constitution, which granted citizenship to all persons born in the United States (except Indians on reservations), established penalties for states that prevented freedmen from voting, and put civil rights under the protection of the federal courts. Johnson opposed the amendment but failed to prevent its passage by the Senate and ratification by the states.

Passage of the Fourteenth Amendment to the Constitution was, in part, a result of Johnson's having appointed governments in the South which passed "Black Codes" intended to lock the freedmen into second-class status.

THE "SWING AROUND THE CIRCLE"

In 1866, when Johnson was invited to Chicago to participate in the laying of the cornerstone for a monument to Stephen A. Douglas, he lit on the idea of creating a full-scale campaign trip, a "swing around the circle," with sharp "stump" speeches. This would take the place of a vacation, for it would invigorate him.

The itinerary included Baltimore, Philadelphia, New York, Albany, Niagara Falls, Buffalo (where former president Millard Fillmore greeted him), Cleveland, Chicago, Springfield, Illinois, St. Louis, Indianapolis, Cincinnati, Columbus, and Pittsburgh. Although he was greeted by cheering crowds at some stops, his off-the-cuff speeches rambled, were sometimes blasphemous, and were frequently impolitic. By the time he returned to Washington, on September 15, the campaign trip was widely considered a disaster. In November 1868 General Grant won the election in a landslide.

In the November election, Republicans won in a landslide. Within a year they brought a bill of impeachment against Johnson. Although it failed, the House did vote for impeachment the following spring. Johnson's failure to abide by the Tenure of Office Act, passed in 1867, was the proximate cause. It had been passed to prevent him from firing Secretary of War Edwin Stanton (a Lincoln holdover). On March 5, 1868, the Senate convened as a court of impeachment. It voted on three articles, all of which failed to pass by a single vote.

Johnson had run with Lincoln on a "National Union" ticket in 1864, a fusion of Republican and anti-secession Democrats. With Johnson at loggerheads with the Republicans, Johnson no longer had a political base. The Democrats nominated former New York governor Horatio Seymour; the Republicans, General Ulysses S. Grant. Grant won the election in a landslide.

THE FINAL MONTHS

On Christmas Day 1868, Johnson issued an unconditional amnesty for all Confederates. On December 30, he celebrated his sixtieth birthday with a party for nearly three hundred children, his grandchildren among them. Two days later he greeted a large group of guests—including several former political adversaries—at the White House New Year's Day reception.

On Inauguration Day, the Johnsons proceeded to the home of a friend, where they stayed for two weeks. On March 11, he boarded a special train provided for him by the Common Council of Baltimore, which he addressed and which feted him royally.

A week later, the Johnsons left for Greeneville. There were receptions at stops along the way, as if this were a victory tour. After a bout with kidney stones, he sensed an opportunity get back into politics in Tennessee and embarked on a statewide speaking tour. Soon thereafter, son Robert, in the grip of alcoholism, committed suicide. Following a period of bereavement, he left for Washington to attend the graduation of another son, Andrew, Jr. (nicknamed "Frank"), from Georgetown College.

Over the years Johnson had built a modest fortune and managed it well. He and Eliza had purchased a fine Greek Revival home in 1851. It was occupied by troops during the war but was now restored. He was the owner also of a 350-acre farm a few miles from Greeneville. It had two flour mills and was profitable.

In 1874, the Tennessee legislature elected Johnson to the U.S. Senate. He took the oath of office in the U.S. Capitol on March 5, 1875.

In late June, while at Carter Station in East Tennessee to visit his daughter Mary and her family, he had a stroke after supper and another one two nights later. He died early in the morning of July 31.

———•◦•———

The Andrew Johnson National Historic Site in Greeneville, Tennessee, is operated by the National Park Service. Covering sixteen acres, it includes the Johnson Homestead, a Visitor Complex (including his tailor shop and a museum), and the Andrew Johnson National Cemetery (where he, his wife, one son, and a son-in-law are buried). The grounds are open from 9 a.m. to 5 p.m. every day except Thanksgiving, Christmas, and New Year's Day. One-hour tours of the Homestead are guided. (Sign up at least fifteen minutes in advance at the visitor center.) For directions visit the website, www.nps.gov/anjo, or telephone 423-638-3551. Address: 121 Monument Avenue, Greeneville, TN 37743.

Chapter Eighteen

---◆---

ULYSSES S. GRANT

THE 18TH PRESIDENT

March 4, 1869—March 4, 1877

"Failures have been errors of judgment, not intent." On that sad note, President Ulysses S. Grant wrote to Congress near the end of his second term. He had gone from being the nation's most popular person in 1865 to one deeply tainted by scandals a decade later.

Grant neither sought nor needed the presidency. As commanding general of the United States Army, he brilliantly led the Civil War to a successful conclusion. The grateful citizens of his sometime hometown, Galena, Illinois, gave him a handsome house. In 1866 he was promoted to General of the Army, earned a comfortable salary, and could look forward to a career in the peacetime army.

EARLY DAYS

Born Hiram Ulysses Grant on April 27, 1822, in Point Pleasant, Ohio, he was the eldest of six children born to Jesse Root Grant and his wife, Hannah Simpson Grant. (In practice, "Hiram" was soon dropped.) Jesse was a tanner by trade, who with energy and determination built his business so that it became a leading leather goods supplier for a large area.

When Ulysses was a year and a half old, the family moved to Georgetown, Ohio. After local schooling he was given an appointment to the U.S. Military Academy at West Point, New York, by the local congressman, Thomas L. Hamer. Grant was seventeen. He added the middle initial "S." at that time and many of his classmates called him "Sam" because, to them, U.S. stood for "Uncle Sam."

He was a middling student, but an expert horseman. Although he preferred the Cavalry, he was assigned as a lieutenant to the Quartermaster Corps.

He saw front-line action in the Mexican War. In 1848, Grant and Julia Boggs Dent were married. They had three sons and a daughter. He stayed in the army and was assigned to the West Coast, first to Fort Vancouver in the Oregon Territory. He could not support a family in the wild west on his pay, so Julia stayed home in St. Louis with her parents.

In 1854 he was promoted to captain and assigned to command an infantry company at Fort Humboldt on the northwest coast of California. After a few months he resigned his commission.

The story goes that he had been drinking heavily and the commanding officer threatened him with a court-martial if he did not resign. He did, and his official record remained clear.

FIVE DIFFICULT YEARS

Out of the army at age thirty-two, he and his family experienced real poverty for the next several years. They moved to a small farm near St. Louis owned by his father-in-law, who was a slave owner. Grant had slaves working along with him, but the farm did not prosper. Two years later he built a rustic cabin for Julia, but she did not like it. Its name, "Hardscrabble," summed up its lack of attractiveness. In 1858 he became a bill collector in St. Louis. After two years, he gave it up and went to work for his father's busy tannery in Galena, Illinois.

The firm, Grant & Perkins, purchased hides locally and sold finished leather goods in the immediate area and beyond. He was hired as a clerk but spent much of 1860 and 1861 on the road selling leather. In Galena, Grant rented a small brick house for his family.

BACK TO THE ARMY

At the outbreak of the Civil War in 1861, Grant rejoined the army. He quickly showed his courage and leadership and was given successively larger commands.

He led the Battle of Shiloh near the Tennessee River in April 1862. The Union forces were pushed back, then moved forward. The carnage was great on both sides. But Grant went on to engineer the Union victory at Vicksburg, Mississippi. This gave the Union control of the Mississippi River, effectively cutting the Confederacy in two.

Grant received much praise, but criticism, too. Military rivals passed the word to newspaper correspondents that Grant had been drunk several times. Lincoln, on hearing of this, is said to have commented, "Find out what brand of whiskey he drinks so I can send a barrel of it to each of my generals."

In late 1863, after his major victory at Chattanooga, Grant was promoted to lieutenant general and put in charge of the entire Union army. He met with Lincoln in Washington to plan the final strategy. In April 1865, his forces captured Richmond.

General Robert E. Lee surrendered his forces at Appomattox Court House, Virginia, on April 9.

Lincoln was assassinated five days later. In July, Congress promoted Grant to the new rank of General of the Army.

A HERO'S HOMECOMING

On August 18, 1865, the Grants returned to Galena and a tumultuous homecoming. Julia wrote later of it, "There was a tremendous and enthusiastic outpouring of people to welcome him. . . . After a glorious triumphal ride around the hills and valley, so brilliant with smiles and flowers, we were conducted to a lovely villa exquisitely furnished with everything good taste could desire." The house was a gift of the people of Galena.

This was their home until his election as president in 1868. After that, they visited occasionally, though it was always kept in a state of readiness. During an 1873 visit he said, "Although it is probable I will never live much time among you, but in the future be only a visitor as I am at present, I hope to retain my residence here. I expect to cast my vote here always." The last time he visited the house was in 1880.

THE PRESIDENCY: MIXED RESULTS

Supporters of Grant had good reasons to expect his presidency to be a great success. The Republican Party had, in effect, saved the Union, made African Americans free, and ushered in an era of great industrial expansion. A railroad would now link the two oceans. The nation would now be led by a man who had become a legend in his time: strong, determined, personally modest. He was expected to reform the government and reunite the nation.

There was another aspect of Grant that the public did not see. At forty-seven, he was at that time the youngest man to hold the office. He had endured years of failure and developed a sense of inferiority, which he concealed with silence. He was inexperienced in the field of civic and public affairs. He knew nothing of the give-and-take of politics. He expected unquestioning loyalty from those around him, and he gave it in return. Two former generals, Ben Butler and Orville Babcock, had great influence with him. He succumbed to the flattery of various captains of industry.

Scandals swirled, although Grant's personal honesty saw him through reelection in 1872.

He presided over the second half of Reconstruction and signed the Amnesty Act of 1872, which codified his support for amnesty for former Confederate soldiers. He signed the Naturalization Act of 1870, which allowed African Americans to become full-fledged citizens. In 1869 and 1871 he signed bills promoting black civil rights and prosecuting leaders of the Ku Klux Klan. His support for justice for Native Americans was a reversal of past government policy. He had to deal with the Panic of 1873, which led to a worldwide depression that reached the United States three months later and lasted five years.

SCANDALS

Although his personal honesty was unquestioned, altogether there were eleven scandals during his two terms. The first was Black Friday in 1869, in which speculators tried to corner the gold market, a move that had negative effects on the economy for several years. There were scandals involving alleged bribes of government appointees, fraudulent land grants, tax evasion, and extortion. Grant also became defensive when his subordinates were accused of wrongdoing. Despite the spate of scandals, Grant was successful in his bid for a second term in 1872.

AN OCEANSIDE RETREAT

Despite the heavy stresses of his presidential days, Grant was determined to relax with his family every summer. Congress usually adjourned as soon as heavy humidity settled on Washington. The Grants would then leave for Long Branch on the northern New Jersey shore. They found a house they liked for rent on Ocean Avenue, a long street with many such large "cottages" favored by dignitaries from the 1860s until World War I.

Not long after Mary Todd Lincoln had visited Long Branch in August 1861, it became one of the nation's premier summer vacation destinations. Famous Gilded Age families such as the Goulds, Vanderbilts, and Drexels had elaborate summer residences nearby.

Julia Grant noted in her memoirs that their oceanfront summer home was a boon to her husband, with its "health-giving breezes and its wide and restful piazza." The Grants received many guests at the cottage and attended balls at the nearby West End Hotel. They swam in the ocean just across the avenue from their home. Julia wrote of "glorious drives on that enchanted beach."

Grant was widely known as Long Branch's First Citizen during and after his presidency. Residents and tourists would stroll by the cottage in the hope of catching a glimpse of the president and his family sitting on the veranda.

Grant made a habit of playing poker with friends every Friday evening. His daily routine involved his taking their carriage out for a twice-a-day drive along Ocean Avenue. At the end of his morning drive he would have breakfast and read his mail on the veranda.

If the Grants arrived in time for July Fourth festivities, they would attend, enjoying the display of cannons firing, church bells ringing, and fireworks exploding in the air in the evening.

Their son Jesse wrote in his memoirs that his mother was the most relaxed and happiest when they were at Long Branch and that his father enjoyed his "working vacations" there. He noted that one time his mother, after being teased by the president about spending too much time sitting on the porch, showed her physical fitness by vaulting over the veranda railing.

Most Thursdays during their vacations, the Grants would go by boat to New York City for sightseeing.

They continued to rent their vacation cottage until 1884.

POST-PRESIDENCY

After they left the White House, Ulysses and Julia Grant spent more than two years traveling the world. Large crowds greeted them almost everywhere they visited. Queen Victoria had them to dinner at Windsor Castle. In Germany they dined with Otto von Bismarck. They called on Pope Leo XIII at the Vatican, then toured Russia, the Holy Land, Thailand, Burma, and China. In Japan they were cordially received by the emperor and empress. A tree planted by Grant in Tokyo's Shiba Park still stands.

Grant was not nominated by his party for another term as president in 1880. Instead Grant, the good soldier, campaigned for James Garfield.

The long trip around the world had greatly depleted Grant's savings. He needed to find new income. In 1881, they bought a house in Manhattan and invested nearly all their other assets in an investment banking partnership with Ferdinand Ward at the recommendation of their son Ulysses "Buck" Grant, Jr., who was himself successful on Wall Street. Unfortunately, Ward swindled Grant and other investors and the firm went into bankruptcy in 1884. Ward fled. Grant had to sell his Civil War mementoes to raise $150,000 to repay William Vanderbilt, one of his creditors.

At that time, Grant learned that he had throat cancer. Nearly destitute, he wrote several articles about his Civil War campaigns for the *Century Magazine*. These were well received and brought in enough money to clear the bankruptcy. Mark Twain then offered Grant a contract to publish his memoirs, permitting him to keep 75 percent of the royalties from sales. Congress then restored Grant to General of the Army with full retirement pay.

Friends lent him the use of a cottage at Mount McGregor near Saratoga Springs, New York, where he finished his *Memoirs* just days before he died on July 23, 1885. He was sixty-three. The book sold more than three hundred thousand copies and brought his family more than $450,000. It is widely regarded as one of the finest military memoirs ever written.

As the train carrying Grant's casket passed by West Point, the entire undergraduate battalion, led by Cadet Captain John J. Pershing, stood at present-arms.

The General Grant National Memorial ("Grant's Tomb") is a mausoleum in which both Grant and his wife (who died in 1902) are entombed. It is located in Riverside Park in the Morningside Heights section of Manhattan, New York City. It overlooks the Hudson River. It was built by public subscription and opened in 1897. It fell into disrepair and was restored in the 1930s by the Works Progress Administration. The National Park Service took over management in 1958.

By the 1970s it had been seriously vandalized and defaced with graffiti. Congressional legislation in 1994 called for restoration and perpetual care of the site, which reopened in 1997.

Also restored is the Overlook Pavilion across the street. It is a visitor center, with interpretive exhibits, a bookstore, and restrooms. Free talks by rangers are available there Mondays through Sundays at 11:15 a.m. and 1:15 and 3:15 p.m. The memorial itself is open daily from 9 to 5, but closed on Thanksgiving, Christmas, and New Year's Day.

Ulysses S. Grant Home, Galena, Illinois, was restored to its 1868 appearance in 1955, with much of the Grants' furniture and furnishings. Open April through October, Wednesday through Sunday, 9 a.m.–4:45 p.m.; November through March, 9–4. Closed Monday and Tuesday and the following days: New Year's Day, Martin Luther King Day, Presidents' Day, Veterans' Day, General Election Day, Thanksgiving, and Christmas. Location: Galena State Historic Site, 500 Bouthillier Street, Galena, IL 61036. Tel. 815-777-3310. Email: granthome@granthome .com.

Ulysses S. Grant Memorial, Washington, DC. The world's third-largest equestrian statue sits on a base of Vermont marble 252 feet long and 71 feet wide. The statue of Grant, on his horse Cincinnati, is seventeen feet high. The overall memorial depicts Grant leading his troops in battle. Planning for it began in 1902. It was dedicated on April 27, 1922, the centennial of Grant's birth. Location: Below the west front of the U.S. Capitol, on the National Mall, First Street between Pennsylvania and Maryland Avenues.

Long Branch, New Jersey, sites. The Grants' summer home was demolished in 1963. The Church of the Presidents, where seven presidents worshipped (including Grant on his post-presidency visits), was consecrated in 1879 as St. James Protestant Episcopal Chapel. Designed in Carpenter Gothic style, it was a seasonal church, open for the summer. It was deconsecrated in 1953 and acquired by the Long Branch Historical Museum Association and opened as a museum (it included President Grant's gun cabinet). It was closed in 1999 because of the need for structural repairs. Restoration work has been ongoing ever since, though it is not yet open to the public. Location: 1260 Ocean Avenue, Long Branch, NJ.

Seven Presidents Park is an oceanfront park commemorating the visits to Long Branch and its environs by seven presidents: Grant, Hayes, Garfield, Arthur, Benjamin Harrison, McKinley, and Wilson. It encompasses thirty-eight acres, including a mile of public beach for swimming and surfing. Many species of birds may be seen there. It is maintained by the Monmouth County Park System.

Chapter Nineteen

RUTHERFORD B. HAYES

THE 19TH PRESIDENT

March 4, 1877—March 4, 1881

Both gallant warrior and successful politician, Rutherford Hayes was determined when he became president to achieve reforms in education and civil service, even prisons. However, he made a campaign promise he would later regret. That was the promise to serve only one term.

It was not enough time to accomplish everything he wanted to.

EARLY YEARS

Rutherford's parents moved from Vermont to Ohio in early 1822, but his father died three months before his birth on October 4. His mother was Sophia Birchard Hayes, who along with her younger brother, Sardis Birchard, raised Rutherford, the fourth of the Hayes children (a brother died at age ten in 1825, a sister at age four in 1821, and another sister at age thirty-six in 1856). Nicknamed "Ruddy" as a boy, later "Rud," he was schooled at the Methodist Academy in Norwalk, Ohio; Isaac Webb's School in Middletown, Connecticut; Kenyon College in Gambier, Ohio; and Harvard Law School. In 1850 he moved his law practice to Cincinnati. Criminal defense work became a specialty and he defended a number of escaped slaves who had come from across the river in Kentucky, a slave state.

He courted Lucy Ware Webb and they were married in 1852. She was a graduate of Wesleyan Women's College in Cincinnati. Later she was to become the first First Lady to have graduated from college. They had eight children.

CIVIL WAR SERVICE

At the outbreak of the Civil War, the governor appointed Hayes major in the 23rd Ohio Volunteer Infantry. He saw active service for the duration of the war and rose to become a brevet major general. He was seriously wounded at the Battle of South Mountain in 1862. He was known for his courage and fortitude and had four horses shot out from under him in battle. Altogether he was wounded four times. During his front line service he took a shine to a bright young messenger, William McKinley, who later became a political protégé and, ultimately, president.

While still fighting in the war Hayes was elected to the U.S. House of Representatives, but he did not take his seat until the war ended in April 1865. He was reelected in 1866. In his first term, he and his fellow Republicans worked to pass the Civil Rights Act of 1866 to protect blacks' civil rights, especially in the South. This put them in conflict with President Andrew Johnson.

Hayes resigned his House seat to run for governor in 1867 and won. In 1873, after retiring as governor, the family moved into Spiegel Grove, near Fremont, Ohio. Sardis Birchard died in early 1874. Sardis had begun construction of Spiegel Grove in 1859. It was originally intended as a summer retreat for the entire family and ultimately expanded to thirty-one rooms. Sardis, who had served as a surrogate father to Rutherford, had in mind that it would one day become the permanent home of Rutherford, Lucy, and their children, and it did. Hayes busied himself with business interests, especially after the Panic of 1873 hurt those interests. He borrowed to overcome the problems and hoped to stay away from politics in order to finish paying the debts.

That was not meant to be. In 1875, the Republican state convention nominated him once again for governor. He had barely occupied the governor's office when his name was floated as a presidential nominee in 1876.

In his campaign, Hayes called for "thorough, radical and complete" reform of civil service and spoke out for education reform. He advocated merit as the basis for government appointments, racial equality in all things, and general improvement of individuals through education.

Hayes took the oath of office in the White House on March 3, 1877. He reformed civil service, and in his first year also had to confront a major railroad strike. In the wake of the Panic of 1873, several railroads had cut workers' wages. The strike and riots consumed most of July 1877. It ended with most of the salary cuts in place, but the public blamed the railroads and they began to improve working conditions and refrained from any further cuts.

LEMONADE LUCY

The First Lady was a temperance advocate and was quickly nicknamed in the press as "Lemonade Lucy." Hayes agreed with her proposal to omit alcohol for all White House events.

She was not, however, a prude, and her warmth and charm made her very popular with Washington society. The costs of White House social events came out of Hayes's pocket and he put the money saved by not serving wine into expanded entertainment for their guests.

Lucy, herself an accomplished contralto, brought in many singers and musicians to perform classical and popular music for guests.

TRAVELS AND RETREATS

Hayes liked to travel. He did a good deal of it and politics was usually involved. He made a point of traveling in the summer and fall of Congressional election years to take his case on the issues directly to the people while incumbents and their opponents were debating them.

In summer 1877 he toured New England, calling at every stop for reconciliation between former Civil War rivals and civil rights for black

Americans. He attended his son Birch's graduation from Harvard Law School and was himself given an honorary degree. Not quite two weeks after returning from that tour, Hayes, his family, and several cabinet officers embarked on a nineteen-day tour of Ohio, Kentucky, Tennessee, Georgia, and Virginia. He was well received everywhere.

From December 21 to 24, Hayes and the First Lady traveled to New York, both to relax and to attend to presidential duties. He participated in the opening of the American Museum of Natural History and they were feted at dinners and receptions.

The next April, he and his wife were in Chester, Pennsylvania, for the launching of a new steamship. In June they sailed up the Hudson River for a visit to West Point. On returning to Washington, they sailed down the Potomac to George Washington's Mount Vernon, where they slept in Lafayette's room.

When an Ohio journalist friend chided Hayes for so many travels, he wrote back, "You have no idea of how much they are needed. . . . Every month a man in this place ought to shake off its oppression. Nothing does it better than . . . a journey."

In September 1878, Hayes traveled by train to the Dakota Territory, by way of Pennsylvania, Ohio, Illinois, Wisconsin, and Minnesota. In July and August 1879 the family moved to the Soldiers' Home in Washington, as they had done before. This is the retreat Lincoln made famous during the Civil War. Hayes had a special reason for liking it. He had contracted malaria during the war and was worried about a recurrence. He was anxious to have Washington's swamps drained to prevent infestations of mosquitoes, but this had not yet happened.

On September 8 he left for the Midwest, stopping first at the Cincinnati Industrial Exposition, then a brief rest at Spiegel Grove. Then he was off to give speeches in Indiana, Illinois, Missouri, and Kansas. He knew well the importance of direct communication to the public. In St. Joseph, Missouri, he told his audience, "It is public opinion that rules in this Republic." At every stop he covered favorite themes, "equal civil and political rights . . . on every inch of American soil" and free public education. He returned to Spiegel Grove in time for his fifty-seventh birthday and to vote in the Ohio state election. He and Lucy remained there for two weeks.

The day after Christmas, worried that former president Grant would seek a return to the job in the 1880 election, Hayes met with him at a friend's home in Philadelphia. For two hours he sought to dissuade Grant, but he was not successful.

In January 1880, burdened by the knowledge that many things he had sought would remain undone and by unhappy memories of the election controversy of 1876, Hayes wrote in his diary, "I am now in the last year of my presidency, and look forward to its close as a school boy longs for the coming vacation."

Expansion of the Hayes home at Spiegel Grove was under way, with son Webb supervising. That summer the Hayeses planned what would be the first presidential trip ever to the West Coast.

The Hayeses and the rest of their party left Washington on August 26, riding in a new private car belonging to the Pennsylvania Railroad's superintendent of inspection. Their first stop was Spiegel Grove, where they stayed for a week and celebrated Lucy's forty-ninth birthday. On September 1, they left Spiegel Grove for California. With them were sons Birch and Rud, niece Laura Platt Mitchell, General William Tecumseh Sherman and his daughter, and Secretary of War Alexander Ramsey. The total party was usually nineteen in number, but that fluctuated as people left the tour and others joined it. After an overnight stop in Chicago, they headed for Salt Lake City. At every stop, Hayes's remarks were brief and informal. Sherman and Ramsey would say a few words and Lucy would be introduced. Hayes discussed broad topics, but not politics; however, his very appearance in so many places served to help nominee Garfield and the Republican Party.

The Hayeses thrilled to the spectacular scenery in Utah. They arrived in San Francisco on September 9, the thirtieth anniversary of California's admission to the Union. There were parades, banquets, receptions, and many other occasions for Hayes and General Sherman to speak. In Sacramento on the twenty-second, Hayes predicted that the three Pacific Coast states would one day have a population of 50 million (that is close to the actual 2010 figures). The scenery, climate, and hospitality continued to please all in the party.

From Sacramento they went north to Redding, where the railroad ended. From there it was a stagecoach ride of 275 miles to Roseburg, Oregon, the next railhead. From there they went to Portland, then across the Columbia River to Vancouver, Washington. They visited an army installation, then went by steamboat and railroad east to Walla Walla, where they were entertained by a group of Umatilla braves doing an hour-long war dance, followed by the First U.S. Cavalry Band playing selections by Wagner and Schubert.

Next they cruised on Puget Sound for a week, then went by ocean voyage back to San Francisco, arriving on October 18. They left immediately for Yosemite (not yet a national park), then south to Los Angeles and east to Tucson, Arizona. On the twenty-fifth they reached the eastern end of the Southern Pacific line and boarded horse-drawn army ambulances for the rugged three-day trip to cover 152 miles to meet the Santa Fe Railroad. It took them to Santa Fe, New Mexico, where a fiesta awaited them. The next day, the twenty-ninth, they left for home in Ohio, via Kansas City.

The night before the election, Hayes gave his one political speech of the season to a large group of Republicans who had marched from Fremont out to Spiegel Grove. He gave a rousing endorsement of Garfield, who won.

With his many journeys he was easily the most-traveled U.S. president up to that time.

POST—WHITE HOUSE LIFE

Rutherford and Lucy Hayes left Washington for Spiegel Grove after Garfield's inauguration.

From there Hayes took up his causes that remained unfinished, initially education. His belief was that universal education—both academic and vocational—was the way to heal rifts in society and allow individuals to make the most of their lives. He sought passage of a bill that would have allowed federal aid to education. It did not pass. He worked on other issues as well, particularly helping veterans obtain their pensions and seeking reform of prison conditions. In April 1886 he went to Chicago to address the fifth congress of the Loyal Legion.

In June the following year he traveled to Malone, New York, for the funeral of his vice president, William A. Wheeler, of whom he wrote, "He was one of the few Vice Presidents who were on cordial terms—intimately and sincerely friendly—with the President."

In May 1889 he and Lucy and daughter Fanny had a happy trip to

New York to attend the centennial events marking Washington's inauguration. He made several short speeches, attended a symposium, and enjoyed social events with his wife and daughter.

Six weeks later, on June 21, on returning from a meeting in Columbus of the Ohio State University board of directors (he had become a member), he learned that his beloved Lucy had suffered a stroke that day. She was partially paralyzed, could not speak, and was unconscious much of the time. Within three days, she was gone. After her passing, he wrote that Spiegel Grove was still beautiful, but "the soul had left it."

After weeks of grieving, in late September Hayes took Fanny with him to Mohonk, New York, to attend an annual conference dedicated to improving conditions for Native Americans. In November they attended the National Prison Association conference in Nashville.

Travel seemed to be good grief therapy, for in March 1890 he took many trips to Ohio cities for various reasons. On April 17 he and Fanny left for an eleven-day trip to Bermuda, where they were feted. In May he was in New York to visit with old friends and attend a conference. He continued to work for education and prison reform, believing that a lack of education prevented children from having economic opportunity and that this led to poverty and often bad behavior based upon ignorance. On October 6, 1892, two days after celebrating his seventieth birthday, he and Fanny left for another Mohonk conference and, in New York City, the naval parade marking the quadricentennial of Columbus's first voyage to the Americas. On February 14, 1893, accompanied by son Webb, Hayes suffered a heart attack at the railroad station in Cleveland, where he had attended a conference. He was confined to bed upon his return to Spiegel Grove. He died three days later.

————•◦•————

The Rutherford B. Hayes Presidential Center on the grounds of Spiegel Grove, near Fremont, Ohio, contains the nation's first presidential library, a museum with permanent and temporary exhibits, and the Hayes's thirty-one-room residence.

The Hayes family, led by the late president's second son, Colonel Webb Cook Hayes, and his siblings, planned for the library and museum. The building was funded by the state of Ohio and opened in 1916. There were major additions in 1922 and 1968. The library contains extensive archival material from the president's military and political careers and more than seventy thousand books bearing on his interest in local history, genealogy, and the Gilded Age in which he lived. It also has collections of the papers of other well-known figures from that period.

Hayes's uncle Sardis Birchard purchased the large wooded property in 1846 but did not begin building the house until 1859. He liked the many tall trees and the reflection of them in the pools collected with each rainstorm. Thus he chose the name Spiegel Grove, for spiegel is the German word for "mirror" and the pools of reflected water reminded him of his youth.

The home is furnished as it was when Rutherford and Lucy Hayes lived there full-time.

Spiegel Grove is open Tuesdays through Saturdays, 9 a.m.–5 p.m. It is closed Sundays, Mondays, and federal holidays. Many events are scheduled throughout the year. Write, call, or email for details. Address: Rutherford B. Hayes Presidential Center, Spiegel Grove, Fremont, OH, 43420. Tel. 419-332-2081. Email: admin@rbhayes.org. Website: www .rbhayes.org.

———•◦•———

Chapter Twenty

JAMES A. GARFIELD

THE 20TH PRESIDENT

March 4, 1881 — September 19, 1881

"*L*awnfield," so dubbed by members of the press, was James Garfield's retreat from 1876 until his death in 1881. Some twenty-five miles east of Cleveland in Mentor, Ohio, the 120-acre farm he purchased had a house on it. He immediately planned a new one (actually, he left the detailed planning to his wife, Lucretia). It was finished by the time of his 1880 presidential campaign. More or less neo-Gothic in style, the large and comfortable home had quarters for his elderly mother as well as the Garfields and their five surviving children.

When he was home in Mentor he busied himself overseeing work on buildings, fences, and orchards. A favorite pastime of his was to take a two-mile carriage or horseback ride through the woods to the shores of Lake Erie for a swim.

THE LAST LOG CABIN PRESIDENT

Garfield was born in a log cabin in what is now Moreland Hills, Ohio, to Abram and Eliza Garfield. His father died when James was seventeen months old. He was raised by his mother, sisters, and an uncle.

From 1851 to 1854 he attended the Western Reserve Eclectic Institute (later renamed Hiram College), in the town of Hiram, about thirty-five miles southeast of Cleveland. He went from there to Williams College in Massachusetts, where he earned his bachelor's degree.

For a short time he preached in Poestenkill, in upstate New York (he was also a minister in the Church of Christ), but decided to seek a career in education instead. He applied for a job as principal of the high school in Poestenkill, but didn't get the job. He returned to Hiram College, where he taught classical languages, then served as president from 1857 to 1860. After their marriage, the Garfields bought a cottage on the college green. By 1860 he decided that an academic career was not what he wanted, so he arranged to "read" law privately and was admitted to the Ohio bar. By 1866 he had argued a case before the U.S. Supreme Court.

POLITICS AND THE ARMY

Garfield was elected to the state senate and served in the years 1859–61. With the start of the Civil War he enlisted in the Union Army. He was made a colonel, assigned to the 42nd Ohio Volunteer Infantry. He distinguished himself leading troops in several battles, including Shiloh, where he was made a brigadier general. In spring 1863 he became chief of staff to General William Rosecrans, commander of the Army of the Cumberland.

While still serving in the field in October 1862, he was elected to the 38th U.S. Congress as a Republican. He served Ohio's 19th Congressional District from then until his election as president; however, he stayed on active field duty in the army until December 1863, fourteen months after his election, for the new Congress did not convene until then. He resigned his commission (by then he was a major general) on December 5, 1863, but was ever after called "General Garfield," even when he was president.

Garfield had long liked the countryside along Lake Erie east of Cleveland. One time in 1865 he was visiting Painesville (a few miles from Mentor) and attended a town meeting. A large group of local temperance advocates had been trying to get rid of a brewery, with no success. Garfield, a temperance man himself, said he would do it within an hour. Thereupon, he paid cash for the brewery and promptly converted it into a cider vinegar factory. It did well and four or five years later he sold it at a profit.

TWO HOMES

The Garfields continued to live in the cottage in Hiram until 1875, when they sold it. For about a year their only home in the congressional district was a summer house Garfield had built on Little Mountain, overlooking a swath of farm country on the shore of Lake Erie. This sufficed until they bought the Mentor farm.

Early in his Congressional career, Garfield had purchased a home in downtown Washington, facing Franklin Square, at the southeast corner of I and 13th Streets. The house was described by contemporary Garfield biographer James D. McCabe as "brick, plain and square, built after the manner of its distinguished owner and occupant." The highlight of the house was the 14-by-25-foot library, with a collection of shelves holding "two to three thousand books." McCabe writes, "Books, books, books. It is the one striking feature. They confront one in the hall upon entering, in the parlor and sitting-room and in the dining room—yes and even in the bathroom, where documents and speeches are corded up like firewood."

Garfield's love of books spilled over to the Mentor farm, where the new house had a "snuggery" for him on the second floor, lined with bookshelves, and where an adjacent building was erected to serve him as a library.

While the Garfields returned to Mentor whenever possible, his duties in Washington made Mentor more a retreat, while the downtown Washington house was their principal home (the site is now occupied by a modern twelve-story office building).

In 1880 the Ohio legislature elected Garfield to take a U.S. Senate seat for the term that would begin March 4, 1881. But at the Republican convention in 1880, Garfield was nominated to be the presidential candidate. He returned to Mentor, where he began the nation's first successful "front porch" campaign for the presidency. He won by barely two thousand votes in November.

(He did not, of course, ever take the Senate seat.)

A STRONG START

The Capitol grounds were covered with snow on March 4, 1881, when Garfield was inaugurated.

In his inaugural address he emphasized civil rights and civil service reform.

ASSASSINATION

Little progress on civil service reform had been made by the time President Garfield prepared for a train trip on July 2 to Massachusetts to speak at his alma mater, Williams College. As Garfield entered the Washington, D.C., station at 9:30 a.m., Charles J. Guiteau, a disgruntled (and probably unhinged) office-seeker, shot Garfield. The first bullet grazed his arm; the second lodged in his spine. The doctors could not find the bullet but put their hope in a metal detector devised by Alexander Graham Bell. Unbeknownst at the time, the metal bed frame caused the Bell device to malfunction.

Infection set in and Garfield's condition worsened. On September 6, his doctors moved him to the cooler New Jersey shore. His condition worsened and, on the nineteenth, he died of a heart attack, after already suffering from blood poisoning and pneumonia. His vice president, Chester A. Arthur, was sworn in as the twenty-first president.

Guiteau was tried, found guilty, and hanged on June 30, 1882.

During his short presidency, Garfield never got away to his beloved farm at Mentor, Ohio. After his death, his widow added a Memorial Library wing to their home to house his papers. This became the model for the many presidential libraries that followed.

———•◦•———

The James A. Garfield National Historic Site in Mentor, Ohio, is operated by the National Park Service. From May 1 to October 31 it is open for tours 10 a.m.–5 p.m., Monday through Saturday and Sunday, noon–5 p.m. From November 1 to April 30 it is open Saturday and Sunday, noon–5 p.m. (closed Monday–Friday). It is closed Thanksgiving Day, Christmas Eve, Christmas Day, and New Year's Day. Contact information: 8095 Mentor Avenue, Mentor, OH 44060. Tel. 440-255-8722. Website: www.nps.gov/jaga.

Chapter Twenty-one

CHESTER A. ARTHUR

THE 21ST PRESIDENT

September 20, 1881 — March 4, 1885

Chet Arthur never wanted to be president. He even did nothing to get on James Garfield's ticket as his candidate for vice president in 1880. Being a loyal party man, however, when Garfield asked him, he said "Yes," and was flattered by the offer.

Arthur was born in Vermont in 1829, one of four children of a Baptist minister and his wife. When his father landed a permanent church assignment in the Hudson River Valley, they moved to New York State and that is where Chester grew up.

He became an ardent abolitionist, something acquired from his father. He joined a New York City law firm and soon learned that political connections helped bring business. He joined the new Republican Party, which had been formed to champion the abolition of slavery.

In 1859, he married Ellen "Nell" Lewis Herndon. They set up home at 34 West 21st Street, in a neighborhood that, except for his White House years, would be his for life.

During the Civil War, Arthur was New York State's quartermaster general, responsible for housing and supplying a large number of New York troops. In 1862 he went back to his law practice.

He held frequent social sessions with friends and colleagues at the Fifth Avenue Hotel, a short walk from his home. It became his favored retreat during his New York days and every time he returned to the city during his vice presidency and presidency. He also frequented Delmonico's restaurant, at Fifth Avenue and 26th Street.

On New Year's Day 1880, Nell Arthur died suddenly of pneumonia. Chet was beside himself over the loss of his wife. They had had two children, Chester Alan and Nell.

When Garfield won the Republican nomination for president, he selected Arthur as his running mate. Arthur raised a good deal of money for the campaign.

On July 2, Garfield was shot at the railroad station, about to board a train to New York. The assassin, Charles Guiteau, yelled, "I am a stalwart and Arthur will be president!" Garfield lingered until September 19, then died. Arthur was at home in New York. A state judge administered the oath of office at 2:15 a.m., September 20.

Once in the White House, Arthur surprised most politicians and the press with his first speech to Congress on December 6. It was comprehensive, detailed, and statesmanlike, and called for civil service reform.

He asked his younger sister, Mary McElroy, to serve as proxy First Lady. Mary also took over the care of Arthur's daughter Ellen, ten years old. White House remodeling ensued under the supervision of Louis Comfort Tiffany. A French chef from New York was hired.

Arthur was a city man, so when he wanted to get away from work he entertained frequently at the White House, either with companions over a quiet dinner or with entertainment. The White House soon became a popular social destination.

The new president kept nine-to-five hours and tried to save time for a walk or a carriage ride every day.

In August, he went to Rhode Island for a vacation. He caused a small "scandal" by refusing to attend the high point of the summer social season, a clambake in Newport. What was not known was that he was suffering from Bright's disease, a kidney disorder. His body could not properly dispose of toxins, resulting in headaches, fevers, and fatigue. He stayed in his rooms, suffering in silence. In September he returned to Washington, feeling better enough to get away late in the month for his favorite outdoor pastime, a fishing trip to upstate New York.

TO FLORIDA FOR HIS HEALTH

In April Arthur took a trip to Florida, hoping the sunshine would improve his health. He traveled to Savannah, Georgia, by private railcar, then by scheduled train to Jacksonville. There he developed such a high fever, his physicians thought it might be life-threatening. He recovered, going to New York City to take part in the ceremonies opening the Brooklyn Bridge on May 24, 1883. He stayed for a few days at his home and enjoyed his old retreat, the Fifth Avenue Hotel.

Yellowstone, which had become the first national park in 1872, was Arthur's destination in July. After a train trip to Cheyenne, Wyoming, he and his party took a 350-mile loop trip by horseback to the park. He spent hours trout fishing in Jackson Lake and the Snake River. Logistically the trip was a major undertaking for the army, and though he had an army security escort, word got to the East of a daring plot to kidnap the president. Allegedly, a gang of desperadoes intended to hide him in a cave until they collected half a million dollars in ransom. The desperadoes were never caught and the story may have been only a western tall tale. In any event, it made good copy in eastern newspapers.

After two months in the wild, Arthur returned to Washington relaxed and in apparent good health.

He gave thought to seeking election to a new term in 1884; however, he had lost his base. He did have some admirers. Mark Twain said of him, "I am but one in 55 million; still, in the opinion of this one-fifty-five-millionth of the country's population, it would be hard to better President Arthur's administration."

In his final year in office, Arthur signed a treaty with Nicaragua for a canal linking the oceans. He signed a bill restoring Ulysses Grant's rank and salary before the former president died of cancer in July that year.

Members of the New York legislature sounded him out about being appointed to the U.S. Senate after his presidency. He declined, having decided to retire to his Lexington Avenue home and resume his law practice. His last White House ball was a gala affair at which Arthur welcomed the president-elect.

Once home, his kidney disorder worsened. At first he resumed his evening gatherings at the Fifth Avenue Hotel. Soon, however, his entertaining began to become less frequent. By 1886 he was confined to bed and a liquid diet. He improved by summer and went to Connecticut for several weeks to visit family. Back home in the fall, however, he died of a cerebral hemorrhage on November 18. He was fifty-six.

Chester Arthur had done the unexpected in his nearly four years in the White House: he signed the Civil Service Reform Act, was a voice of reason in the debate over Chinese immigration, and vetoed the pork-laden Rivers and Harbors Bill.

Through it all, he was always the gentleman.

———•·•———

Chester Arthur's favorite "retreat," the Fifth Avenue Hotel, is long gone. The only reminder of him in the neighborhood is a statue at the northeast corner of Madison Square Park.

In the village of Fairfield, Vermont, there is a 1953 replica of the home into which his family moved shortly after his birth. It was the parsonage for the local Baptist congregation. The actual birthplace, demolished long ago, was a hastily erected cabin. The re-created home and a granite monument dedicated in 1903 are part of the President Chester A. Arthur State Historic Site. It is in northwest Vermont, 3.5 miles east of Fairfield Station on the road leading to Route 108. It is open during summer and early fall. For days and hours consult http://www .historicvermont.org/sites/html/arthur.html, telephone 802-828-3051, or email John.Dumville@state.vt.us.

Arthur and his wife are buried in the Rural Cemetery, Albany, New York.

Chapter Twenty-two

GROVER CLEVELAND

THE 22ND AND 24TH PRESIDENT

March 4, 1885—March 4, 1889;
March 4, 1893—March 4, 1897

Grover Cleveland led the group called Bourbon Democrats, which illustrates how times change. These were fiscal conservatives, opposed to high tariffs, inflation, and subsidies. Himself incorruptible, Cleveland fought for political reform and against patronage and political bossism.

Born in Caldwell, New Jersey, in 1837, Cleveland was the son of Richard Cleveland, a Presbyterian minister, and his wife, Ann. Grover was the first of nine children. During his childhood the family moved three times as his father took on different pastorships. In 1841 it was to Fayetteville, New York, where Grover spent much of his childhood. When he was sixteen his father died, whereupon Grover left school to help support the family. He then moved to Buffalo, where he had an uncle who introduced him to well-connected business and professional people. He became a law clerk and later read law at the firm and was admitted to the bar.

He became an assistant district attorney in the county, then narrowly lost an election for district attorney in 1865. In 1870 he was elected sheriff of Erie County. During those years he personally carried out the hangings of two convicted murderers.

In 1881, the Democrats sought him as a candidate for mayor to run against a slate of Republican machine politicians. He picked his own slate, ran on a platform to clean out corruption, and won.

Cleveland's fame spread. In 1882 he became his party's nominee for governor and won by a large margin. Tammany Hall, the Democratic machine in New York City, was no friend of Cleveland. On the other hand, he gained the support of Theodore Roosevelt and his reform Republican friends.

In his first year in office he was visited by the daughter of his deceased friend Oscar Folsom. Frances Folsom was twenty-one and a college student. Smitten with her, Cleveland asked her mother for permission to correspond with Frances.

He was soon touted as the ideal candidate to run for president in 1884 against Republican James Blaine. For years Blaine had been rumored to be corrupt, profiting for using public office to help two railroads. He denied it, but correspondence turned up tending to verify the rumors. At the bottom of one letter, Blaine had written, "Burn this letter." Democrats seized on this by coining the jingle "Blaine, Blaine, James G. Blaine, the continental liar from the state of Maine. 'Burn this letter.'"

Cleveland's image was one of incorruptibility and high moral standards. The latter was dented when Republicans picked up rumors that Cleveland had fathered an illegitimate child during his earlier years of law practice. The Republican taunt was "Ma, Ma, Where's my Pa?" Cleveland blunted the potential scandal by admitting he had paid child support in 1874 to a woman who was involved with him and several other men at the time. He wasn't sure he was the father; however, he was the only bachelor among the men, so took responsibility. He won the election.

Cleveland and Frances Folsom were married in the White House on June 2, 1886. They had three children: two daughters and a son. The first child was born in 1891, the last in 1903.

Cleveland enjoyed several short hunting and fishing trips while he was president. He liked to go up the Potomac River for bass and out to Chesapeake Bay for bluefish. Cleveland so liked the outdoor life that he arranged for vacations in the Adirondacks or the uplands of the South.

THE FIRST CLEVELAND ADMINISTRATION

During his first term, Cleveland signed an act to create the Interstate Commerce Commission. He also used his veto pen liberally. When it came time for the 1888 election, he won the popular vote, but Benjamin Harrison won the electoral vote.

Frances Cleveland is reported to have said to a staff member, as she was preparing to move out of the White House, "Take good care of the furniture . . . for I want to find everything just as it is when we come back." Asked when that might be, she replied, "Four years from today." Thereupon the Clevelands moved to New York City, where he joined a law firm.

Between his first and second presidency, Cleveland purchased a vacation home, Gray Gables, at Buzzards Bay, Massachusetts. The fishing was good and thereafter he and his wife spent their vacations there. During his second term it became, in effect, the Summer White House.

By 1892 he was increasingly mentioned as a potential nominee for president in that year's election. At the Democratic convention in Chicago he was nominated on the first ballot.

The rematch with Benjamin Harrison was low-key, as Mrs. Harrison lay dying and the president barely campaigned. In deference to the situation, Cleveland did the same. He won convincingly in both the popular and electoral votes.

Shortly after Cleveland's second inauguration, a panic struck Wall Street. The proximate cause was the drain on gold reserves caused by the free coinage of silver. After a contentious debate, the Senate repealed the coinage of silver and gold reserves were restored.

In 1894, workers at the Pullman Palace Car Company struck over wages and working hours. Other unions called for "sympathy" strikes. The nation's railroad network was paralyzed. The railroads carried the mail and Cleveland was determined that service would continue. He called in the army to end the strike.

During this period, a group of Honolulu businessmen had succeeded in overthrowing Queen Liliuokalani and installing Sanford B. Dole as the head of a new government. Shortly after his 1893 inauguration, Cleveland withdrew the treaty for the annexation of Hawaii the Harrison administration had drafted. Opposed to annexation, he finally recognized the new Republic of Hawaii and established diplomatic relations with it.

In June 1893, Cleveland was diagnosed with a epithelioma, a nonmalignant tumor inside his mouth. (His taste for cigars may have played a role.) To avoid alarming the public, Cleveland and his medical advisers agreed on surgery aboard the yacht *Oneida*, owned by a friend, Commodore E. C. Benedict. Announcing that he was going on a vacation, Cleveland left on July 1 with his physician, Dr. Joseph Bryant, for New York, where they boarded the yacht. It sailed off Long Island while the delicate operation was performed. The surgeons removed part of his upper left jaw and hard palate. The procedure left his mouth misshapen. On July 17, also aboard the yacht, a second surgery was performed during which an orthodontist fitted him with a prosthesis, which brought his appearance back to normal. He recovered quickly. All of this was done without the press, the cabinet, the vice president, and the public knowing about it. The cover story that was used was that the president had two bad teeth removed during his "vacation." This seemed to satisfy all curiosity.

A SECOND RETIREMENT

On March 4, 1897, the Clevelands left for retirement at Westland Mansion, an estate they had purchased in Princeton, New Jersey. Cleveland became a trustee of Princeton University. Seriously overweight at 280 pounds, Cleveland soon found his health declining. He died from a heart attack in 1908.

———•◦•———

The Grover Cleveland birthplace, boyhood home, Princeton estate, and vacation homes are either no longer extant or unavailable. Grover Cleveland Park, near the town of his birth, Caldwell, New Jersey, was dedicated in his memory in 1916. It is operated by the nonprofit Grover Cleveland Park Conservancy. Designed by the Olmsted brothers (of Central Park fame in New York City), the park covers forty-one wooded acres. It has tennis courts, baseball fields, a playground, and a pool used for wading in summer and ice-skating in winter.

Chapter Twenty-three

BENJAMIN HARRISON

THE 23RD PRESIDENT

March 4, 1889—March 4, 1893

Short, stocky, and serious. That was one description of Benjamin Harrison, son of a congressman-farmer, grandson of a president, and great-grandson of a governor of Virginia and signer of the Declaration of Independence.

Despite the aristocratic pedigree, Benjamin Harrison's immediate family was not rich. His father, John Scott Harrison, owned and worked a farm in Ohio. Most of his income went to the education of his four sons and four daughters. A childhood friend recalled Ben's early days:

"He was a farmer's boy; lived in a little farm house; had to hustle out of bed between 4 and 5 o'clock in the morning, year 'round to feed stock, get ready to drop corn or potatoes or rake hay by the time the sun was up. He knew how to feed the pigs, how to teach a calf to drink milk out of the bucket; could harness a horse in the dark, and do all the things we, as farmer's boys, knew how to do."

Benjamin first attended a one-room schoolhouse near home, then a tutor prepared him for college. He and his brother enrolled at Farmer's College in Cincinnati. After two years, he transferred to Miami University, after which he read law at a Cincinnati firm.

In 1853 he married Caroline Lavinia Scott, daughter of the Farmer's College president.

The next year they moved to Indianapolis, where he was admitted to the bar and joined a local law office. He joined the Republican Party in 1856 and was elected as city attorney.

In 1862 Harrison helped raise a regiment, and when it left for the war, Harrison joined it and was given the rank of colonel. It was renamed the 70th Indiana Infantry. In 1864, the unit joined General Sherman's Atlanta campaign. Harrison was given command of the 1st Brigade of the 1st Division of the Twentieth Corps, which he led in several battles. In March 1865 he was promoted to brigadier general.

He went on to become a U.S. senator, serving from March 1881 to March 1887. In 1888 he won the presidential nomination. The incumbent, Cleveland, won the popular vote, but Harrison carried the Electoral College. Soon after the inauguration, Caroline Harrison's sister died. The Harrisons took in her ninety-two-year-old father and the sister's daughter, Mary Scott Lord Dimmick, a young widow. The Harrisons also had a married son and daughter, each with children.

THE HARRISON ADMINISTRATION

Civil service reform was a burning issue during much of Harrison's term. He favored a merit system and pushed for the Dependent & Disability Pension Act, which passed. It helped disabled Civil War veterans and also used up some of the federal surplus brought about by high tariffs.

He also commissioned the Edison Electric Light Company to install electric lighting in the White House. Once the work was completed, it is said, the president and his wife were afraid to touch the switches for fear they would be electrocuted. As a result, they often went to bed with the lights on.

The Harrisons did not go home to Indianapolis for vacations, for they had rented out their large home there. During his term, six new states were admitted to the Union: North and South Dakota, Montana, Washington, Idaho, and Wyoming. Harrison visited all of them.

In 1890, the president took hunting and fishing trips on Chesapeake Bay and a short cruise to Fortress Monroe, but had no real vacation until July. Earlier that year, department store pioneer John Wanamaker, along with some other rich Philadelphians, had a twenty-room beach "cottage" built on the shore at Cape May, New Jersey, as a gift for the First Lady. Mrs. Harrison was so pleased with its broad porches open to the breezes that Harrison decided she would have it. He also decided to pay for it, lest it be considered a bribe.

The White House was undergoing extensive repairs, so the Harrisons made plans to spend September renting a cottage in the Poconos at Cresson, Pennsylvania. That fall Secretary of State James G. Blaine also invited the Harrisons to visit him at Bar Harbor, Maine, for several days. Senator Henry Cabot Lodge of Massachusetts was also there. In 1891 the Harrisons again vacationed at Cape May. A typical day included four hours attending to official work and the rest of the time relaxing with ocean fishing, carriage rides, and beach strolls.

THE PRESIDENT LOSES HIS WIFE

After what appeared to be a case of flu in spring 1892, Mrs. Harrison showed signs of lung trouble. In early summer he took her to Loon Lake in New York's Adirondack Mountains, where she stayed until early October. By that time she was in the latter stages of tuberculosis. On her return to the White House, she took to her bed and died on October 25.

With the 1892 election coming, Harrison saw the harbingers of what would become the Panic of 1893. Harrison was renominated in a rematch with Cleveland. Because of his wife's illness and death, Harrison did not actively campaign. This time Cleveland won both the popular and electoral vote.

After leaving the White House in March 1893, Harrison visited the World's Columbian Exposition in Chicago in June, then returned to Indianapolis, adding to his home a Regency-style front porch, electricity, and new plumbing. He joined the board of trustees of Purdue University and resumed his law practice, earning a handsome income. In 1894 he taught at Stanford University. In 1899 he attended the First Hague Conference, a treaty convention in the Netherlands.

In 1896 he married his late wife's niece, Mary Dimmick, twenty-five years his junior. Neither his son, Russell, nor his daughter, Mary, approved of the marriage and neither attended the wedding. The couple had one child, Elizabeth. That year he purchased land at Second Lake near Old Forge, New York, in the Adirondacks and had Berkeley Lodge built there for him. He and his new wife spent several summers there. In February 1901, Harrison developed a cold, which turned into pneumonia. Despite medical care, he died at his home on March 13.

———•◦•———

The Benjamin Harrison Presidential Site in Indianapolis contains the brick home he built in 1874 and in which he died in 1901. Although he was a native of Ohio, he spent his adult life in Indiana and is remembered as the only president from the Hoosier State.

The home is open for guided one-hour tours on the hour and the half-hour from Mondays through Saturdays. It is also open on Sundays in June and July. Visitors see ten of its sixteen rooms.

Furnishings are authentic and there are many historic items from the president's career.

There is no indoor waiting space, so visitors are asked to arrive on time for a tour. The address is 1230 North Delaware Street, Indianapolis, IN 46202. For additional information telephone 317-631-1888 or go to the website, http://presidentbenjaminharrison.org.

Chapter Twenty-four

WILLIAM MCKINLEY

THE 25TH PRESIDENT

March 4, 1897—September 14, 1901

In his pre-presidential political career, William McKinley was a high-tariff man, favoring them to protect American industries. By the time he was reelected for a second term he had become an all-out expansionist, presiding over a brief, successful war against Spain from which the United States, in effect, gained an empire. It was he who saw to it that the United States would become a major naval power.

McKinley did not live to see his handiwork completed. He was cut down by an assassin's bullet six months into his second term. It was left for his successor, Theodore Roosevelt, to send the new "Great White Fleet" around the world just to make sure everyone appreciated the fact of America's military might.

BRAVERY IN BATTLE

William McKinley, Jr., was the seventh of nine children of William and Nancy Allison McKinley. He was born in Niles, Ohio, a suburb of Youngstown. His father was engaged in mining and manufacturing iron. Times were often tough for the family. Young William graduated from the Poland Academy, attended Mount Union College and Allegheny College, but did not graduate. Shortly after the Civil War began he enlisted as a private in the 23rd Ohio Infantry. At the battle of Antietam in 1862, McKinley drove a commissary wagon through battle to bring food to the troops. For his bravery, he was promoted to sergeant. Before long he became a first lieutenant. At coming battles he showed bravery under fire and when he was mustered out in June 1864, he held a commission as a major.

As a civilian again, McKinley enrolled in Albany Law School in Albany, New York. He was admitted to the bar in 1867 and settled in Canton, Ohio. A sister lived there. In 1868 he met the beautiful Ida Saxton, one of two daughters of a prosperous Canton banker. They were married in January 1871. The McKinleys had two daughters: Katherine, who lived less than five years, and Ida, who lived only five months. After the death of the second daughter, Ida contracted phlebitis and had convulsions. Specialists diagnosed her as having epilepsy. She had bouts of depression. Her phlebitis crippled her, making walking difficult and painful. For the rest of her life she was considered an invalid who demanded attention, which her husband willingly gave her.

McKinley served in the U.S. House of Representatives from 1877 to 1882 and 1885 to 1891. He was then elected governor of Ohio for two terms. In 1895, while still governor, he mounted a successful drive to raise the money for food and clothing for ten thousand poor people. After his second term, the McKinleys returned to Canton. They had sold the house her father had given them as a wedding present twenty years earlier. They now heard it was available for rent. They took it.

In 1896 McKinley was nominated for president.

McKinley won a solid victory, carrying the urban vote and that of ethnic workers. On March 1, 1897, the McKinleys and a party of fifty left for Washington aboard a luxurious train provided by the Pennsylvania Railroad. He was inaugurated on March 4.

The new administration and the people were in the mood for expansion. On June 16, a treaty was signed with the Republic of Hawaii to annex it and make its people American citizens. Even though McKinley had been an abolitionist, he was reluctant to use his executive power to enforce the Fifteenth Amendment against the discriminatory "Jim Crow" laws that had cropped up in the South. He did, however, appoint thirty African Americans to executive jobs in his administration. When he first became president he kept a horse in the White House stable and rode often.

"REMEMBER THE *MAINE!*"

On February 15, 1898, the battleship USS *Maine* was in Havana Harbor as a show of strength to the Spanish, who owned Cuba. That day the *Maine* exploded and sank. The cause of the disaster was never learned. "Remember the *Maine!*" became an oft-repeated cry. In late April Congress declared war on Spain. The navy was ready, as were many national guard and militia units. Theodore Roosevelt and his "Rough Riders" volunteered. His fame spread when they saw service in the Battle of San Juan Hill in Cuba. Spain's fleet was sunk in battle. The war was over in 118 days. In the peace treaty that followed, the United States acquired the Philippines, Guam, and Puerto Rico, as well as economic control over Cuba.

McKinley won reelection in 1900 by a greater margin than in 1896. This time Theodore Roosevelt was McKinley's running mate.

From 1887 through 1901, the McKinleys spent their vacations at the McKinley Farm. The plain, two-story, white clapboard house of eleven rooms had been purchased with outbuildings and 164 acres of land by Mrs. McKinley's grandfather in 1857. (In later years, Ohio newspapers referred to the McKinleys' farm as "McKinley's Camp David.") Life at the farm was simple and unhurried. McKinley entertained political friends and visiting dignitaries there. The McKinleys spent much of July and August of 1901 at the farm and were there just ten days before their trip to Buffalo to attend the Pan-American Exposition.

ASSASSINATION

On September 5 McKinley gave a speech, and the next morning he visited Niagara Falls. That afternoon he was scheduled to be at the Temple of Music to shake hands with well-wishers. He began the process as a Bach sonata was being performed in the background. There was a large crowd in single file. At 4:07 p.m. Leon Frank Czolgosz stepped forward with a handkerchief over his right hand, concealing a pistol. He fired at the president twice. The first bullet grazed his shoulder, but the second penetrated his stomach, pancreas, and kidney before settling in his back muscles. Later, doctors found the first bullet when it dropped out of McKinley's underwear. They operated but could not extract the second. Conditions in the exposition's first aid station worked against them. There was no electricity inside, and the doctors were reluctant to use candlelight lest it ignite the ether they were using as an anesthetic. X-ray machines were then very new and there was one on the premises, but they worried that it might create adverse side effects for the patient.

The doctors were optimistic that he would recuperate. By the morning of September 12 he felt well enough to sit up and take his first food; however, that afternoon he began to go into shock. He died at 2:15 a.m. on the fourteenth. His last words were, "It is God's way; His will be done, not ours." He was fifty-eight.

Czolgosz, an anarchist, was tried, found guilty, and executed by electric chair on October 29 that year. Ida McKinley returned to Canton to the family home. She sold the farm in 1903. In 1905 she participated in the laying of the cornerstone of the McKinley Memorial in Canton. She died in May 1907.

The William McKinley Library & Museum has a collection of McKinley artifacts and memorabilia, and its library holds documents of the McKinley career. The Stark County Historical Society owns and operates both the Library & Museum and the imposing McKinley Memorial. The library and museum are located at 800 McKinley Monument Drive N.W., Canton, OH 44708–4832. Telephone: 330-455-7043. Email: library@mckinleymuseum.org. Website: www.mckinleymuseum.org.

The McKinley home on North Market Street was demolished in 1935. Its site is marked by a plaque.

The McKinley Farm for several years became the Westward Frontier Museum. The farm was purchased in 1973 by Robert Lozier, a local farm implement dealer. His dream was to create in the farm's ten outbuildings a museum featuring his large collection of early vehicles and tools. It would also feature restoration of the farmhouse to the time of McKinley. It opened in 1976, the nation's bicentennial year. Attendance did not meet expectations, however, and it closed in 1981. Most of the contents were sold at auction.

Chapter Twenty-five

THEODORE ROOSEVELT

THE 26TH PRESIDENT

September 14, 1901 — March 4, 1909

"*I* wonder if you can ever know how I love Sagamore Hill," Theodore Roosevelt said to his wife, Edith, the day before he died. From the day he purchased the land in August 1880 until his death in 1919, this was the place most favored by this well-traveled leader. For eight years it became the Summer White House.

For Theodore (called "Teedie" by the family), his older sister Anna, his younger brother Elliott, and other sister Corinne, their first summer at Oyster Bay on the north shore of Long Island, in 1874, was pure heaven. Theodore was sixteen. They spent the time together with cousins and friends swimming, rowing, hiking, horseback riding, and picnicking. Their base was "Tranquility," the house their father, Theodore, Sr., had rented that year. Their grandfather and two uncles had owned houses in Oyster Bay from the 1860s. Many other happy summers were to follow.

By 1880, young Theodore bought land near Tranquility on which to build a house. He persuaded his fiancée, Alice Hathaway Lee, that Oyster Bay was the perfect place to raise a family. The next year they were married. He ordered plans for a large house with a working farm on the property. The first structure to be built was the stable with a lodge and office for the farm manager. It was completed in 1883. The next year, tragedy struck. Shortly after their daughter (also named Alice) was born, his wife died of undiagnosed kidney failure. By happenstance, Theodore's mother died on the same day, of typhoid fever. He went west to deal with his grief. In time, he decided to keep the Oyster Bay property and returned to New York in 1886. Late that year he went to London, where he married Edith Carow, a childhood friend. They honeymooned in Europe, and while there he climbed the Matterhorn.

Theodore Roosevelt was born October 27, 1858, to Theodore, Sr., and Martha ("Mittie") Bulloch Roosevelt in New York City. His Dutch ancestors settled in New York in the mid-seventeenth century and prospered. By the nineteenth century the family was rich and influential. Theodore, Sr., was a partner in the family's long-established glass-importing business and a leading philanthropist.

Young Theodore suffered from asthma as a child and was not robust. He was bright and had an inquiring mind. His lifelong interest in zoology began when he was seven. He and two cousins created their own "Roosevelt Museum of Natural History," and filled it with animals they caught or killed, then studied. He was encouraged to exercise regularly so he took up boxing lessons.

Roosevelt's lifelong interest in travel was developed on family trips to Europe in 1869 and 1870 and to Egypt in 1872 and 1873. Mostly homeschooled by tutors, he was well-read, especially in history, geography, and biology. He entered Harvard College in 1876 and graduated Phi Beta Kappa in 1880. He then entered Columbia Law School, but dropped out the next year to run for a state assembly seat, which he won and to which he was later reelected.

Roosevelt liked the outdoor life. He subsequently went to the Dakota Badlands, bought a ranch, and became a deputy sheriff. When the severe winter of 1886 wiped out his cattle herd, he returned to New York City. In 1891, President Harrison appointed him to the U.S. Civil Service Commission, where he served through 1895. He then moved on to become president of the New York City Board of Police Commissioners.

In 1897, President McKinley appointed Roosevelt assistant secretary of the navy. Roosevelt was acting secretary on the afternoon the battleship *Maine* exploded in Havana Harbor. He lost no time in alerting all navy units to prepare for war. When war was declared in 1898, he resigned from the Navy Department to form the 1st U.S. Volunteer Cavalry Regiment. The newspapers dubbed the group the Rough Riders. On July 1, 1898, Roosevelt led his Rough Riders in charges up Kettle Hill and San Juan Hill in Cuba and prevailed in both.

In 1898, Roosevelt ran for governor of New York and won. Two years later he was McKinley's reelection running mate. In the six months he served as vice president, his most memorable statement was "Speak softly, but carry a big stick," said at the Minnesota State Fair in a speech extolling a robust foreign and military policy. On September 6, 1901, at the Pan-American Exposition in Buffalo, McKinley was shot by an assassin.

Initial reports indicated he would recover, so Roosevelt carried out plans to go to Mount Marcy, New York's highest peak, for a climb and camping. On his way back, he received a telegram that McKinley was near death. Roosevelt immediately left for Buffalo. En route he received another telegram notifying him McKinley had died. Roosevelt was sworn in when he reached Buffalo. At forty-two, he was the youngest president ever to take office. After winning a full term of his own in 1904, he pushed for passage of the Meat Inspection Act (1906) and the Pure Food and Drug Act. With his love of the outdoors, he made conservation a national issue. He was a significant force in the creation of 150 national forests, five national parks, and eighteen national monuments. Altogether, his actions were instrumental in the conservation of some 230 million acres.

In the wake of the Spanish-American War, Roosevelt wanted the world to know that the nation would be playing a major role on the world stage. He was convinced that for both commerce and security, the nation needed a shortcut between the Atlantic and Pacific oceans, and so he made sure that construction of the Panama Canal would proceed. In 1905 he served as a volunteer mediator between the Russians and Japanese over their war. For this he received the 1906 Nobel Peace Prize.

SUMMERS AT SAGAMORE HILL

As soon as Congress adjourned for the summer the Roosevelt family left for Sagamore Hill. The first year, 1902, Edith and the children went ahead, while Theodore gave a Fourth of July speech in Pittsburgh. He arrived at Oyster Bay two days later. For these sojourns the White House, in effect, moved with the president until they returned to Washington in early September. The presidential staff had summer offices in the village of Oyster Bay and also took over the library of the main house. There was a single telephone line at home, but multiple lines at the office, where most communication from Washington was conducted. Couriers from Washington regularly brought the president documents for his signature. The Summer White House saw many visitors. In 1905, the Japanese and Russian delegations stopped for a visit. Various cabinet members also called on the Roosevelts.

Sagamore Hill was a working farm, as well as the family's home and retreat. There was a small dairy herd, a pigpen, horse pastures, a flower and vegetable garden, fields planted to wheat, rye, and barley, and an apple orchard. The resident staff included the manager, gardener, and a coachmen. There were also day workers, but Roosevelt would sometimes pitch hay, chop trees, and do other strenuous work for exercise.

In 1909 Roosevelt went on an extensive safari expedition to sub-Saharan Africa, with a large entourage. The party killed or trapped more than eleven thousand animals, from insects to elephants. Skins and specimens were salted for mounting by the Smithsonian Institution, which then shared many with other museums. He gave a full account of the safari in *African Game Trails*, one of eighteen books he wrote.

SEEKING THE WHITE HOUSE AGAIN

In 1912 Roosevelt decided to seek the presidency again. In typical TR style he campaigned energetically. In Milwaukee on October 14, 1912, one John Schrank shot him. His steel eyeglasses case and a folded copy of his speech in his pocket apparently stopped the bullet. Roosevelt reasoned that because he wasn't coughing up blood, the bullet had not gone through his chest wall, so he spoke to the crowd for ninety minutes. Later examination showed that the bullet had in fact lodged in his chest muscles. The doctors decided that removing it would be more dangerous than leaving it, so Roosevelt carried the bullet in him for the rest of his days.

Undaunted by his failure to win the presidency again, Roosevelt embarked in 1913–14 on a scientific expedition to South America with Brazilian explorer Candido Rondon. The American Museum of Natural History provided funding. Accompanying Roosevelt and Rondon were the Roosevelts' twenty-four-year-old son, Kermit; a naturalist; a Brazilian army officer; a physician; and sixteen paddlers and porters. Their goal was to find the headwaters of Brazil's Rio da Duvida, the "River of Doubt," then trace it north to the Amazon. They made this strenuous trip of discovery, but on the way downriver Roosevelt contracted malaria and sustained a minor leg wound, which became infected. He wrote extensively about the expedition in his book *Through the Brazilian Wilderness*.

In 1918, during World War I, the Roosevelts' youngest son, Quentin, an aviator, was shot down and died behind German lines. TR's grief over this loss contributed to his declining health. On January 6, 1919, he died in his sleep of a heart attack, at Sagamore Hill. At his death, son Archie cabled his brothers, "The Old Lion is dead." He was not quite sixty-one. Edith Roosevelt died in 1948. They are buried at Young's Cemetery, on a hillside overlooking Oyster Bay, a mile from Sagamore Hill.

———•◦•———

After Mrs. Roosevelt's death in 1948 the family and the Theodore Roosevelt Association opened Sagamore Hill to the public. In 1963 it was given to the nation. As the Sagamore Hill National Historic Site, it is maintained and operated by the National Park Service.

Admission to the main house is by guided tour only (no more than fourteen persons to a tour). Tickets are available at the Visitor Center 9 a.m.–5 p.m., daily. Tours are conducted on the hour, beginning at 10 a.m. The last tour of the day begins at 4 p.m.

Sagamore Hill is closed Thanksgiving, Christmas, and New Year's Day. Location: 20 Sagamore Hill Road, Oyster Bay, NY 11771. Tel 516-922-4788. Website:: www.nps.gov/sahi.

The Theodore Roosevelt Birthplace National Historic Site is also administered by the National Park Service. It is in Manhattan in New York City. It is open Tuesday–Saturday, 9 a.m.–5 p.m. Guided tours of the historic rooms are conducted at 10 and 11 a.m. and 1, 2, 3, and 4 p.m. Visitors may also browse the ground-floor gallery, which contains many original items from Roosevelt's life.

Location: 28 East 20th Street, New York, NY 10033. Tel. 212-260-1616. Website: www.nps.gov/thrb.

———•◆•———

Chapter Twenty-six

WILLIAM HOWARD TAFT

THE 27TH PRESIDENT

March 4, 1909 — March 4, 1913

*W*illiam Taft did not want to be president. He wanted to be a justice of the Supreme Court. He was—ultimately— but not until after he ran for and won the presidency in 1908.

Scion of an illustrious Cincinnati family, Taft was born on September 15, 1857, to Alphonso and Louisa Torrey Taft. Alphonso served as secretary of war and attorney general to President Ulysses S. Grant. Taft attended Woodward High School, then, in the family tradition, went on to Yale, where he acquired the nickname "Big Lub," reflecting his already considerable girth. He graduated, then earned his law degree at Cincinnati Law School in 1880. After he was admitted to the Ohio bar, he was appointed as an assistant prosecutor in Cincinnati's county, Hamilton. He then became the area's collector of internal revenue.

In 1886, Taft married Helen Herron (know as "Nellie" to family and close friends), whom he had been courting for some time. The next year, his career began to advance significantly. The governor appointed him a judge of the superior (county) court. In 1890, President Benjamin Harrison appointed him solicitor general of the United States. A year later, the president nominated him and the Senate confirmed him for a seat on the new U.S. Court of Appeals, Sixth Circuit.

In 1904, he was asked to join the Roosevelt cabinet as secretary of war.

He met with the emperor of Japan and learned about a coming war between that country and Russia. In 1906, he was sent to Cuba to become temporary governor and negotiate a peaceful end to a revolt. He then participated in supervision of the building of the Panama Canal. At one point he was also acting secretary of state. Although Taft repeatedly expressed his desire to be on the Supreme Court, and especially chief justice, Roosevelt had other plans, wanting him to be the next president so that he could carry on Roosevelt's progressive approach. Taft won an easy victory.

As president-elect Taft traveled by ship (January 29–February 7, 1909) to inspect construction of the Panama Canal.

TIME OFF

For fourteen years prior to his election, Taft and his family had vacationed at Murray Bay, a fashionable resort on the St. Lawrence River northeast of Quebec City. Much as they liked the summer life there, Taft thought it would not be proper for a U.S. president to vacation outside the United States. Thus they began looking for a new location. Friends John H. and Natalie Hammond recommended the North Shore of Massachusetts—the coastline north of Boston—and especially the oceanside town of Beverly.

After looking at several possible homes to rent, they chose a green, shingled fourteen-room "cottage" known as Stetson Hall. It was located on Woodbury Point, overlooking the ocean. In 1909 it was owned by Robert Dawson Evans and was the guesthouse for Dawson Hall, just across the lawn.

Dawson had, over time, risen to be president of U.S. Rubber (later Uniroyal). He and his wife, Marie Antoinette Evans, used the "cottage" for their own summer guests but consented to rent it for two years to the new president.

On May 18, less than ten weeks after the inauguration, Helen Taft, at age forty-eight, suffered a stroke. It took her a year and much therapy to regain the ability to fully speak. Newspapers reported her condition as a "nervous breakdown." She stayed away from Washington until October that year. On returning she only appeared at ceremonial functions in which she had no speaking role.

The first family settled in for a restful summer vacation. Anchored offshore was the presidential yacht, the *Mayflower*, although Taft did not use it much that summer, preferring automobile trips. The *Mayflower* was 273 feet from stem to stern and had a crew of two hundred (sea and land) and a sixteen-piece band. There was also the small yacht USS *Sylph* for short cruises. During his Beverly summers, Taft almost always followed the same daily routine. He played golf in the morning, then had lunch, followed by a nap, then reading or visiting and, after dinner, playing bridge. Taft loved golf and had joined both the Myopia Hunt Club and the Essex Country Club. His friend John Hammond was his favorite golfing companion. There were other Beverly summer residents he also saw, including Justice Oliver Wendell Holmes and the industrialist Henry Clay Frick.

The Tafts' summer stay at Stetson Hall in 1910 was the second and last. The Tafts soon found a new home for the summers of 1911 and 1912 (with a provision for additional rentals there if he were reelected in 1912). It was Parramatta, an eighteen-room "cottage" belonging to the widow of Henry B. Peabody. It was three-quarters of a mile inland from Stetson Hall but had a view of the ocean. The Tafts left Beverly for the last time on October 26, 1912, and when they did, four years of Summer White Houses on the Massachusetts North Shore came to an end.

SIDELIGHTS

Helen Taft, after visiting Japan in earlier years, got the idea to have flowering cherry trees planted along the reflecting pool by the Jefferson Memorial in Washington. Her efforts resulted in the gift of the trees from the Japanese government in 1912. They have been a major attraction in the spring for all the decades since.

The Tafts were the first presidential family to own automobiles. They owned four. To house them, Taft had an area of the White House stable remodeled. He was especially fond of driving fast (probably fifteen miles per hour at the time).

President Taft began what became a tradition at baseball games, the seventh-inning stretch. He liked to attend baseball games and one day stood up at that point. Soon everyone else in the ballpark was doing the same.

AFTER THE WHITE HOUSE

In 1912, Taft was defeated by Woodrow Wilson in his bid for reelection. Soon after leaving Washington, he became a professor at Yale Law School. He was also elected president of the American Bar Association. He wrote extensively on American legal philosophy. He also favored the concept of a league of nations, long before one was formally proposed. When the chief justice of the Supreme Court died in 1921, President Harding appointed Taft to replace him. Thus he achieved his long-held ambition. He is the only man to have been both president and chief justice. In his new role he officiated at the swearing-in ceremonies of Presidents Coolidge and Hoover. Taft was happy on the bench and was respected by his fellow justices. In 1929 Taft led the successful effort to house the Supreme Court in a new building of its own, so that it could move out of the Capitol, Congress's domain. The new Court building, still used today, was not completed until after Taft's death.

FAMILY LIFE

Soon after leaving the presidency, Taft began to lose weight, going from a high of 340 pounds down to about 250. The sleeplessness he had suffered disappeared, his blood pressure dropped, and his energy level went up. This prompted him to take a trip to Alaska. From 1913 on, the Tafts returned to Canada's Murray Bay in Quebec for their summer vacations.

He retired from the bench on February 8, 1930, and died just a few weeks later, on March 3.

Helen Taft lived on until 1943. Both are buried in Arlington National Cemetery.

The William Howard Taft National Historic Site is operated by the National Park Service. It is Taft's birthplace and the house in which he grew up. Guided tours are conducted every thirty minutes, on the hour and half hour (the last one of the day is at 3:30 p.m.). Tours are available seven days a week, year-round, except for Thanksgiving, Christmas, and New Year's Day.

Address: 2038 Auburn Avenue, Cincinnati, OH 45219. Telephone: 513-684-3262, ext. 201. Website: http://www.nps.gov/wiho.

———◆———

Chapter Twenty-seven

WOODROW WILSON

THE 28TH PRESIDENT

March 4, 1913 — March 4, 1921

Thomas Woodrow Wilson was not all things to all people. He was self-righteous, stubborn, reserved, uncompromising. He was also idealistic. With people with whom he was close, Woodrow (he dropped his first name early on) could be warm, humorous, even romantic. His eight years in the White House were marked by great sadness, great changes in policy, a world war, and ultimately a dogged campaign to make the League of Nations a reality. After all that he suffered the ravages of a stroke.

Wilson was born in 1856 in Staunton, Virginia, to Joseph Wilson, a Presbyterian minister, and his wife, Jessie. He had two sisters and a brother. His primary schooling was by tutors, followed by Davidson College, Princeton University, and the University of Virginia Law School. In 1882 he began a law firm in Atlanta and passed the bar examination. The next year he enrolled in Johns Hopkins University to earn a doctoral degree in political science. He is still the only U.S. president to hold a Ph.D. In 1885, Wilson married Ellen Louise Axson of Savannah, Georgia. They had three daughters: Margaret, Jessie, and Eleanor.

After receiving his Ph.D., Wilson had short academic stints at Cornell, Bryn Mawr, and Wesleyan University in Connecticut. In 1890 he joined the faculty at Princeton and he was appointed president there in 1902. In 1910 Wilson became governor of New Jersey.

Two years later he ran for president and won. When war broke out in 1914 he was determined to keep the United States out of it. He offered to mediate between the Allied and Central powers, but neither accepted the offer. Also in 1914 the Panama Canal opened. He pushed the switch that blew up an earthen plug in the canal, opening it to ships.

His wife, Ellen, in failing health for some time, died on August 6, 1914, of Bright's disease. She was fifty-four. After her death, Wilson's cousin Helen Bones took over the duties of official White House hostess. On December 18, 1915, Wilson married Edith Bolling Galt, a socially prominent widow. They spent a two-week honeymoon at Hot Springs, Virginia, and the Greenbrier resort in West Virginia.

A SECOND TERM—WAR

In 1916, Wilson campaigned vigorously on his avoidance of U.S. involvement in the war. Nevertheless, in his nomination acceptance speech he warned that if German submarines attacked American ships, we would respond. He won reelection. When Germany moved to unrestricted submarine warfare and attempted to enlist Mexico as a war ally, Wilson decided the time had come for the United States to become engaged. On April 2, 1917, he addressed Congress with his War Message, describing how we would enter a "war to end all wars" to make "the world safe for democracy." Congress moved a declaration of war two days later.

THE PEACE CONFERENCE, 1919

In January 1918, Wilson gave his "Fourteen Points" speech, calling for a League of Nations and the right of peoples to determine their independence within respected boundaries. He led the U.S. delegation to Paris for the conference that was to negotiate a peace treaty. After six months, the conferees came up with the Treaty of Versailles, which included a charter for the League of Nations. In 1919, his peace treaty effort netted Wilson the Nobel Peace Prize.

On October 2, 1919, Wilson suffered a severe stroke at the White House that paralyzed his left side. It was soon clear that he would be fully incapacitated for some time. Mrs. Wilson prevailed upon Dr. Cary Grayson and Joseph Tumulty, Wilson's loyal secretary (comparable to today's chief of staff), to make only general statements about Wilson's condition. Edith Wilson determined who would see her husband and what matters would be put before him. She seemed to be, in effect, a shadow chief executive. On leaving office, Wilson and his wife retired to a Washington, D.C., home they had bought in the Embassy Row area. He lived there quietly until his death on February 3, 1924. He was sixty-seven.

SUMMERS AT SEA GIRT

In 1887 the state of New Jersey purchased 120 acres near the shore in Sea Girt on the northern coast of the state for a National Guard training camp (it's still in use today). It also included a house to be used as the Summer Capital by the governor. During Wilson's two years as governor the family stayed there to combat the summer's heat. There he could indulge his love of bicycling (earlier he went on several cycling vacations in England's Lake District). The Wilsons were at Sea Girt when he was nominated for president. Soon a brass band arrived, as did a string of automobiles and buggies. The band played "Hail to the Chief" and Princeton's "Old Nassau."

TO AN ARTISTS' COLONY

Ellen Wilson was an accomplished painter. In June 1913, she and the girls went to Haarlachen, an artists' colony in Cornish, New Hampshire, where the family rented a cottage. The president joined them briefly in July.

CHRISTMAS ON THE GULF SHORE

A few days before Christmas in 1913, the Wilsons and two of their daughters boarded a train for Pass Christian, Mississippi, a seaside resort on the Gulf of Mexico, where they rented a large, airy house near the water and a golf course. After three relaxing weeks they returned to the White House—and a city now in the midst of its busy social season.

SHADOW LAWN—
THE SUMMER WHITE HOUSE

Set on a low hill in West Long Branch, New Jersey, not far from the ocean, Shadow Lawn was an imposing fifty-two-room "summer" mansion on forty acres of landscaped grounds. The owner in 1916, Captain Joseph B. Greenhut (a Civil War veteran), offered Shadow Lawn as a Summer White House for President Wilson. He accepted.

As it turned out, it was more of a Fall White House for Wilson as he campaigned from there for reelection to a second term.

———————

Woodrow Wilson House in Washington, D.C., is the home to which the Wilsons retired at the conclusion of his second term. Built in 1916 in Georgian Revival style, it is fully furnished as it was then. Mrs. Edith Wilson lived on until 1961 and bequeathed it to the National Trust for Historic Preservation, which operates it. It is open for tours Tuesday through Sundays, 10 a.m.–4 p.m. (closed Mondays and major holidays). The ground floor contains a gallery featuring changing exhibits. Address: 2340 S Street, N.W., Washington, DC 20008. For information call 202-387-4062. Website: www.woodrowwilsonhouse.org.

The Woodrow Wilson Presidential Library and Museum in Staunton, Virginia, consists of the home that was his birthplace and an adjacent building with many artifacts from his life and career. Included is the new 1919 Pierce-Arrow limousine that awaited him in New York as he returned from Paris after helping to negotiate the Treaty of Versailles. There are also library floors and archives. Tours of the Manse (birthplace) take place from November through February and are offered every forty-five minutes, from 10 a.m. to 4 p.m. Mondays through Saturday and noon to 4 p.m. on Sunday. From March through October tour hours are 9 a.m.–5 p.m. Monday through Saturday and noon–5 p.m. Sunday. Address: 20 North Coalter Street, Staunton, VA 24401. Telephone: 540-885-0897 or toll-free 888-496-6376. Email: info@ woodrowwilson.org. Website: www.woodrowwilson.org.

Chapter Twenty-eight

WARREN G. HARDING

THE 29TH PRESIDENT

March 4, 1921 — August 2, 1923

*I*t was quite a sight: a motorcade of fifty automobiles leaving Washington on July 24, 1921, to take the President Harding, Thomas Edison, Henry Ford, Harvey Firestone, and assorted friends and staff members to a retreat at Firestone's Masons' Woods property on Licking Creek in rural Maryland. This was the latest iteration of what had become an annual event called Nature's Laboratory. It had been started several years earlier by naturalist John Burroughs and continued after his death. It was billed as a week away from "fictitious civilization." Harding was the honored guest on this trip. He brought with him his Secret Service detail and a radio car in which rode a cipher operator who stayed in contact with the State Department.

At Masons' Woods, the group lived in what has been called "primitive luxury" under canvas tents and on canvas cots. They used portable washstands. As for dining, there was a kitchen crew on duty. Harding took walks in the wood with Edison and Ford, chopped wood (presumably for the kitchen and the evening campfires), and, to use his favorite word, "bloviated" (that is, engaged in unstructured conversation).

THE EARLY YEARS

Warren Gamaliel Harding was born in Marion, Ohio, on November 2, 1865, to Dr. George and Phoebe Harding. He was the eldest of eight children. Phoebe later obtained a medical license, but George was restless as a medical practitioner and also tried farming and schoolteaching. He then bought a weekly newspaper in Caledonia, Ohio. There, at age ten, Warren began to learn about journalism. Then, at Ohio Central College, he studied printing and the newspaper business. Upon graduation at age seventeen he sold insurance and taught for a while. Then, with some friends, he purchased Marion's newspaper, the *Daily Star*. In 1891 he married Florence Kling DeWolfe. She was five years Harding's senior, a no-nonsense, controlling woman (he nicknamed her "the Duchess"). His affable manner contrasted with hers and the match seemed to work for both.

INTO POLITICS

In 1914, Harding was elected U.S. senator. Noncontroversial and friendly to all his colleagues, Harding saw his popularity grow. He was the chairman of the Republican convention in 1916 and delivered its keynote address. He was elected president in 1920. Inclement weather caused most of the inaugural festivities to be canceled. The swearing-in ceremony and a reception were held at the White House. In his inaugural remarks, Harding said, "Our most dangerous tendency is to expect too much from the government and at the same time do too little for it," foreshadowing a remark by John F. Kennedy forty years later. After eighteen months of a "closed" White House during Wilson's illness, the Hardings threw open the doors for regular hours for ordinary citizen visitors and reestablished the annual children's Easter Egg Roll.

In April 1921 he laid out an ambitious program: creation of a Bureau of Veterans Affairs, development and regulation of radio, lower federal tax rates, new protectionist tariffs, a new approach to farm loans and regulation, peace with former enemies Germany and Austria, anti-lynching legislation, and a larger merchant marine—among other things. He created the Bureau of the Budget (today's Office of

Management and Budget) and signed the Federal Highway Act of 1921. He took the leadership in organizing a multination naval conference in 1921–22 that produced six treaties and twelve resolutions, which lasted until Japan invaded Manchuria in 1937.

TRAVELS WITH WARREN

For relaxation, Harding as president developed the habit of playing golf two afternoons a week.

His first official trip was with his wife in April 1921 to New York City in a ten-car motorcade.

In May he took the presidential yacht *Mayflower* to New York Harbor to greet a freighter arriving with the remains of 5,212 American soldiers from Europe. He gave a speech at the dockside memorial service. On July 2, during a golfing weekend in New Jersey, he signed the Congressional joint resolution ending the state of war with Germany. The weekend after his 1921 Nature's Laboratory sojourn he was aboard the *Mayflower* again, this time heading for Plymouth, Massachusetts, to commemorate the three hundredth anniversary of the landing of the Pilgrims.

Whenever he could in the warm, humid summer months, Harding liked to slip away on the *Mayflower* with a group of friends.

In October 1921 he traveled to Atlanta and Birmingham, where he gave a remarkable speech. His theme: Democracy was a lie without political and economic equality for black people.

The following March the Hardings left for several weeks in Palm Beach, Florida, with Ned and Evalyn Walsh McLean (she of the Hope Diamond). On July 1 the Hardings left by motorcade to take part in Marion, Ohio's centennial celebration. The three-day trip included a first night stop at Gettysburg, where they witnessed a reenactment of Pickett's Charge. The second day they stopped at Point Pleasant, Ohio, to visit Grant's birthplace. In early September the Duchess developed a bad cold, followed by an attack of kidney trouble. By mid-month the crisis had passed and a long, slow recovery began.

President Washington's bedchamber, the room in which he died.
Mount Vernon Ladies' Association

Bird's-eye view of the mansion at Washington's Mount Vernon estate.
Mount Vernon Ladies' Association

FACING PAGE TOP TO BOTTOM:
The Hermitage, President Andrew Jackson's home and
retreat in Nashville, Tennessee. *The Ladies' Hermitage Association*

Bronze statue of President Lincoln and his horse. Behind is the main
building at the Soldiers' Home, Washington, D.C. The Lincolns spent
their summers at a cottage in front of the statue. *Irene Hannaford*

President Benjamin Harrison's controversial seaside cottage at Cape May, New Jersey. *Benjamin Harrison Presidential Site*

The McKinley Farm, near Canton, Ohio, President McKinley's "Camp David," where he spent several weekends and vacations. *William McKinley Presidential Library and Museum*

Sagamore Hill, President Theodore Roosevelt's home and retreat at Oyster Bay, Long Island, New York. *Peter Hannaford*

President Rutherford Hayes's longtime retreat (and home),
Spiegel Grove, Fremont, OH. *The Hayes Presidential Center*

The main lodge at Camp Rapidan, the retreat President Hoover built in Virginia's Shenandoah Valley. *Shenandoah National Park, National Park Service*

President Truman disembarks from the USS *Williamsburg*. *Copyright unknown; courtesy of Harry S. Truman Library*

The "Texas White House" at the LBJ Ranch. President Johnson's office is off to the left. *Peter Hannaford*

President Reagan signs the historic across-the-board tax-cut bill on the patio of his ranch house, August 1981.

Ronald Reagan Presidential Library and Museum

THE VOYAGE OF UNDERSTANDING

Despite the rumors of various scandals, Harding was determined to run for reelection in 1924. He decided that an extensive rail trip to the West, with many stops and speeches, would revive his personal support. He traveled to Utah, Montana, Idaho, Washington, and Alaska.

One of his colleagues had purchased several large crabs before they left Alaska. One late evening, he and Harding sat at a dining table gorging themselves on crab meat and butter.

Later, in Seattle, he nearly collapsed during his speech. On the train to San Francisco, however, he had cramps and indigestion. His doctor thought they were caused by the rich seafood Harding had eaten. Two doctors aboard were convinced that Harding's heart was dangerously enlarged. They arrived in San Francisco on Sunday and went directly to the Palace Hotel. On Monday, his condition worsened and the rest of the public schedule was canceled. On Tuesday, Harding began to feel better. On Thursday evening, the Duchess came in to read a complimentary story about him in the *Saturday Evening Post*. She then returned to her room.

The duty nurse left to get him a glass of water for his nighttime medicine. When she returned, he was slumped over, dead. It was 7:32 p.m., Pacific time, on August 2, 1923.

———•◦•———

The Hardings' home in Marion, Ohio, was designed by Warren and Florence Harding in 1890. They oversaw its construction. The two-and-a-half-story home is in the Queen Anne style. The facade is dominated by a large porch, from which Harding conducted his 1920 "Front Porch" campaign for president. It was their home for thirty years.

Mrs. Harding willed the house and its furnishings to the Harding Memorial Association. Today it is operated for the Ohio Historical Society by Marion Technical College. Fully restored, it is open from late May until early September (Mondays and Tuesdays by appointment; Wednesdays–Sundays, noon–5 p.m.; Memorial Day and July 4, noon–5 p.m.). Address: 380 Mount Vernon Avenue, Marion, OH 43302. Telephone: 740-387-9630 (toll-free 800-600-6894). E-mail: shall@hardinghome.org. Website: www.hardinghome.org.

The Harding tomb, a circular monument of white Georgia marble, is the resting place of both Hardings. It resembles a Greek temple and is set in ten acres of landscaped grounds. It is open all year during daylight hours. Address: Corner, State Route 423 and Vernon Heights Boulevard in Marion.

Chapter Twenty-nine

CALVIN COOLIDGE

THE 30TH PRESIDENT

August 3, 1923 — March 4, 1929

alvin Coolidge had plenty of opportunity to turn his thoughts to the flowing streams near the farm village where he was born, Plymouth Notch, Vermont, when he was vacationing there in the summer of 1923. He had been vice president of the United States for nearly two and a half years. He and his wife, Grace, were looking forward to spending most of July and August there, visiting his father and settling into the quiet rural life "Silent Cal" so enjoyed. Reared on a Yankee regime of hard work and self-reliance, Coolidge did not let the summer days slip by in idleness. He worked on the farm nearly every day and considered a few hours in a nearby fishing stream a reward for doing useful things on the farm.

This idyll was to end abruptly the night of Thursday, August 2. The family had retired at 9 p.m. They were awakened about 2 a.m. when a messenger brought a telegram from the nearest town (the farm had neither electricity nor a telephone). President Warren Harding was dead. Coolidge's father, in addition to being a farmer and former state legislator, was a justice of the peace. At 2:47 a.m., Friday, August 3, in the farmhouse dining room, he administered the oath of office to his son as the thirtieth president of the United States—by the light of a kerosene lantern. Later that day Calvin and Grace Coolidge left by train for Washington.

YANKEE UPBRINGING

John Calvin Coolidge, Jr., was born on July 4, 1872, the son of John, Sr., and Victoria (who died when the boy was twelve). Their daughter Abigail died at age fifteen in 1890. His father remarried in 1891. Always known as Calvin, he had deep roots in New England. His first ancestor to come to America from England landed in Massachusetts around 1630. Farming in the rocky soil of New England was not easy and Calvin did farm chores from an early age. He attended school at the Black River Academy in Ludlow, about ten miles from Plymouth, then Amherst College in western Massachusetts. After college he moved to nearby Northampton, where he read law at a local firm. He was admitted to the bar in 1897 and opened his own law office the next year.

In 1905 he met Grace Goodhue, also a Vermonter, who was a teacher. With very different personalities, the two were attracted to one another and were married later that year. Grace was outgoing and talkative; Calvin was studious and serious, and measured his words with such care that he came to be known as "Silent Cal." They had two sons, John, in 1906, and Calvin, Jr., in 1908. Theirs was a happy marriage.

UP THE POLITICAL LADDER

In 1906 he won election to the Massachusetts House of Representatives, then later to the state senate, and he was eventually elected governor. In 1920 he was presidential candidate Warren Harding's running mate. The ticket won in a landslide. The new president invited Coolidge to attend cabinet meetings, a first for a VP. Coolidge gave many speeches, but otherwise his two and a half years were uneventful. However, he heard with concern rumors about corrupt doings of some members of the Harding administration.

On July 8, 1923, the Coolidge family drove to Plymouth Notch where they planned to spend several weeks at his father's farm. On July

30, news accounts noted that Harding had suffered apparent ptomaine poisoning on a ship in Alaska and had been taken by train to San Francisco. His condition was supposedly improving. Harding died at 7:32 p.m., Pacific time, August 2. By the time Coolidge took the oath of office it was early morning, Friday, August 3.

THE THIRTIETH PRESIDENT

When Coolidge arrived in Washington later that day, he was sworn in a second time, this time by a justice of the District of Columbia Supreme Court. On December 6 he addressed Congress, echoing many Harding themes. This was the first presidential speech to be broadcast nationally by radio.

The family had planned to spend most of the summer in Washington, with several trips down the Potomac on the *Mayflower*. A few days after the convention, the Coolidges' younger son, Calvin, developed an infection from a toe blister acquired from a tennis game on the White House court. Blood poisoning resulted. He died on July 7. Coolidge later said to a visiting friend, ". . . when I look out that window I always see my boy playing tennis on that court out there." And, several years later, he wrote in his autobiography, "When he went, the power and the glory of the presidency went with him."

He conducted a subdued campaign for a full term, partly because of his grief. He nonetheless won in a landslide.

As president, Coolidge was the antithesis of the Roaring Twenties. He embodied thrift, dignity, industriousness, modesty, morality, and civility. These qualities, combined with the widespread and growing prosperity, made him respected and admired.

MOVABLE RETREATS

Although he always considered the farm at Plymouth Notch as home, Coolidge as president did not have one retreat to which he and his family always returned. They began to make frequent use of the presidential yacht, the *Mayflower*. They took their first cruise on it in September when their sons were home from school for a few days. Three friends accompanied them. By spring 1924 the Coolidges had developed the habit on Sundays after church of going aboard the *May-flower* for an afternoon cruise down the Potomac. When they spent an occasional weekend on the yacht, they arranged for church services aboard.

The death of young Calvin affected both of them deeply. On July 10, 1924, they went to Northampton for his funeral and then to Plymouth where he was buried. From there they went to the seaside town of Swampscott, Massachusetts, to spend a few days with their friends the Stearns. In early August they left Washington again for Plymouth. Among their guests there were Henry Ford, Thomas Edison, and Harvey Firestone.

The next year, the Coolidges left Washington for Swampscott on June 22 to spend most of the summer at White Court, a rented residence that was to become the Summer White House. This was the first time since Theodore Roosevelt's summers at Sagamore Hill and Woodrow Wilson's sojourn at Shadow Lawn that a president had established a seat of government away from Washington. From this time on, wherever the president went a staff went with him and telephone lines were set up to keep him in touch with the White House. Offices for the staff were set up in an office building in nearby Lynn. The Coolidges lived quietly, but also took a number of short cruises on the *Mayflower,* which was anchored at Marblehead harbor.

On July 5, 1926, the president gave a speech in Philadelphia to commemorate the 150th anniversary of the Declaration of Independence. From there the Coolidges went to White Pine Camp, a rustic but luxurious summer retreat of a Kansas City newspaper owner. On a beautiful lake, it was not close to roads, so privacy was assured. The staff set up offices in a hotel in the nearest town. Occasional bits of news drifted out of the camp about the president's frequent fishing sessions. They returned to Washington on September 19 to find that the White House's first elevator had been installed.

In 1927, the Coolidges decided to vacation in the Black Hills of South Dakota. They arrived on June 15. The state game lodge became the Summer White House. It had twenty rooms (including a large living room with a massive stone fireplace) and twelve miles of trout streams. The staff office was located in Rapid City, thirty-two miles away. Always happy to accommodate constituents, Coolidge wore a ten-gallon hat and a cowboy costume presented by a group of cowboys, and was "adopted" by the Sioux Indians as "technical chief" of their tribe. On August 17 he addressed some ten thousand tribe members.

"Speculation was rife that he would run for reelection the next year. He arranged to have the press meet him at noon on August 2, the fourth anniversary of his becoming president. He wrote out this sentence, 'I do not choose to run for President in nineteen twenty-eight,' had copies made, and silently handed them to reporters. They, of course, went wild, scrambling for telephones."

On August 31 the Coolidges left for Yellowstone National Park, where Grace and son John went sightseeing while Coolidge fished. They returned a week later to the lodge, where, on September 2, Charles Lindbergh flew low over Rapid City in tribute to the Coolidges, whose guest he had recently been in Washington. They returned to the White House on September 11. The president was rested, tanned, and comfortable with his decision not to run for reelection.

For his last summer in office, Coolidge arranged for the use of Cedar Island Lodge on an island in the Brule River, thirty-five miles from Superior, Wisconsin. (The traveling staff, now eighty-eight in number, was located in a high school building in Superior.) As he arrived on June 15 he learned that Herbert Hoover had been nominated to succeed him. He then changed into khaki trousers, waders, and a ten-gallon hat and was soon out on the river fly-casting. Before evening he landed several steelhead trout.

The Hoovers briefly visited them at the camp on July 18. The Coolidges returned to Washington on September 12. Coolidge began to be worried about his health. In late November the couple spent several days at the Swannanoa Country Club, in the Blue Ridge Mountains of Virginia. A month later they traveled to Sapelo Island, off the Georgia coast, where, at the behest of his host, he took up shooting and bagged a number of quail.

On January 15, 1928, he left Washington for Havana, Cuba, and the Sixth Pan-American Conference. The First Lady accompanied him. One newspaper report noted that on his arrival he was "wildly cheered by enthusiastic Cubans."

POST-PRESIDENCY

At the conclusion of his term, the Coolidges retired to Northampton, where they bought a good-sized home, The Beeches. He took space for an office in his former law firm and wrote his autobiography, besides penning a daily newspaper column for a year. He died of a heart attack on January 5, 1933, six months shy of his sixty-first birthday.

The Coolidge home village, Plymouth Notch, Vermont, has been preserved much as it was the day he took the oath of office as president. The entire village and surrounding land are part of the President Calvin Coolidge State Historic Site. Included are the general store owned by his father (with his birthplace behind it), a cheese factory his father established, the Union Christian Church, barns with period farm equipment, and the Coolidge Homestead. The store's second floor is the town social hall and served as the Summer White House office when the Coolidges were in residence. The site is open daily, 9:30 a.m.–5:00 p.m., from late May to mid-October. Telephone: 802-672-3773. Email: william.jenney@state.vt.us. Mailing address: P.O. Box 247, Plymouth Notch, VT 05056. Also on site is the Calvin Coolidge Museum & Education Center, owned by the Calvin Coolidge Memorial Foundation, www.calvin-coolidge.org.

Inside the Forbes Public Library in Northampton, Massachusetts, is the Calvin Coolidge Presidential Library & Museum, containing private papers and memorabilia of Coolidge. Address: 20 West Street, Northampton, MA 01062. Telephone: 413-587-1013.

The Coolidge presidential papers are at the Library of Congress.

———◆—◆———

Chapter Thirty

HERBERT HOOVER

THE 31ST PRESIDENT

March 4, 1929 – March 4, 1933

$\mathscr{A}$fter his election victory in November 1928, President-elect Hoover asked his secretary, Lawrence Richey, to find for him a site for a country retreat within one hundred miles of Washington, at an elevation of at least 2,500 feet (to avoid mosquitoes and heat), and with a good trout stream.

Virginia's Governor Harry Byrd, a strong supporter of the creation of a Shenandoah National Park, had the chairman of his state's Commission on Conservation and Development carry out the search. In January 1929, Hoover and his wife, Lou Henry, visited the Blue Ridge Mountains, west of Washington, and which the Virginians thought would provide a good site. In late March, just three weeks after Hoover's inauguration, they recommended a site where two streams joined to form the Rapidan River, and the Hoovers accepted.

Thus the Camp Rapidan retreat was built. It was the first specifically built presidential retreat since Thomas Jefferson created Poplar Forest. Hoover paid for the camp's 164 acres and the building materials out of his own funds. The Hoovers were looking for rusticity, as the two of them had spent ten years in mining camps in various parts of the world during the years of his very successful engineering career.

A crew from the U.S. Marine Corps built the camp's thirteen buildings as a "military exercise."

There were sleeping cabins, a lodge, "town hall" for meetings, two mess halls, and a large outdoor fireplace for conversational gatherings. In addition, the marines constructed hiking trails and a trout pool. To cover the cost of the camp's operations, Hoover decommissioned the presidential yacht *Mayflower*. Its crew members were transferred to the camp.

ROAD TO THE WHITE HOUSE

Herbert Clark Hoover was born August 10, 1874, in West Branch, Iowa. He was to become the first president born west of the Mississippi River. His parents were Quakers, Jesse Clark Hoover, a blacksmith, and Hulda Minthorn Hoover. They died when Herbert was six and ten, respectively. For a time he lived with an uncle in West Branch, then moved to Newberg, Oregon, to live with another uncle, who was both a physician and owner of a real estate office.

For two years Herbert attended Friends Pacific Academy, then worked in the real estate office. He learned math, typing, and bookkeeping in night school.

In 1891, he entered Stanford University in its first year of operation. He graduated four years later with a degree in geology. In 1899 he went to Australia for Bewick, Moreing & Company, a London mining company. There, he scouted mine sites for the company. That year, he married his Stanford sweetheart, Lou Henry. Two years later he was made a partner. They had two sons. They went to China, where he was the company's lead engineer. While there, both Hoovers learned Mandarin Chinese. Then, back in Australia, he developed a process for extracting zinc—otherwise lost—from lead-silver ore. He became a mining consultant in 1908 and had a busy, lucrative practice until World War I began. He and his wife translated into English a sixteenth-century Latin text on mining.

HOOVER THE HUMANITARIAN

He soon found himself immersed in helping others. In August 1914, he led a crew of five hundred volunteers to arrange for more than one hundred thousand Americans then in Europe to return to the United States. The Hoovers distributed steamship tickets, clothing, food, and emergency cash.

He next found himself as chairman of the Commission for the Relief of Belgium (CRB), which undertook the task of feeding all Belgians for the duration of the war. His organization raised from governments and private donors some $11 million a month for the CRB to buy and ship several million tons of food, which was then distributed by the country's own relief committee.

When the United States entered the war, President Woodrow Wilson recruited Hoover to become head of the U.S. Food Administration. He created the slogan "Food Will Win the War" and put it into action by promoting such things as Meatless Monday and Wheatless Wednesday to reduce overall home consumption, thus to better feed the troops overseas. Government rationing never became necessary.

At the war's end he was named to head the American Relief Administration, which organized food for millions of Europeans in need. This included Germans and Russians living in areas controlled by the Bolsheviks. In this work, he enlisted the help of the then-new Quaker organization the American Friends Service Committee. The *New York Times* included him in its list of the "Ten Most Important Living Americans."

Returning to the United States in 1919, he donated his files from the relief programs, along with an endowment, to establish the Hoover War Collection at Stanford University. It later became known as the Hoover Institution on War, Peace and Revolution as its scholars amassed the most comprehensive collection of material on Soviet communism outside the Soviet Union itself.

Today, the Hoover Institution is known as one of the nation's leading think tanks for the study of public policy.

POLITICS AND PUBLIC SERVICE

President-elect Harding appointed Hoover as secretary of commerce (although he'd given Hoover a choice between that post and the Interior Department). Hoover oversaw an "Own Your Own Home" campaign to promote home ownership. He also promoted American movies for overseas distribution and held major conferences on radio and air transportation in order to expand these important new elements in American life.

THE 1928 ELECTION

Hoover's reputation as a wonder-worker and national efficiency expert, combined with his general popularity, helped lead to his election as president. His campaign also made much of his position on Prohibition. Hoover was publicly "dry" (though he often stopped at the Belgian embassy on the way home for a cocktail, for it was technically foreign territory).

WEEKENDS AT CAMP RAPIDAN

As soon as construction was completed at Camp Rapidan the Hoovers began using it. At that time it took three hours or more to reach it from the White House. Sometimes the Hoovers would picnic by the roadside on the way there.

While President Hoover and particularly Mrs. Hoover enjoyed horseback riding at camp, he did not want to ride a horse in order to get to it from the access road. The state of Virginia thus created a one-mile unpaved extension from the access road. He was also a fishing enthusiast, like his predecessor Coolidge. Actual fishing expeditions by Hoover and his guests were to streams outside the campgrounds, for the stream in it had fish that he described as "tame."

FAMOUS GUESTS

Because it was both secure and far from "civilization," Camp Rapidan proved to a popular place for statesmen to discuss business with the president and for other famous people to visit for relaxation. British prime minister Ramsay MacDonald, for example, held serious discussions with Hoover while sitting on a log. In exchange for forgiving Britain's World War I debts, Hoover proposed that Britain give to the United States Bermuda, Trinidad, and British Honduras (now Belize). MacDonald declined, but the two did agree on the basis for the 1930 London Naval Treaty (they reached the agreement shortly before the October 1929 Wall Street crash). MacDonald's daughter was also a guest during her father's visit.

Other famous visitors included the Lindberghs, Supreme Court justice Harlan Stone, Winston Churchill (then chancellor of the exchequer), Edsel Ford (son of Henry Ford), Henry Luce, Thomas Edison, and Theodore Roosevelt, Jr., and his wife.

Hoover staff members, cabinet secretaries, and other senior officials were often invited to the camp, both to discuss business and to enjoy a retreat from daily work. Hoover considered it a place to find relief from the stresses of the Great Depression. Hoover's physician, Dr. Joel Boone, felt the camp was important to the president's health. He said, "The president could recuperate from fatigue faster than anybody I have ever known. . . . He had tremendous power of relaxation once he surrendered himself to taking periods to relax and rest mentally and physically."

Business nevertheless went on at the camp. Under the hemlock trees, Hoover and his associates discussed major issues without interruption, although the camp did have telephones in both his cabin and the Secret Service's duty station. Every day he was there, an airplane dropped a bundle of newspapers and other material for the president as it flew over the Marine detachment's nearby camp.

ADDITIONAL CAMPS

About two miles down the river from the main camp, Secretary of the Interior Ray Lyman Wilbur and Secretary of Agriculture Arthur Hyde had the marines construct a camp in 1930 for members of the Hoover cabinet. It was built on land expected to be incorporated into a Shenandoah National Park but still owned by a timber company. There was only an oral agreement, which led to a well-publicized dispute over that camp's ownership. It was settled with an agreement that the cabinet officers could use it throughout Hoover's time in office, but it would be returned to the owner when he left office. When that time came, the National Park Service did not have the funds to buy it from the owner.

Hoover's Rapidan Camp was allowed to decay. In 1953, a group of fourteen families calling themselves Rapidan Camps purchased the Cabinet Camp and rehabilitated the cabins. The group's membership has grown to one hundred families who use it as a seasonal retreat. It has three of the four original Hoover cabinet cabins and two newer ones in similar style. On hiking maps it is shown as "Rapidan Family Camp" to avoid confusion with the National Park Service's presidential camp, Rapidan Camp.

About a mile east of the main camp the marines had originally constructed a camp for themselves. It consisted of a mix of tents and wooden cabins. Many marines were selected for their skills in electrical work, carpentry, and plumbing. A detail of 150 or more was on duty when the president was in camp. A wintertime crew consisted of only a handful of marines. (This camp was demolished in 1944.)

RUSTIC COMFORT

The main camp consisted of thirteen buildings, connected by paths and bridges constructed by the marines. The most prominent was the President's Cabin, dubbed the Brown House. A guest cabin was called the Prime Minister's Cabin. Another was the Creel Cabin. The Town Hall was the main meeting place for everything from serious business meetings to Ping-Pong. There was a Mess Hall for breakfast and dinner (lunches were often taken outdoors). The Secret Service had its duty station cabin and another, facetiously called the Slums, housed Mrs. Hoover's secretaries.

Over the four years they had Camp Rapidan, the Hoovers stayed there seventy times, for a total of 209 days. In addition, Mrs. Hoover visited the camp a number of times with friends and youth groups.

ANOTHER RETREAT

In 1929, Hoover's aide Lawrence Richey purchased 1,500 wooded acres in Frederick County, Maryland, about an hour's drive northwest of Washington, to create his own fishing camp on Little Hunting Creek. He called it Trout Run. He built a stone-and-timber main lodge and several cabins (one of which he named after Hoover) for friends to use. The creek was said to have some of the best trout fishing in Virginia. Hoover visited a number of times to enjoy fly-fishing (strictly catch-and-release).

DARK CLOUDS

The Wall Street market crash in October 1929 led to a series of events that caused the Great Depression.

Hoover tried a number of things to improve the economy. But by 1932, unemployment had reached 24.9 percent. Added to this was a drought in parts of the Midwest and Southwest. Many homeowners were defaulting on mortgage loans and more than five thousand banks had closed. Thousands of citizens who had become homeless gathered in urban shantytowns soon dubbed Hoovervilles. Hoover was unenthusiastic about standing for reelection, but did. He suffered a crushing loss to Franklin Delano Roosevelt.

CAMP RAPIDAN AFTER DEFEAT

After the election, the Hoovers donated Camp Rapidan to the federal government with the expectation that it would become part of the new Shenandoah National Park. They hoped the camp would be used by subsequent presidents. President Roosevelt visited the camp in 1933 with that possibility in mind; however, he found the trails too rough for a wheelchair or even walking with crutches. And the streams were too cold for the kind of therapeutic warm water he needed for swimming. Nevertheless, Roosevelt cabinet ministers used the camp, especially Secretary of the Navy Claude A. Swanson, who died there in 1939. After that, it ceased being used.

In 1946, the park superintendent cited lack of funds in his request to demolish the camp.

Instead, the Boy Scouts of America signed a twenty-year lease on it. By 1958, however, the BSA found it too costly and withdrew. The National Park Service then demolished all but three of the original buildings. Thereafter, until 1992, the camp was used as a vacation place for high-ranking federal officials. Jimmy Carter was the last president to visit it. Among other visitors were Vice Presidents Walter Mondale and Al Gore. In 2004, the national park completed restoration of the camp, with the three buildings returned to their 1931 condition. It is open to the public.

HOME TO CALIFORNIA

Shortly after leaving the White House, the Hoovers moved to their home in Palo Alto, California. From there they took many auto trips throughout the West, frequently in search of good fishing streams. In 1946, President Truman asked Hoover to travel to Germany to assess the food supply situation there. The next year, he oversaw the creation of a program in the U.S. and British zones of Germany to feed 3.5 million children. Both Truman and Eisenhower asked him to head commissions to identify waste and inefficiency in the federal government.

Hoover spent much time writing in his late years, including *The Ordeal of Woodrow Wilson*, which became a bestseller, and *Fishing for Fun—And to Wash Your Soul*.

Herbert Hoover died on October 20, 1964, at age ninety. He is buried alongside his wife, who died in 1944, at the Hoover Presidential Library in West Branch, Iowa.

Camp Rapidan is open with guides on duty for much of the year. It is located in the central section of Shenandoah National Park in Virginia, approximately sixty miles west of Washington, D.C. For information on schedules, hours, and fees, call 540-999-3283. For information and background, see the website: www.nps.gov/history/nr/travel/presidents/hoover_camp_rapidan.html.

The Herbert Hoover Presidential Library & Museum is in West Branch, Iowa, the town of his birth. It is located within the 187-acre Herbert Hoover National Historic Site, administered by the National

Park Service. It is open 9 a.m.–5 p.m. year-round except for major holidays. The museum contains permanent exhibits on the life and times of President Hoover, as well as changing exhibits. The library contains his public papers, which are now online as well.

On the grounds of the site are also Hoover's birthplace cottage, a Quaker meetinghouse, and a blacksmith shop—all to create the atmosphere of his early years. The Hoovers' graves are also on the site. Address: 210 Parkside Drive, West Branch, IA 52358. Tel. 319-643-5301. Website: http://hoover.archives.gov/info/index2.html.

Chapter Thirty-one

FRANKLIN D. ROOSEVELT

32ND PRESIDENT

March 4, 1933 — April 12, 1945

He was a playboy, a rich dilettante, scoffed the Democratic Party's veterans. Franklin Roosevelt, scion of an old-money New York Hudson River Dutch family, had gone to Groton and Harvard. It didn't help their opinion to know that he was tall, good-looking, poised, charming, and athletic. He would never make it in politics, they concluded. What they didn't realize was that he was smart and very determined.

BORN TO PRIVILEGE

Franklin Roosevelt was born in Hyde Park, New York, in 1882, the only child of James and Sara Delano Roosevelt ("Delano" had been Anglicized from "de la Noye," the surname of the first French Huguenot to land in the New World). Sara was a strong-willed woman. She saw to it that Franklin was well traveled and learned French and German. He also learned to ride horseback, shoot, row, swim, and play polo and golf. He was ebullient and enthusiastic about many things. As a young man, he never had to worry about money, because of the family's wealth. On the other hand, Endicott Peabody, the renowned headmaster at the Groton School, in Massachusetts, drummed into him the belief that Christians had a duty to help those less fortunate.

THE POLITICS "BUG"

Franklin caught the politics "bug" when the local state senate seat was up for grabs in 1910. This district included Springwood, the family's Hyde Park estate along the Hudson River, as well as most of Dutchess County. It had not elected a Democrat since 1884. He astonished local party leaders by winning. On taking office in Albany he quickly became a leader of a group called the Insurgents. They were dedicated to opposing the Tammany Hall machine, which had dominated the state party. Roosevelt played a strong role in preventing its candidate from winning a U.S. Senate seat (then still filled by state legislatures) in 1911. His popularity grew and he won a second term.

Roosevelt resigned in 1913 to become assistant secretary of the navy in the administration of Woodrow Wilson.

MARRIAGE

In 1902, for the first time since childhood, he met his fifth cousin once removed, Eleanor Roosevelt, at a White House reception. She was a niece of Theodore Roosevelt, who was then president. Romance blossomed and they were married on March 17, 1905. His outgoing nature was very different from Eleanor's. She was shy and lacked self-confidence (her mother had once called her "an ugly duckling"—a phrase that haunted her for years).

They had six children in succession (one died after a few months; the rest lived to ripe ages).

In 1904 Franklin entered Columbia Law School but he left three years later, without completing his studies, when he passed the bar exam and went to work for a Wall Street law firm.

His mother had opposed the marriage and she and Eleanor struggled to influence Franklin. This went on for years, although a truce prevailed for much of that time. At one point Sara had twin side-by-side brownstone town houses built for her and them on East 65th Street in Manhattan. There were connecting doors between the houses and the elder Mrs. Roosevelt never hesitated to drop in one them. She doted on her grandchildren and they loved her.

MOVING TO WASHINGTON, D.C.

Eleanor's Aunt Bye, a sister of Theodore Roosevelt, owned a house at 1733 N Street in Washington and lent it to them. He loved the sea and enjoyed his work in the Navy Department.

Eleanor, as a new official's spouse, strove to become used to the obligatory rounds of formal calls on leading Washington wives, and so engaged a part-time social secretary, Lucy Mercer. Franklin was taken by Lucy's good looks and warm personality.

One weekend in June 1916 he planned a trip down the Potomac on the *Sylph*, the yacht used by Presidents McKinley, Theodore Roosevelt, and Taft, and which was now in the possession of the secretary of the navy's office. He invited some friends and Lucy Mercer. Unaccountably, Eleanor did not make the trip.

Gradually, Lucy and Franklin's friendship developed into an affair. One day in 1918 Eleanor came upon some letters that had passed between the two and confronted her husband about it. It is said she offered him a divorce. His mother said if that happened she would cut him out of her will. They made what amounted to a compact. They would no longer have conjugal relations, but would stay married, with him pursuing his career and her supporting him, while she could develop her own interests. It was agreed that Lucy would leave. She did, but a friendship with Franklin was renewed many years later.

Eleanor had always lived in subordination to the agenda of others. She had borne six children without knowing anything of contraception and was worn-out from the experience. She had low self-esteem but high intelligence. She wanted to develop a personality of her own—and did in the coming years.

Franklin greatly enjoyed his job in the Navy Department and became a lifelong champion of the navy. He resigned in 1920 to accept the Democratic Party's nomination as vice presidential running mate to James M. Cox, governor of Ohio. Warren Harding, the Republican candidate, won and Roosevelt took his family back to New York City to resume his law practice.

A FATEFUL RETREAT ON CAMPOBELLO ISLAND

Since he was an infant, Franklin Roosevelt had vacationed at the family's homes on Campobello Island, off the New Brunswick shore and hard by the easternmost point of Maine. His parents had first built a summer home there in 1883, along with other wealthy easterners. He acquired his own thirty-four-room "cottage" on reaching adulthood and took his own family there every year.

One August day in 1921, after several days of strenuous activity, he took some of his children on a hike and swim on the other side of the island. On returning, he fell ill with a fever and found himself paralyzed. At first the several doctors who were summoned diagnosed this as polio. Later, other medical experts concluded that because of his age at the time, thirty-nine, and the symptoms, it was more likely Guillain-Barré syndrome. In any case, he was permanently paralyzed from the waist down. His innate optimism and determination led him to try various treatments, including hydrotherapy. He exercised intensely, building up his torso and arms and learning to lift himself.

THE CAMPAIGN TO WALK AGAIN

Roosevelt had acquired a virtual alter ego, a short, disheveled man named Louis Howe, during his Navy Department days. Howe was to be with him from then on, single-mindedly devoting himself to the advancement of Roosevelt's political career, culminating in the presidency. Howe worked for him at the law office but spent much of his time planning and scheming in the political arena. A former newspaperman, he had many connections in that field. Roosevelt also acquired an efficient, comely secretary, Margaret "Missy" LeHand. Between them, Howe and LeHand made a formidable backup team for their boss.

In his determination to walk, he purchased—along with former classmate and friend John Lawrence—a down-at-heel houseboat in early 1924 to use as a base from which to rebuild his leg muscles. They renamed it *Larooco* (a mix of their names). They parked it in Florida for long winter retreats. He found he could make full use of his legs swimming in the ocean every day.

Friends would come and go for jolly visits. Fishing, poker, lounging on the deck were regular pursuits, in addition to swimming. Eleanor came sometimes, but Missy LeHand more often. She was becoming part of the family. Eleanor thought of her almost as a daughter, although she must have realized that Franklin and Missy had become more than boon companions.

DISCOVERING WARM SPRINGS

In early summer of 1924, Roosevelt's friend George Foster Peabody wrote to tell him of a dilapidated resort in Georgia that had warm waters and had apparently restored to a crippled young New Yorker the ability to walk, with the help of canes. Peabody was so impressed he bought a half interest in the place. Another part owner was the former editor of the *Atlanta Constitution,* Tom Loyless, who called on Roosevelt to tell him of the "miracle" of Warm Springs. Loyless arranged for the disabled young man to meet with Roosevelt, who was impressed.

It was October before he could arrange to visit the place. What he found was a hotel and some cottages in advanced stages of decay, set in a weed-choked acreage. Both Eleanor and Missy accompanied him on the trip to try the waters. A spring flowed into pools at a constant 88 degrees. Mineral-laden, the water was buoyant. He found he could swim for along periods of time without becoming tired. Generations previously, the therapeutic value of the waters had been discovered by Indians. By the late nineteenth century, the place was a popular resort, now abandoned except for occasional visitors who had heard about its seemingly magical properties.

Eleanor disliked the place, though she appreciated the therapeutic benefits he was getting. She returned to New York, where she was planning to build her own cottage, Val-Kill, about two miles from Springwood. Tom Loyless wanted to restore the old Warm Springs hotel, as did Peabody. Roosevelt asked Howe to spread the word. He drummed up some publicity and inquiries began to pour in. Roosevelt and Missy stayed until mid-November.

At Warm Springs, Roosevelt began conducting swimming exercise classes for the growing number of visitors. He put the *Larooco* on the market, hoping to use the proceeds toward purchase of the old resort; however, a hurricane carried it from its moorings and inland four miles. He let the captain dispose of it for whatever he could get. Roosevelt made a last entry in its log, "So ended a good old craft with personality."

He worked energetically to raise money to buy Warm Springs and finally acquired it in April 1926 for a purchase price of $201,667, which he borrowed on a demand note that was finally paid off after his death, from the proceeds of a life insurance policy.

ALBANY, THEN WASHINGTON

Roosevelt was elected governor of New York in 1928 and then re-elected by a large margin in 1930. He thus became a favorite for the 1932 nomination for president. Under the banner of the New Deal (from a phrase in a campaign speech), he was forging a new political coalition that would dominate American politics for years to come. He won the presidency in 1932. The next phase was "recovery," and public works played a large role in his strategy. He was able to make some spending reductions and supported repeal of Prohibition. He also over-saw the creation of Social Security. Unemployment stayed stubbornly high through the late 1930s and did not come under full control until the production demands of World War II.

TAKING TIME OFF

During his first two terms in office, Roosevelt took eleven vacation trips, most of them to go fishing, a sport he could enjoy even with the constraints of paralysis. As president-elect, he went fishing in the Bahamas in February 1933. He repeated this in April 1934 and again in April 1936. He spent three vacations at Campobello Island. The last of these, August 14–16, 1939, was combined with a fishing trip to the Bay of Islands and Bone Bay in Newfoundland.

In these early days of long-distance air travel, he combined several "business" stops with vacations. He made informal visits to Haiti, Panama, and Colombia en route to a July 1934 vacation in Hawaii. As president, in August 1938 he called on then-president Juan Arosemena of Panama during a Caribbean vacation. In February 1940 he met with then-president Augusto Boyd of Panama under the same circumstances.

During and after those years, his favorite retreat was to Warm Springs for the restorative qualities of its mineral waters. From late 1940 on he made many trips outside the United States, all of them for meetings with Allied leaders to advance war plans.

SECOND AND THIRD TERMS

Roosevelt had won reelection in 1936 in a landslide. This time, he won all but Maine and Vermont. In 1940 he broke the two-term presidential tradition and easily won renomination. As storm clouds gathered in Europe, followed by the Munich appeasement, Roosevelt worked quietly to find ways to help the Allies without violating U.S. neutrality laws. He devised the Lend-Lease program, offering the British navy—and later the Soviet Union—a number of obsolescent warships and other equipment.

On the heels of the Japanese attack on Pearl Harbor, December 7, 1941, which Roosevelt called "a date which will live in infamy," Congress declared war against Japan. Soon we were officially at war with all three of the Axis powers: Germany, Italy, and Japan. Roosevelt poured all his energy into creating winning strategies in the war on two fronts. Up to the time of the Japanese attack, a strong isolationist segment of the population fought Roosevelt's efforts to help the Allies.

In the months leading up to war he continued what had become a tradition: radio "fireside chats" to the American people. His use of the medium was masterful—personal, reasonable, never histrionic.

FOURTH TERM; A LAST VISIT TO
HYDE PARK AND WARM SPRINGS

There was no question among Democratic Party leaders and—in November—the voting public that 1944 was not the time to change leaders. (Vice President Henry Wallace, however, was replaced by Senator Harry Truman as running mate.) Roosevelt had been instrumental in forging the strategy for winning the war. He was planning a meeting of Allied heads of state in the coming February and the formation of the United Nations later in 1945.

The leaders met at Yalta on the Crimean Peninsula in the USSR. The main topic was the new order in Europe after the defeat of Germany. Before long, great controversy erupted over what had been agreed to at the conference. Roosevelt departed February 12 aboard the destroyer USS *Quincy*. In Egypt, aboard ship he met separately with the king of Egypt, Emperor Haile Selassie of Ethiopia, King Abdulaziz ibn Saud of Saudi Arabia, and British prime minister Winston Churchill, who had also been at Yalta.

Back in Washington, Roosevelt addressed Congress on March 1. He looked ill, very tired, and old (though he was only sixty-three). He sat during his speech, contrary to his customary insistence on always standing when giving a speech. He called for "a universal organization in which all peace-loving nations will finally have a chance to join." That month he sent sharply worded messages to Soviet leader Joseph Stalin accusing him of breaking commitments he had made at Yalta.

After a brief visit to Springwood, the family's Hyde Park estate, he left on the twenty-ninth for Warm Springs, to rest before the conference in San Francisco that was expected to result in the formation of the United Nations. Missy LeHand had died of a stroke the year before; however, Roosevelt's daughter, Anna Boettiger, had moved into the White House to give her father added support. She also arranged for him to meet with his former mistress, Lucy Mercer, now a widow. Lucy was with him on April 12 when he complained of a sharp pain in his head and fell unconscious. He died of a stroke that afternoon. He is buried at Hyde Park. Eleanor lived on until 1962 and is also buried at Hyde Park.

Warm Springs, about seventy miles north of Atlanta, continued to flourish after Roosevelt's death; however, by the time the Salk and Sabin vaccines were widely used and polio more or less eradicated, it changed its mission. Today it is the Roosevelt Warm Springs Institute for Rehabilitation, a state-run center for victims of stroke, brain and spinal cord injuries, and severe arthritis.

The Roosevelt family estate, Springwood and its land, has become the Franklin D. Roosevelt National Historic Site. It also includes the Franklin D. Roosevelt Presidential Library & Museum.

Springwood was purchased in 1866 by Roosevelt's father, James, who enlarged the house. In 1915, Franklin and his mother, Sara, added two fieldstone wings, doubling the size of the house.

They added a tower and a third story, flat-roofed. The facade was changed from clapboard to stucco to complement the stonework. The finished mansion was one of Colonial Revival style.

Between 1911 and Roosevelt's death in 1945, some four hundred thousand trees were planted on the grounds. In 1943, he gave the estate to the nation, retaining a life interest for his family. After his death, the family relinquished this right. Since then, the property has been administered by the National Park Service. The Presidential Library and Museum are operated by the National Archives and Records Administration.

The museum is open from 9 a.m. to 5 p.m. from November through April and 9 a.m.–6 p.m., May through October. It is closed on Thanksgiving, Christmas, and New Year's Day. The research room of the library is open 8:45 a.m.–5 p.m., Monday through Friday, but closed on national holidays.

Address: 4097 Albany Post Road, Hyde Park, NY 12538–1997. For information email roosevelt.library@nara.gov or telephone 880-FDR-VISIT. Website: http://www.nps.gov/hofr/index.htm.

Chapter Thirty-two

HARRY S. TRUMAN

THE 33RD PRESIDENT

April 12, 1945—January 20, 1953

*I*t wasn't long after Harry Truman became president upon the sudden death of Franklin D. Roosevelt that he developed a fondness for short weekend cruises on the presidential yacht, the USS *Williamsburg*. No wonder, for no president before or since has confronted so many momentous decisions in such a short period of time. No one could begrudge him a few hours' relief from them.

During the eighty-two days Truman was vice president, Roosevelt rarely contacted him, thus he was not privy to Roosevelt's ideas and commitments regarding a post–World War II globe. He quickly got down to business. Secretary of War Henry L. Stimson briefed him on the Manhattan Project, which had produced the atomic bomb. It was news to Truman.

He asked the Roosevelt cabinet to stay but made it clear he would be the decision-maker. From this came the slogan he put on a plaque on his desk, "The Buck Stops Here."

He then went to Potsdam, a suburb of Berlin, to meet with Stalin and British prime minister Clement Attlee to write the Potsdam Declaration. It called for all parties to recognize democracy in the lands previously conquered by the Nazis and for Japan's unconditional surrender. The Japanese turned this down, so Truman approved the use of atomic weapons to shorten the war and prevent the death of thousands of American troops in a land invasion of Japan. The first bomb was dropped on Hiroshima on August 6, 1945; the second on Nagasaki on August 9. In a 1963 letter to a Chicago columnist, Truman wrote, "I knew what I was doing when I stopped the war. . . . I have no regrets and, under the same circumstances, would do it again."

Next came the launching of the United Nations, which Truman strongly supported. Stalin soon abandoned the commitments he had made at Potsdam and the USSR began the takeover of central and eastern European nations, to make them into a buffer between Russia and the West.

The communists soon fomented a civil war in Greece and made efforts in Iran and Turkey. The Cold War was beginning. In this climate the Truman Doctrine was created. Its purpose was to contain the advance of Soviet communism. With strong bipartisan support in Congress, this was followed by the huge Marshall Plan, a program to rebuild the shattered cities and countries of Western Europe.

The big decisions kept on flowing from Truman's Oval Office. The National Security Act of 1947 created a new Department of Defense, under which the armed services were placed. The Army Air Force was hived off to become a separate branch, the U.S. Air Force. The act also created the Central Intelligence Agency.

His secretary of state, George Marshall, and other senior officials argued that the United States should not recognize the state of Israel; that it would destabilize the region and was, in any case, secondary to combatting Soviet expansionism. A UN committee was formed that recommended dividing Palestine into two states. Truman supported this plan. The General Assembly approved the plan on November 29, 1947. The Arabs declined to accept it. Conflict ensued. On May 14, 1948, the State of Israel declared itself a nation. Eleven minutes later, Truman announced U.S. recognition of it.

In June 1948, the USSR blocked ground access to the three sectors of Berlin held by the United States, the United Kingdom, and France. The purpose was to squeeze out the three allies. Truman approved a daring plan to supply West Berlin by air. On June 25, the Berlin Airlift began, delivering food, clothing, even coal. It continued for over a year, even after the Soviets lifted their blockade.

All this time, demobilization of our wartime armed forces proceeded. Ships were mothballed or sold; units were reduced in strength. The White House's defense budget requests declined until June 1950, when North Korean troops invaded South Korea.

A HEARTLAND BEGINNING

Harry S. Truman (he had no middle name, just the initial) was born May 8, 1884, in Lamar, Missouri, the eldest of three children of John A. and Martha Ellen Young Truman. This was an American heartland family. John was a farmer and livestock dealer. They lived on a succession of farms, settling on his grandfather's six-hundred-acre farm in Grandview in 1887. They then moved to Independence. Young Harry was especially interested in history, reading, and music. He studied music into his teen years and awoke at five every day to practice the piano.

His first brush with politics was as a page at the 1900 Democratic National Convention. After high school graduation he worked as a railroad timekeeper, office clerk, and newspaper mailroom clerk. In 1906 he moved to the Grandview farm, where he lived and worked until he went into the army in 1917. He was in the Missouri National Guard from 1905 to 1911. With U.S. entry into the war, he rejoined, bound for France after training. As a captain he led a battery in an artillery regiment. In one battle, his troops began to fall back. Using the most colorful cuss words he could muster, he ordered them back in line and led them to safety. By the time he left the army he had risen to the rank of colonel.

INTO BUSINESS AND POLITICS

After the war, Truman briefly attended a business school, then a night law school, but dropped out. In 1919 he married Bess Wallace. They had one daughter, Mary Margaret (known as Margaret). That year he also opened a men's clothing store in downtown Kansas City with Eddie Jacobson, an army buddy. The business failed in the recession of

1921. Truman paid off the last of its debts in 1934. He became active in
Freemasonry and remained so throughout his life.

In the army he also came to know James M. Pendergast, nephew of
Kansas City's Democratic political boss, Thomas Joseph ("T.J.") Pendergast. With the help of Pendergast's machine in 1922 he was elected
judge of the Jackson County Court. This was not a judicial position
but was akin to county commissioner/supervisor in counties elsewhere.
He lost his bid for reelection in 1924, but was elected again in 1926, this
time as presiding judge, and reelected in 1930. In this position he oversaw a ten-year plan to add new roads and public buildings to Kansas
City.

After Roosevelt's 1932 election, Pendergast, who controlled federal patronage in the area, saw to it that Truman was appointed state
director of the Federal Reemployment Program. The following year,
Pendergast supported him for a U.S. Senate nomination over two other
Democrats. Truman won and then unseated an incumbent Republican.
During his first term he followed the New Deal line. In 1943 he was
named to head a special committee, which came to be known as the
Truman Committee, to ferret out waste and mismanagement in the war
effort. He proposed numerous sensible measures for saving money for
the military and gained national attention as a result.

VICE PRESIDENT

By mid-1944, Democratic Party leaders were greatly worried by President Roosevelt's declining health. They wanted the very liberal vice
president Henry Wallace off the ticket. Robert Hannegan of St. Louis
was Democratic national chairman. While Roosevelt agreed to drop
Wallace, he wanted the convention to pick his replacement and indicated that either Truman or Supreme Court justice William O. Douglas
would be satisfactory. Hannegan and others wanted Truman, who had
done nothing to campaign for the position. They invited him to a meeting at Chicago's Blackstone Hotel (scene of the Harding "smoke-filled
room" twenty-four years earlier) to listen in on a telephone conversation between them and Roosevelt. Unbeknownst to Truman, the
conversation had been rehearsed. In it, Roosevelt asked the party leaders if Truman would accept the nomination. They said he would not,

whereupon FDR sharply accused Truman of endangering party unity. He hung up. Truman, being a loyalist, decided he had no choice but to agree to go on the ticket, which went on to defeat New York governor Thomas Dewey and his running mate, Ohio senator John Bricker, by 432 to 99 electoral votes.

On April 12, 1945, Truman, as vice president and thus also president of the Senate, had adjourned the body for the day and set out for House Speaker Sam Rayburn's office for a drink when he got the news to go to the White House. There, Eleanor Roosevelt told him of her husband's death.

PRESIDENTIAL DOMESTIC TROUBLES

In July Truman was in Germany for nearly two weeks at the Potsdam Conference, where he discussed the future of Germany and Europe with British prime minister Clement Attlee and Soviet leader Joseph Stalin. In early August he also had to make the final decision on the use of the atomic bomb. He had to weigh the probable loss of tens of thousands of American soldiers in an invasion of Japan against the likely number of civilian deaths from the bomb.

While Truman was making momentous—and courageous—decisions on the world stage, things were bumpy at home. The conversion of the nation from a wartime to peacetime economy brought many stresses. Inflation moved upward. Long-dormant labor-management disagreements surfaced in strikes in several industries. The biggest was a national railway strike in 1946. Freight and passenger traffic ground nearly to a halt. When workers rejected a settlement proposal, Truman temporarily nationalized the railroads and threatened to draft railway workers into the army to run them. He addressed Congress to get support for this when news came that the strike had been settled in the way he wanted. He received great credit for this, although he lost some labor support in the process.

In the 1946 Congressional elections, voters, tired of wartime constraints, elected Republican majorities in both houses. They lowered tax rates and ended wartime price controls—to the dismay of Truman. While he and the Republicans cooperated on foreign policy matters, they were adversaries on nearly every domestic issue.

By 1948, Truman's support in the polls had declined steadily (to 36 percent) and it was widely believed he would be defeated for election in his own right. When the party's national convention passed a strong civil rights plank, two southern states' delegations walked out.

Truman liked the plank, however, and two weeks later signed an executive order desegregating the armed services.

The worries of party leaders that this would cause a southern revolt were realized when South Carolina governor Strom Thurmond declared he would be a candidate on what became known as the Dixiecrat ticket. Meanwhile, former vice president Wallace had gone far left and became the candidate of the Progressive Party. The Democratic Party seemed on the verge of disintegrating. During this dark time, Truman's line, "If you can't stand the heat, get out of the kitchen," gained wide circulation.

Truman embarked on a nationwide whistle-stop train campaign. He drew large, enthusiastic crowds. He railed against the "Do-nothing Congress," earning the cheer "Give 'em hell, Harry." Major polling firms, which ceased surveying weeks before the election, failed to detect the growing momentum for Truman. On election day he and his running mate, Kentucky senator Alben Barkley, won 303 electoral votes, crushing the ticket of Dewey and California governor Earl Warren, which had 39. Henry Wallace received none.

THE SECOND TERM

In 1949, Truman secured Senate approval for creation of the North Atlantic Treaty Organization (NATO). When, in that same year, the Chinese communists under Mao Zedong succeeded in winning the civil war for mainland China and Chiang Kai-shek's Nationalist government decamped for Taiwan, Truman ordered the U.S. Seventh Fleet into the Taiwan Strait to prevent both a communist invasion of the island and a Nationalist attempt to attack the mainland.

On the home front, growing concerns over the expansion of Soviet communism as well as the specter of a communist-ruled China surfaced in accusations of communist infiltration of U.S. institutions, such as the film industry and the federal government. Investigations ensued and Wisconsin's senator Joseph McCarthy dramatically claimed to have a list of communists in influential jobs in the Department of State. The Whittaker Chambers–Alger Hiss case erupted during this time. Truman counterattacked, but it was not until 1954, after he had left office, that McCarthy was discredited in public hearings.

THE KOREAN WAR

In late June 1950, when North Korea attacked its southern neighbor and pushed its defense forces out of its capital city, Seoul, Truman immediately sought a U.S. naval blockade, but he found that cutbacks in the navy made this impossible. He then obtained UN Security Council approval for armed UN intervention—a first. This was made possible because the Soviet Union was boycotting the UN at the time and was not there to exercise a veto.

At first, U.S. land forces were not fully prepared to push back the North Koreans. Truman brought in General Douglas MacArthur, hero of World War II, who devised a surprise amphibious landing at Inchon that resulted in the North Korean forces being pushed back almost to that country's northern border, the Yalu River. Then, in November, China sent in thousands of its troops, pushing the UN forces back to approximately the 38th parallel, the original post–World War II boundary.

There the war settled into a stalemate.

MacArthur wanted to bomb Chinese supply points. Truman met with him on Wake Island in the Pacific. Worried that the USSR might be drawn into the war, he turned MacArthur down. MacArthur took his proposal to the Republican House leaders, who leaked it to the press. This was too much for Truman. On April 11, 1951, he relieved MacArthur of command—a very unpopular decision. The president's approval ratings dropped sharply and there were calls for his impeachment.

MacArthur landed in San Francisco to a hero's welcome. His flair for drama made his speeches popular with his audiences and the general public.

Truman's popularity never recovered. He had hoped to run for another term in 1952 (he was "grandfathered in" under the Twenty-second Amendment, which was ratified in 1951 and limited presidents to two terms). He changed his mind after Tennessee senator Estes

Kefauver beat him in the New Hampshire primary. In February that year, his Gallup Poll approval rating was only 22 percent. On March 29, he announced he would not run. Illinois governor Adlai Stevenson went on to win the nomination.

OTHER TROUBLES

In November 1950, two Puerto Rican nationalists attempted to assassinate Truman, who was residing in Blair House, across the street from the White House, which was undergoing extensive renovations. One of them shot and killed a White House policeman and was killed himself. The other was sentenced to life imprisonment. Truman, his instinct for fairness undimmed, authorized a plebiscite to be held in Puerto Rico to determine the wishes of its people in their relationship to the United States.

Truman's role as a loving parent came to the fore when a *Washington Post* music critic panned a vocal concert by his daughter, Margaret. Truman shot back a letter that noted, among things, "I hope to meet you. When that happens, you'll need a new nose, a lot of beefsteak for black eyes and perhaps a supporter for below!"

Several members of his administration were caught up in scandals. One intimate, Harry Vaughan, military aide, was involved in several influence-peddling schemes, which embarrassed Truman, who was not aware of them. Several dozen Internal Revenue Service employees resigned or were discharged.

ANCHORS AWEIGH

The USS *Williamsburg* was a convenient means for the president to leave the cares of office behind, even if only for a day or so. He made more than two hundred short cruises and three longer ones on it.

In his oral history for the Truman Presidential Library, Gerald P. Pulley, a navy photographer, said, "The President liked to get away. And he'd get away from the press [that way]. He loved to get on that *Williamsburg*."

From August 16 to September 2, 1946, Truman and twelve guests took a vacation cruise, first up the coast to Rhode Island, then to

Bermuda. According to the ship's log some of the guests were only aboard for the first part. Among the guests were Truman's press secretary, Charles Ross; Robert Hannegan, by then the postmaster general; Harry Vaughan, whose wheeling and dealing later caused his boss much grief; and Secretary of the Treasury John Snyder. Aboard also was a rotating Secret Service detail of six to eight men.

In addition to the ship's crew, commanded by Captain Charles L. Freeman, the staff for the presidential party included a movie operator, a secretary, a navy aerographer, the president's valet, a photographer, and a musician. Following the *Williamsburg* was an escort ship, the USS *Weiss,* with the news media aboard: fifteen newspaper and wire service reporters, four radio correspondents, three still photographers, and one newsreel cameraman.

Truman took another vacation cruise on the *Williamsburg* in 1949, from August 20 to 29. It cruised the Chesapeake and Delaware bays.

FLYING DOWN TO RIO

In summer 1947, the president accepted an invitation to make a state visit to Brazil. He, Mrs. Truman, Margaret, and the rest of their party flew in the presidential airplane (a propeller plane) from Independence, Missouri, to Brazil. Upon their arrival in Rio they found approximately one million people lining the streets to greet them. Truman addressed an Inter-American Conference then under way and also a joint session of the Brazilian Congress. He was host to Brazilian president Eurico Dutra and six hundred other guests for lunch aboard the USS *Missouri.* President Dutra entertained the Truman party at a state dinner. On his last day there, President Truman reviewed a military parade commemorating the 125th anniversary of Brazil's independence.

On September 7, with the Truman party aboard, the *Missouri* weighed anchor for Norfolk, Virginia. It arrived on the nineteenth. There the presidential party transferred to the *Williamsburg* for the final leg home to Washington, arriving early the next morning.

Truman had made two earlier trips by air in 1947: a three-day state visit to Mexico in March and a two-day official visit to Ottawa, Canada, in June. For his remaining five years and four months in office after the Rio trip, Truman did not leave the United States.

CARIBBEAN TRIP

From February 20 to March 5, 1948, Truman and a party visited Puerto Rico, the Virgin Islands, the U.S. naval base at Guantanamo Bay in Cuba, and Key West, Florida. They first flew to Key West, then to San Juan, Puerto Rico. There they boarded the *Williamsburg* for the Virgin Islands and "Gitmo," then returned to Key West for a week before flying back to Washington.

A HAVEN IN KEY WEST

After his first visit to the Key West Naval Base in 1946, Truman liked it so well he returned ten more times during his presidency. Altogether, he spent 175 days at the Key West retreat. All his visits took place between November and March. Key West afforded him peace and quiet. The Secret Service liked it, too, because its acreage was surrounded by a high fence and the president could stroll the grounds at his leisure in complete safety.

His quarters (except for the first trip, when his party stayed at a submarine base) were a second-floor suite in a building that was dubbed the Winter White House. He and his party would enjoy balmy weather by the beach and swim in the ocean. He responded to his daily mail and messages, had telephone conversations with cabinet secretaries back in Washington, and met, as needed, with members of his party on presidential business matters. The visits were, however, intended to be relaxing and they were. Truman took to wearing loose-fitting Hawaiian print short-sleeved shirts, not tucked into his trousers. After photographs of him in this attire swept the country, so did a rush in men's stores for Hawaiian shirts.

PURE BUSINESS TRAVEL

For the Big Three conference in Potsdam, just outside Berlin, President Truman crossed the Atlantic on the heavy cruiser USS *Augusta*. The trip covered the period July 6–August 7, 1945. For his climactic meeting with General Douglas MacArthur on the mid-Pacific island, Wake, he flew. That trip covered the days October 11–18, 1950.

POST-PRESIDENCY

After General Eisenhower was inaugurated on January 20, 1953, the Trumans returned to their home in Independence, Missouri. Four months later, they took a trip that would be unthinkable today for a former president. The two of them, unescorted, drove in their new Chrysler sedan to Philadelphia, where he addressed the Reserve Officers Association. They made stops along the way to see sights and visit friends, including days in Washington. (The trip is recounted in detail in Matthew Algeo's 2009 book, *Harry Truman's Excellent Adventure*.)

Back home, he raised the money to build his presidential library, which was donated to the federal government. He eschewed offers to join corporate boards and had only his small monthly army pension. This was later remedied when Congress passed legislation to provide all former presidents an annual pension.

In 1956, the Trumans traveled to Europe, where the former president received an honorary degree at Oxford and met with Winston Churchill.

Harry Truman died in Kansas City on December 26, 1972, at the age of eighty-eight. Bess died nearly ten years later, on October 18, 1982. Both are buried at the Truman Library.

———•·•·•———

The Harry S. Truman Presidential Library and Museum holds the public papers of President Truman as well as regular and changing exhibits. Operated by the National Archives and Records Administration, it is open Mondays through Saturday, 9 a.m.–5 p.m.; Sundays, noon–5 p.m.

Closed Thanksgiving, Christmas, and New Year's Day. Address: 500 W. U.S. Highway 24, Independence, MO 64050–1798. Telephone: 800-833-1225 or 816-268-8200. Email: truman.library@nara.gov. Website: www.trumanlibrary.org.

The USS Williamsburg *was decommissioned by President Eisenhower in 1953.*

The naval station in Key West, Florida, was an active installation from 1823 to 1957. When it was deactivated, the area was named the Truman Annex. A portion was developed into a private gated community. The rest is now part of a National Register Historic District.

Chapter Thirty-three

DWIGHT D. EISENHOWER

THE 34TH PRESIDENT

January 20, 1953—January 20, 1961

As a cadet at West Point, Dwight Eisenhower had his heart set on making the baseball team. He wasn't chosen; however, he did become a member of its football team and was on the varsity squad as both a linebacker and running back in the 1912 season. Knee injuries in both boxing and horseback riding, however, put an end to his running career. Years later he took up golf with single-mindedness and played when he could in his military years and frequently as president. Most of his favorite retreats were close to golf courses, and he even had a putting green installed at Camp David.

A POOR FAMILY

Born October 14, 1890, Dwight David Eisenhower (originally David Dwight, but he transposed the names when he entered West Point) was the son of David J. and Ida Stover Eisenhower. His father had an engineering degree but never prospered, so the family was always poor. Dwight was born in Denison, Texas, where his father worked temporarily. Two years later they moved to Abilene, Kansas, where he attended public schools, graduating from high school in 1909.

He went to work as a night foreman at a local creamery, largely to help support his brother's college education. He then sought and obtained a recommendation from one of Kansas's U.S. senators for admission to the U.S. Military Academy. He was accepted in 1911 and graduated from West Point four years later as a second lieutenant.

Eisenhower was assigned to an army camp in Texas. There he met Mamie Geneva Doud, a native of Boone, Iowa. They were married on July 1, 1916, in Denver where her family lived.

They had two sons. Doud died of scarlet fever at age three. John, born in 1922, had a successful army career (retiring as a brigadier general) and became an author. He also served as ambassador to Belgium from 1969 to 1971. John's son, David, married Julie Nixon, the younger daughter of Richard Nixon.

MILITARY CAREER MOVES

During World War I, Dwight Eisenhower was part of the leadership of the new tank corps. He trained tank crews near the site of the Gettysburg battlefield. Neither he nor his tank crews saw combat. He was then posted to Camp (now Fort) Meade, Maryland, until 1922. After that he was appointed executive officer to the commander of the Panama Canal Zone.

Next came the Command and General Staff College at Fort Leavenworth, Kansas, where Eisenhower finished first in his class of 245. This was followed by his assignment as executive officer to the assistant secretary of war (1929–33), then chief aide to General Douglas MacArthur, who was the army chief of staff until 1935. That year, MacArthur went to the Philippines as chief military adviser to its government and Eisenhower was his deputy. In time, he and MacArthur disagreed strongly over the role of the Philippine Army's approach to leadership. Their disagreements were never resolved.

In 1936, Eisenhower was promoted to lieutenant colonel, after many years as a major. In 1939 he returned to the United States. In 1941 he became chief of staff to the commander of the Third Army, based in Texas. By then he had also attained the rank of brigadier general.

Following the Japanese attack on Pearl Harbor he was assigned to the Army General Staff in Washington, D.C., working on overall plans to defeat Germany and Japan. By mid-1942 he was based in London as Commanding General, European Theater of Operations, then Supreme Commander, Allied Force of the North African Theater of Operations. He had to deal with the strong personalities of Prime Minister Winston Churchill and British Field Marshal Bernard "Monty" Montgomery.

After the Allied forces defeated the Axis in North Africa, Eisenhower commanded the invasion of Italy. Late in 1943, President Roosevelt designated him as the Supreme Allied Commander in Europe, in charge of planning and executing the invasion of Normandy and carrying the war to victory in Germany. The invasion, Operation Overlord, took place on June 6, 1944, D-Day, and the war in Europe ended with the surrender of Nazi Germany on May 8, 1945.

By now holding the rank of General of the Army, Eisenhower was put in charge of the U.S. Occupation Zone in Germany. He saw to the filming of evidence at Nazi concentration camps and brought in large amounts of food for the undernourished civilian population. From late 1945 to 1947 he was back in Washington as Army Chief of Staff, overseeing the demobilization of several million troops.

POLITICS

He became president of Columbia University in 1948. In 1952 a strong push developed to draft Eisenhower as the Republican presidential candidate that year. His followers rallied around the theme of "I Like Ike." With Richard Nixon as his running mate, he went on to defeat the Democratic ticket of Illinois governor Adlai Stevenson and Alabama senator John Sparkman with 57.6 percent of the popular vote and an electoral vote of 457–74.

THE PRESIDENCY, 1953–61

On December 2, 1952, before he was inaugurated, Eisenhower did go to Korea to set in motion negotiations to end the war there. A cease-fire took place the following July.

He did not seek to dismantle New Deal social programs, but rolled them into a new Department of Health, Education and Welfare (today the Department of Health and Human Services, with a separate Department of Education since the Carter administration). Through his leadership Congress passed the Federal Highway Act of 1956, which created the Interstate Highway System.

In foreign affairs, Eisenhower embraced a "containment" policy toward the Soviet Union, even though in the late 1940s he had been skeptical about such an approach. The CIA was involved in several covert operations, such as the replacement of Guatemalan and Iranian governments. Eisenhower's administration also planned the Bay of Pigs operation to overthrow Cuban communist leader Fidel Castro, although it was the Kennedy administration that carried it out, in 1961 — with disastrous results.

In 1956, when Hungarians rose up against the Soviet puppet government and Soviet armed forces invaded the country, Eisenhower felt there was nothing he could do but condemn the action. Also that year, the French and British launched a joint invasion of Egypt to ensure that the Suez Canal would remain open to them. Eisenhower condemned this action, feeling he could not condemn the Russians and condone actions by his allies that looked similar on the surface. Long afterward he said that the decision to condemn the Suez invasion at the United Nations was the biggest mistake of his presidency.

In 1957 and 1958 his administration sent aid to the government of Jordan. It also sent several thousand U.S. marines to Lebanon on a peacekeeping mission to bolster that country's pro-Western government. These actions had the effect of pushing back at the anti-Western actions of Gamal Abdel Nasser's Egypt and a pro-Soviet Syria.

In 1953 the French asked Eisenhower to support them in their war in Indochina against communist insurgents. He agreed to send military advisers to South Vietnam's army. By the time he left office there were nearly nine hundred such U.S. advisers on the ground in Vietnam.

Domestically, Eisenhower took bold action in 1957 when Arkansas governor Orval Faubus refused a federal court order to integrate his state's schools in the wake of the historic *Brown v. Board of Education* decision in 1954 by the U.S. Supreme Court. In what became known as the Little Rock Nine crisis, Eisenhower signed an executive order putting the Arkansas National Guard under federal control and also sending U.S. Army troops to escort nine black students into Central High School in Little Rock.

Eisenhower was far more open than his predecessors about his health. In late September 1955, during a Colorado vacation, he had a heart attack. He was at Fitzsimmons Army Hospital in Denver from September 24 to November 11. During his recuperation, his cardiologist, Paul Dudley White, held regular media briefings about Ike's condition. In June the next year the president had surgery to clear a bowel obstruction. In November 1957 he suffered a mild stroke. After that he remained in good health throughout the rest of his time in office. In the interest of his health he had stopped smoking in 1949.

TRAVELS WITH IKE

For the first five of his eight years in the presidency, Eisenhower traveled in propeller-driven aircraft. In 1958 the air force acquired three Boeing 707 jets. Whichever one he was on was designated Air Force One.

As president-elect, he kept his promise to go to Korea by traveling there in early December 1952. After his inauguration he took only seven propeller-era trips. Only two were long-distance. The first was to Geneva, July 16–23, 1955, for a summit conference with British prime minister Anthony Eden, French premier Edgar Faure, and Soviet premier Nikolai Bulganin. The second was to Paris, December 14–19, 1957, for a conference of the heads of state of NATO's member countries. The other trips during that time were much shorter, such as to Mexico and Canada.

On the new jets Ike became a globe-trotter. In ten trips over three years he met with heads of state and other leaders in Canada, Mexico, West Germany, Britain, France, Italy, Turkey, Pakistan, Afghanistan, India, Iran, Greece, Tunisia, Spain, Morocco, Brazil, Argentina, Chile, Uruguay, Portugal, Philippines, the Republic of China (Taiwan), and Korea. He also met the pope at Vatican City. On one trip to England and France, he took a three-day break to play golf and relax at Culzean Castle, on the coast of Scotland.

A SECOND TERM

In 1968, the Eisenhower-Nixon ticket defeated Adlai Stevenson by a larger margin than in 1952, 457–73 electoral votes. Senator Estes Kefauver of Tennessee was Stevenson's running mate.

R&R

According to Dick Snyder, son of Eisenhower's White House physician, Howard Snyder, his father saw health benefits for the president in "periodic escapes from White House pressures."

Dick Snyder writes, "The Augusta National Golf Club, the El Dorado Country Club in Palm Springs and the Cherry Hills Golf Club in Denver were favorites, as was the fine trout fishing not far from the Denver residence of his mother-in-law, Mrs. Doud. Camp David, with its easy commute from Washington, was also an Eisenhower favorite." Dr. Snyder was very much aware of the effect of Eisenhower's legendary "short fuse" on his blood pressure, so he endorsed these relaxing activities.

Ike took what the archivists at his presidential library call "extended vacations" every year in office; however, nearly all of these involved some official appointments or official documents, so they were actually working vacations. Altogether he spent 456 days on such sojourns, a yearly average of 57.

In the first three years of his presidency, he and the First Lady took their vacations at her mother's home in Denver or the Summer White House at Lowry Air Force Base, also in Colorado. He played 69 rounds of golf at the aforementioned Cherry Hills County Club there. The president also visited several times at the Aksel Nielsen Ranch near Fraser, Colorado, to fish in St. Louis Creek.

He also made short visits to Denver in 1958, 1959, and 1960.

In Eisenhower's second term, the naval base at Newport, Rhode Island, became the Summer White House. The First Family was provided with living quarters there and the White House staff had a nearby office on the base. The Eisenhowers were there September 4–30, 1957; August 29–September 23, 1958; and July 7–August 7, 1960. Golf, as usual, figured prominently in Ike's off-hour activities. He played fifty rounds over those three visits, at the Newport Country Club.

In 1950, the Eisenhowers purchased their farm adjacent to the Gettysburg, Pennsylvania, Civil War battlefield. From 1955 until the completion of his second term in 1961, the president made 118 visits there. Some were only for a few hours, some for several days. In 1959, the Eisenhowers had one of their longest stretches there, August 7–23.

Another Eisenhower favorite was the Augusta National Golf Club in Georgia, famous as the home of the Masters tournament. He made twenty-eight visits there during his White House years and played 211 rounds of golf. His stays ranged from a few days to two weeks. The club was so pleased to have the president as a guest that it built a special cottage for him and the First Lady along the first fairway. It was soon dubbed "Mamie's Cabin."

Every February from 1954 to 1959, "Ike" spent from three to twelve days hunting quail at Secretary of the Treasury George Humphrey's Milestone Plantation near Thomasville, Georgia.

Ike made four visits to the Palm Springs area of Southern California. From February 17 to 23, 1954, he stayed at Smoke Tree Ranch and played golf at the Tamarisk and Thunderbird country clubs.

From September 30 to October 8, 1959, and January 28 to February 1, 1960, he stayed at the La Quinta residence of longtime friend George Allen and played golf at the El Dorado Country Club. That year, from October 18 to 24 he stayed in Palm Springs, played golf at La Quinta, and gave some campaign speeches on behalf of Richard Nixon, his vice president, who was then running to succeed him.

Eisenhower made one- or two-day visits to Custer State Park, South Dakota; Parmachenee Lake, Maine; Hianloland Farms, Rhode Island; and Little Hunting Creek Lodge, Thurmont, Maryland.

After John F. Kennedy's inauguration on January 20, 1961, the Eisenhowers retired to their Gettysburg farm. In 1964, he spoke at the 1964 Republican National Convention and later appeared in a television spot with nominee Barry Goldwater that was filmed at the Gettysburg farm.

Dwight Eisenhower died of congestive heart failure on March 28, 1969, at Walter Reed Army Hospital in Washington, D.C. He was seventy-eight. He is buried in the small chapel at the Eisenhower Presidential Library in Abilene, Kansas, as is his wife, Mamie, and son Doud, who died as a young child.

In 1967 the Eisenhowers made a gift of their Gettysburg farm to the National Park Service, retaining the right to live there for the rest of their lives. Mrs. Eisenhower died in 1979. It opened to the public the next year.

In 1950 they purchased what was then a 189-acre farm, with buildings much in need of repair.

In 1953, much of the main residence was demolished and rebuilt. Since it was the first home the couple had ever owned, Mrs. Eisenhower decorated it with all the furnishings they had had in storage for several years.

When the restoration was completed, the Eisenhowers invited the entire White House staff to a house-warming party there.

The Eisenhowers increased the acreage to 230.

They installed a putting green and a skeet-shooting range. In the home, they spent much of their time in a glass-enclosed porch reading, playing cards, and visiting with friends. Among the famous visitors to the farm were Soviet leader Nikita Khrushchev, French president Charles de Gaulle, British prime minister Winston Churchill, and California governor and future president Ronald Reagan.

The Eisenhower National Historic Site now covers 690 acres and includes four farms, three of which Eisenhower used to raise his show herd of Black Angus cattle. Today, visitors see the home as it was when they lived there.

Tickets for tours of the farm are available at the Gettysburg National Military Park Visitor Center and Museum, 1195 Baltimore Parkway, Gettysburg, PA 17325. Visitors take a shuttle bus to the farm. Buses leave throughout the day from 9 a.m. to 4 p.m. Plan on spending one and a half to two hours for the visit. (Closed Thanksgiving, Christmas and New Year's Day.)

Telephone: 717-338-9114. Website: www.nps.gov/eise/index.htm.

The Dwight D. Eisenhower Presidential Library and Museum, part of the National Archives and Research Administration system, features permanent exhibits about the president's life, changing exhibits throughout the year, and a research room.

The museum is open 9 a.m.–4:45 p.m. every day, except Thanksgiving and New Year's Day.

Summer hours (Memorial Day through mid-August) are 8 a.m.–5:45 p.m.

Research Room hours are Monday through Friday, 8:30 a.m.–noon and 12:45–5:15 p.m. (Closed on all federal holidays.)

Address: 200 S.E. 4th Street, P.O. Box 339, Abilene, KS 67410. Telephone: 785-263-6700, 877-RING-IKE. Email: eisenhower.library@ nara.gov. Website: www.eisenhower.archives.gov.

Chapter Thirty-four

JOHN F. KENNEDY

THE 35TH PRESIDENT

January 20, 1961 — November 22, 1963

*L*ike his brothers and sisters, "Jack" Kennedy was taught to strive for excellence and he did, academically and in war service. Nevertheless, it was his older brother, Joseph, Jr., who their father had expected to take up the mantle of politics after World War II. In the midst of that war, however, Joe was lost in August 1944, so the mantle passed to Jack.

BORN TO SUCCEED

John Fitzgerald Kennedy was born May 29, 1917, in Brookline, Massachusetts, an inner suburb of Boston, to Joseph, Sr., and Rose Fitzgerald Kennedy. He was the second oldest of four sons and five daughters of the couple. Rose was the daughter of John "Honey Fitz" Fitzgerald, onetime mayor of Boston and three-term member of Congress.

When John was ten, the family moved to Riverdale in the Bronx, New York City, then Bronxville. There he was a Boy Scout (he was the first president to have been one). Summers were spent at the family's home in Hyannis Port, Massachusetts, at the base of Cape Cod.

Christmas and Easter holidays were spent at the family's Palm Beach, Florida, home.

When John reached ninth grade he was sent to Choate school in southern Connecticut. There his older brother, Joe, was a popular football star. Living in his brother's shadow, John became something of a hell-raiser, but one prank nearly got him expelled, so he settled down to the school routine. After recovering from colitis, he graduated in June 1935. The yearbook named him "Most Likely to Succeed" of the graduating seniors.

TO LONDON

In September that year he accompanied his parents to London. His plan was to enroll at the London School of Economics, but a month later he returned to the United States and enrolled at Princeton. Six weeks later, he was hospitalized for what the doctors thought might be leukemia. It wasn't, and after being hospitalized in Boston he convalesced at Palm Beach. The next spring he worked on a large cattle ranch in Arizona. He spent the summer of 1936 mostly racing sailboats off Hyannis Port.

In September 1936, he enrolled at Harvard College. He produced a theatrical review and made the varsity swim team. The next summer he and his convertible coupe shipped out to France and, along with a school chum, he spent the season driving around Europe.

He accompanied his father and brother Joe to London in June 1938, where Joseph, Sr., had been appointed Ambassador to the Court of St. James's. They were to be among his assistants. In August, the family took a villa on the French Riviera.

In the next year, 1939, after the spring semester he traveled to the Soviet Union, the Balkan republics, parts of the Middle East, Czechoslovakia, and Germany for research on his Harvard senior honors thesis. He returned to London the day Nazi Germany invaded Poland—September 1, 1939. From London, Jack took his first transatlantic flight back to the United States.

Jack finished his thesis in his senior year, 1940. It was titled "Appeasement in Munich." He graduated cum laude from Harvard with a degree in international affairs. His father thought the thesis should be published and helped him find a publisher. It came out as *Why England Slept* and became a bestseller.

IN THE NAVY

In fall 1941, John was disqualified from army service because of chronic back problems. With the influence of his father, however, he was able to join the U.S. Navy as an ensign. Initially, he served in the office of the secretary of the navy. After Pearl Harbor he trained with the Naval ROTC and Torpedo Boat Squadron Training Center. He was first assigned to Panama, then the South Pacific, where he commanded a PT (patrol torpedo) boat. These boats were made of plywood and each was powered by two Packard engines. They were light, fast, and highly maneuverable.

In August 1943, Kennedy's PT-109 was on nighttime patrol in the Solomon Islands when it was rammed by a Japanese destroyer. He gathered his crew around the wreckage and they decided to swim to a small island nearby. One crewman was badly burned. Though Kennedy had suffered a new back injury from the crash, he swam toward the island towing the other man by holding a strap of his lifejacket between his teeth.

For his heroic actions, Kennedy later received the Navy and Marine Corps Medal, the Purple Heart, and several other medals.

Later that year, he took command of a PT boat that had been converted for use as a gunboat. It took part in a rescue of a U.S. Marines group from an island. He was discharged in 1945, shortly before Japan's surrender.

ELECTED TO CONGRESS

Back home, he found that James Michael Curley was going to run for mayor of Boston and thus would give up his seat in the U.S. House of Representatives. Kennedy ran for it and won easily. He served in the House for three terms, without rising to any leadership position and sometimes not voting his party's position on bills.

In 1952, he campaigned for U.S. Senate to unseat Republican

senator Henry Cabot Lodge, Jr., the son of Woodrow Wilson's late adversary. Kennedy succeeded. The next year, he and Jacqueline Bouvier were married. They had two children, Caroline and John, Jr.

In 1953 and 1954, Kennedy had several spinal operations and frequently missed Senate days and votes. In 1956, while convalescing, he wrote (with adviser Theodore Sorensen) *Profiles in Courage,* which examined several senators who had risked their political careers over principles. In 1957, Kennedy was awarded the Pulitzer Prize for Biography for the book.

In 1954, the Senate's censure of member Joseph McCarthy of Wisconsin was a dilemma for John Kennedy.

His father had been a McCarthy supporter and his brother Robert had worked for a McCarthy subcommittee. When the censure vote came up, Jack Kennedy was in the hospital. He never said how he would have voted, though he could have paired a censure vote with an opposite one of another senator, but did not do so. His inaction angered many liberals.

In 1956 he was nominated for vice president at the Democratic National Convention. He finished second to Tennessee senator Estes Kefauver.

RUNNING FOR PRESIDENT

The Kennedys decided 1960 was to be Jack's year. He ran in several primaries, defeating Senator Hubert Humphrey in Wisconsin and West Virginia and Senator Wayne Morse in Oregon and Maryland. At the Democratic National Convention in Los Angeles, his main opponent was Senator Lyndon Johnson of Texas. Adlai Stevenson had his hat in the ring again, as did several others, but Kennedy prevailed and was nominated. Needing strong southern support, he asked Johnson to be his vice presidential running mate.

In the campaign, Kennedy addressed the issue of Catholicism by speaking at a convention of Protestant ministers in September. He said, among other things, "I do not speak for my Church on public matters—and the Church does not speak for me." As it turned out, he had laid the issue to rest.

Kennedy and opponent Richard Nixon appeared in the nation's first televised presidential campaign debates. These events proved the power of television imagery. Kennedy, who took the facial makeup offered, looked composed and relaxed. Nixon, tired from a long campaign trip, nursing a sore leg, and showing a "five o'clock shadow," skipped makeup and looked uncomfortable, with perspiration showing. Television watchers, when polled, said Kennedy was clearly the winner. Radio listeners hearing the debate scored it for Nixon.

On November 8, Kennedy edged Nixon by 49.7 percent to 49.5. There were allegations of vote fraud in Chicago. Some of Nixon's advisers wanted him to legally challenge the results. He decided against it, concluding that it would be a long affair, distracting attention from the nation's business and dividing the country. The results were so close that Kennedy, when asked by a reporter to comment on his "mandate," quipped, "It's more like a boydate."

In his inaugural address, Kennedy uttered his now-famous phrase, "Ask not what your country can do for you; ask what you can do for your country."

"THE NEW FRONTIER"

That's the slogan Kennedy gave his plans. After a brief and mild recession toward the end of Eisenhower's tenure, Kennedy made much of "getting the country moving again" as well as the "missile gap" with the Soviet Union, as if the nation had been complacent and languishing. Many young voters—and news reporters—seemed to agree and there was enthusiasm in the air for the young new president and his good-looking, stylish wife. She redecorated the White House and gave a televised tour that was very popular.

Kennedy began his term by reorganizing the White House decision-making structure. Instead of one based on a military-inspired hierarchy, he fashioned his more like a wheel, with himself as the hub and the various offices within it reporting to him. He did not shun making many quick decisions.

He proposed federal funding for education, medical support for older citizens, rural aid, and an end to racial discrimination. Few of his plans were passed during his thirty-four-month presidency, but most did come to fruition in 1964 and 1965.

In his 1963 State of the Union address, Kennedy, with the help of his Treasury secretary, C. Douglas Dillon, proposed a major reduction in income tax rates. At the time, the range was 20–90 percent. His plan proposed 14–65 percent and a corporate rate reduction from 52 percent to 47 percent. In a speech to the Economic Club of New York in 1963, he said, "[T]he paradoxical truth [is] that tax rates are too high and revenues too low; and the soundest way to raise revenue in the long term is to lower rates now." When the measures passed, he proved correct. The new revenue contributed to steady economic growth, which held inflation in check.

From 1961 to late 1963 the gross domestic product grew by an average of 5.5 percent. Inflation was held to approximately 1 percent during that period.

In spring 1962 America's major steel companies raised their prices a few days after settling union negotiations that resulted in a 2.5 percent wage increase. This was the first price increase in three years. Kennedy was furious, thinking it would cause inflation. He launched an administration-wide campaign against the steel companies, charging collusion by them. Attorney General Robert Kennedy had a grand jury called to indict U.S. Steel. Succumbing to pressure, U.S. Steel announced it would not activate the price increase.

When it came to civil rights, Kennedy spoke out for ending discrimination against African Americans in all its forms, but he was skittish about support of grassroots campaigns for fear they would alienate southern lawmakers, who would sink any civil rights legislation. However, while still a candidate, Kennedy had used his influence to have Dr. Martin Luther King, Jr., released from jail.

Early in his administration he founded the Peace Corps and put his brother-in-law Sargent Shriver at the head of it. It grew quickly and, in the fifty years since it began in 1961, some two hundred thousand Americans have been volunteer members, serving in 139 countries.

The space program drew a negative response from Kennedy when he was in the Senate, and early in his presidential term he considered shutting down the Apollo program. However, he had put Vice President Johnson in charge of the U.S. Space Council and held off on his decision. Johnson was an enthusiast for the space program, partly because NASA had proposed putting the Manned Spacecraft Center in

Houston. He helped change Kennedy's mind. In his 1961 State of the Union address, Kennedy called for international cooperation in space. He then twice brought up the subject to Nikita Khrushchev. On April 12 that year, the USSR's Yuri Gagarin became the first person to fly in space. This hastened Kennedy's commitment to the space program.

The next month he told a joint session of Congress, "I believe this nation should commit itself to achieve the goal, before this decade is out, of landing a man on the Moon and returning him safely to the Earth. No single space project in this period will be more impressive to mankind, or more important for the long-range exploration of space; and none will be so difficult or expensive to accomplish." The goal was met after his death, but within the decade, in July 1969.

FOREIGN POLICY

U.S.-Soviet relations occupied much of the Kennedy administration's time. The president met his counterpart in Vienna on June 3–4, 1961. On the way, he stopped in Paris to meet with Charles de Gaulle, who advised him not to be thrown off by Khrushchev's contentious talk. Khrushchev lost no time in bullying Kennedy. He brought up a proposed treaty between the Soviet Union and East Germany. Kennedy said in response that any treaty that interfered with U.S. access to Berlin would constitute an act of war. He left Vienna downbeat and angry at the way things had gone. Khrushchev told associates that Kennedy was quite intelligent, but young and weak.

Shortly after that "summit," the Soviets announced they would do as they wished when it came to East Berlin. Kennedy was angry and considered this a mandate to prepare for war. As many as twenty thousand East Berliners fled west after the Soviets made their announcement. Kennedy, in a July speech, said the United States would send two hundred thousand more troops to West Berlin to protect it in case of war.

He had solid public support for his position.

Within a month Soviet and East German officials put up barbed wire fences between East and West Berlin and quickly replaced them with the Berlin Wall. Access to the west from the east was blocked.

Meanwhile, Kennedy approved activation of the Eisenhower

administration's plan for the CIA to arm 1,500 U.S-trained Cubans to invade the island to generate an uprising to topple the communist Fidel Castro regime. On April 17, 1961, the Bay of Pigs invasion took place, but without U.S. air support. Within two days, the Cuban government had killed or captured the invaders. The Kennedy administration then found itself negotiating for the release of 1,189 surviving prisoners along with a payment by the United States of $53 million in food and medicine. Kennedy suspected the plan had been designed to fail, but he took responsibility for the fiasco.

On October 14, 1962, CIA U-2 spy planes took photos of intermediate-range ballistic missile sites being built in Cuba. The USSR was building these and would supply the missiles. The National Security Council concluded that these were offensive in intent. The alternatives: attack the sites and risk nuclear war or do nothing and increase the risk of threats or actual unilateral attack by the Soviets. Kennedy's decision was a naval quarantine of Cuba, by which the U.S. Navy would inspect all ships heading toward Cuban ports, commencing October 24. He notified Khrushchev of this and told the American public by television. He received unanimous support from the membership of the Organization of American States.

On October 28, it took only one Soviet ship to be stopped and boarded to persuade Khrushchev we meant business. He said they would dismantle the missile sites. For its part, the United States promised never to invade Cuba. What had become the Cuban Missile Crisis was thus over. Kennedy's public approval rating went from 66 percent to 77 percent, almost overnight.

The Kennedy administration continued the Eisenhower policy of providing military trainers and economic aid to South Vietnam. Activities by the Communist Viet Cong forces based in the north continued to escalate and the government of South Vietnam wanted more help. After the Viet Cong seized a provincial capital, the aid came. First it was in the form of a campaign to defoliate forests along the footpath supply routes of the Viet Cong.

When South Vietnam's leader, Ngo Dinh Diem, and his brother, Ngo Dinh Nhu, who led the armed forces, ordered troops into Buddhist temples, leading to the killing of several monks, Washington decided Diem needed to get rid of his brother. Nothing happened. Two

U.S. fact-finding missions were made to assess the situation there. They had contradictory reports, even as rumors of a coup persisted. In time, South Vietnamese General Duong Van Minh ("Big Minh") was to be given covert assistance to launch a coup, but not to assassinate either of the Ngos. This occurred on November 1, 1963. Minh asked the CIA field office for transportation to send the Ngos out of the country. When he was told it would take twenty-four hours to get a plane, he said he couldn't wait and had them shot. Kennedy was shocked. As things turned out, it was left for Lyndon Johnson to deal with the growing mess.

The administration made another bad bet in 1963. It supported a coup to replace Iraq's General Abdel Karim Kassem, who himself had led a 1958 coup to overthrow the monarchy. The CIA's objective was to rid Iraq of suspected Communists by using the Ba'ath Party to stage a new coup. It did—with gusto. Hundreds of intellectuals and professionals were killed. Saddam Hussein is said to have carried out some of the killings himself. He emerged as the new head man.

A nuclear test ban treaty was discussed by Kennedy and Khrushchev at their 1961 summit. They agreed in principle, but then the Soviets conducted a new test. In response, the United States did, too. In July 1963 actual negotiations began. The Soviets held out against inspections. Finally, the Soviet Union, United States, and United Kingdom signed a treaty prohibiting aboveground and underwater testing, but not underground testing. The U.S. Senate ratified it.

THE DIPLOMATIC JET SET

According to his logs, President Kennedy took forty-six presidential business trips in the United States and abroad, with a total mileage of 147,611. Eight of these were outside the United States and dealt with foreign policy. His first was in May 1961 to Canada, where he addressed a joint session of parliament in Ottawa. Next was his Vienna summit with Khrushchev, with a stop in Paris on the way and visits with Queen Elizabeth II and Prime Minister Harold Macmillan on the way back.

Other trips took him to Venezuela and Colombia (twice); to Bermuda (twice) and the Bahamas (twice) to meet with Macmillan; to

Mexico; to Costa Rica for a conference of presidents of the Central American republics; to Germany; to Ireland; to the United Kingdom again (to Birch Grove, Macmillan's home in Sussex); and to Italy and Vatican City. His final overseas trip was in early July 1963. His various bilateral meetings were with heads of state.

U.S. RETREATS

In 1960, when he was still a U.S. senator, Kennedy leased Glen-Ora, a well-established four-hundred-acre farm near Middleburg, Virginia, in the state's horse country. This was so that he and his wife could easily get away for relaxed weekends and she could ride her horses. This continued through early 1963. Altogether they spent thirty-six weekends and two "working" vacations at Glen-Ora for a total of ninety-five days.

Hyannis Port, Massachusetts, however, was where he spent the most days away from the White House. It became his Summer White House. He spent thirty-four weekends and four working vacations there—a total of 113 days. In one 1963 sojourn his guest was Canadian prime minister Lester Pearson.

John Kennedy was a very good sailor and spent many days aboard his sailboat in Nantucket Sound. After one fall 1962 visit to the compound he went to Hyde Park, New York, to attend Eleanor Roosevelt's funeral.

In 1926, Joseph Kennedy had rented a summer cottage on Marchant Avenue in Hyannis Port, on the south shore of the base of Cape Cod, facing Nantucket Sound. In 1928, he and his wife bought the 1904 house and enlarged it to fit their family of nine children. It was there the children acquired their love of sailing, touch football on the lawn, and other sports.

In 1956, John Kennedy purchased a house close to the main one and brother Robert later bought one adjacent to it. These two, along with the main house and guest houses, make up the six-acre Kennedy Compound. Young brother Edward (Ted) considered the main house his principal residence from 1982 until his death in 2009.

The main house has seven bedrooms, four servants' rooms, a motion picture theater, wine cellar, sunroom, sewing room, and utility rooms—among others. Like the other houses, it is a frame structure, faced with white clapboard and typical of New England. They are surrounded by lawns and gardens and command fine views of the ocean. The grounds include a swimming pool, tennis court, boathouse, and two guesthouses. Nearby are other summer homes belonging to other family members.

The Kennedy family also had a winter home in Palm Beach, Florida. As president, John used it for only one weekend, but eight times for "working" vacations, almost always coming or going to conferences and events, such as a speech in Miami, another after a goodwill trip to South America, and another after a conference in San Jose, Costa Rica, with the presidents of the Central American republics. He spent a total of fifty-one days there.

He also spent five weekends and three working vacations at Hammersmith Farm in Newport, Rhode Island. This is a twenty-eight-room "summer cottage" built in 1887 by John W. Auchincloss for his family. When Jacqueline Bouvier, daughter of Mrs. Hugh Auchincloss, married John Kennedy, their wedding reception took place at Hammersmith Farm. The couple liked to visit the farm for its peacefulness, paths through the woods, broad lawns, and well-tended gardens. In September and October 1962, the president used it as a base for five speaking trips in twenty-two cities during that year's election campaign for Congressional candidates. He also left from there to take part in the Columbus Day parade in New York City. Altogether, they made five visits to Hammersmith Farm and spent a total of twenty-one days there.

On three trips west, Kennedy spent weekends at the home of Bing Crosby in Palm Desert, California, near Palm Springs. In 1962, he spent a weekend at the John's Island home of Gene Tunney, off Boothbay Harbor, Maine.

In early 1963 the Kennedys made their first visit to Camp David and their last to Glen-Ora. They had bought thirty-nine acres of farmland near Middleburg to build a home of their own, "Wexford." It is said the First Lady had persuaded the president to build it, for she did not like Camp David at first. After he had riding trails put in there for Jackie and their daughter, Caroline, she grew to like it and they spent fourteen weekends there. Once Wexford was completed, they were able to spend only two weekends there, in early November 1963. (Coincidentally, for the fall 1980 presidential campaign, Ronald and Nancy Reagan leased Wexford from its then-owner.)

THE FINAL TRIP

Looking ahead to a reelection campaign in 1964, Kennedy planned a goodwill trip to Texas.

It was to be a two-day visit to the state's largest cities, ending with a gala barbecue at LBJ Ranch, the home of Vice President Johnson and his wife, Lady Bird Johnson, in the hill country outside Austin.

On November 21, the president dedicated the Aerospace Health Center at Brooks Air Force Base in San Antonio. That evening, he spoke at a dinner honoring Representative Albert Thomas at the Houston Coliseum. The next day he spoke at a breakfast of the Fort Worth Chamber of Commerce and addressed a rally outside the Texas Hotel in that city. Then it was on to Dallas. After they landed at Love Field, his motorcade proceeded through the heart of the city. He was riding in an open convertible sedan and was shot by Lee Harvey Oswald from an upper floor of the Texas School Book Depository Building. The president died at 1 p.m. at Parkland Hospital, Dallas. Lyndon Johnson was sworn in as the thirty-sixth president later that day on Air Force One.

President Kennedy is buried at Arlington National Cemetery, Virginia. His grave is lit with an "eternal flame." Jacqueline and their two deceased minor children were buried with him later. His brothers Robert, also felled by an assassin, and Edward are buried nearby.

———————

The John F. Kennedy Presidential Library and Museum is located in a ten-acre park at Columbia Point on Boston's waterfront. Designed by architect I. M. Pei, it is part of the presidential libraries system operated by the National Archives and Research Administration.

The park is landscaped with pines, shrubs, and wild roses, which evoke the Cape Cod landscape that Kennedy so enjoyed. There is a Harbor Walk and picnic areas on the grounds. From May to October, Kennedy's twenty-six-foot sailboat Victura *is on display.*

The museum re-creates the life and times of John F. Kennedy through films, period settings, and twenty-five multimedia exhibits. The library has the papers of John F., Robert F., Joseph P., and Rose F. Kennedy, as well as some six hundred collections from other family members, authors, politicians, and public figures bearing on the life of the thirty-fifth president. It also houses the Ernest Hemingway Collection.

The museum is open seven days a week, 9 a.m.–5 p.m. The last introductory film is shown at 3:55 p.m. (Closed Thanksgiving and Christmas Days.) The library's research room is open 8:30 a.m.–4:30 p.m. by appointment only. It is closed on weekends and federal holidays. To talk with a member of the research staff, call 617-514-1629. Address: Columbia Point, Boston, MA 02125. Telephone: 617-514-1600 or 866-JFK-1960. Website: www.jfklibrary.org.

Chapter Thirty-five

------·•·------

LYNDON B. JOHNSON

THE 36TH PRESIDENT

November 22, 1963 — January 20, 1969

$\mathcal{A}$ bone-jarring ride at sunset over open pasture land in one of Lyndon Johnson's convertible four-door Lincolns was a favorite way of showing his beloved LBJ Ranch to his guests—and he had many guests. Often they were given Stetson hats as mementoes of their visit.

In 1951, Johnson and his wife, Claudia (known by most everyone as Lady Bird), bought from his aunt Frankie Martin what was then a 250-acre ranch on the north shore of the Pedernales River. By then he was a United States senator. Near the village of Stonewall and not far from Johnson City and Fredericksburg, the LBJ Ranch is in the Texas hill country, with the hills interspersed with open plains.

The main part of the ranch house was built of stone in 1895. Gradually, additions were made until there were twenty-eight rooms. Over the years, the Johnsons added to the land itself until the ranch reached its present size of 2,800 acres. It was a working cattle ranch during LBJ's lifetime and still is. The property is now part of the Lyndon B. Johnson National Historical Park. The cattle herd numbers as many as 160 at any one time, including seventy mother cows, as well as bulls, heifers, and calves.

In 1955, Johnson added a three-thousand-foot airstrip to the property. It could only be used by light aircraft until 1961, when he extended the runway to 6,154 feet to accommodate corporate-type jets. By then he was vice president and used a Lockheed JetStar to travel from Washington and back. (The JetStar is parked at the runway to this day.) While the strip was by then long enough for large jets, such as the Boeing 707 that served as Air Force One, its underlying base was not deep enough to accommodate their weight. Once he became president, he would fly on Air Force One to Bergstrom Air Force Base in Austin. There either the JetStar or a helicopter would ferry him to the ranch.

From the time the Johnsons purchased the ranch, LBJ always thought of it as his home, since it was so closely tied to his birth and growing-up years.

A TEXAS BEGINNING

Lyndon Baines Johnson was born to Samuel Ealy Johnson, Jr., and Rebekah Baines Johnson on August 27, 1908. He was the eldest of five children. He had one brother and three sisters. He was born in a small farmhouse on the Pedernales River (his birthplace is on the LBJ Ranch today).

Johnson City, nearby, was named after a cousin of his father.

Tall and awkward, he nonetheless showed early signs of leadership and was elected president of his high school junior class. In school he was active in debate and baseball. He went on to Southwest Texas State Teachers' College (now a campus of the state university system). He became editor of the campus newspaper and was active in debate and student government. Following graduation he became a teacher. At his third school, a Houston high school, he taught public speaking.

INTO POLITICS

Johnson's father had served five terms in the state legislature and was close to Congressman Sam Rayburn, who became Speaker of the U.S. House of Representatives. After campaigning for a state senator, Johnson was recommended to a congressman as his legislative secretary.

While in that job, Johnson was elected "speaker" of the "Little Congress," an informal group of Congressional aides. This broadened his circles of friends and contacts to include members of Congress, journalists, lobbyists, and aides to President Franklin Roosevelt.

In 1935 he received an appointment as head of the Texas National Youth Administration. In this job he had government resources with which to create job opportunities for young people.

Ambitious, he decided to run for Congress in 1937. He won a special election in the 10th Congressional District (Austin and environs). His platform was that of Roosevelt's New Deal. Lady Bird campaigned with him.

He served in the House for twelve years. He made himself useful to the Roosevelt administration, keeping it abreast of Texas politics, especially those involving FDR's vice president, John Nance Garner, and Speaker Rayburn, who considered Johnson to be his protégé. Johnson's ambition remained unquenched. In 1941, he ran for U.S. Senate in a special election against the sitting governor. He lost.

JOINING THE WAR EFFORT

After the nation entered World War II in 1941, Johnson obtained a commission in the U.S. Naval Reserve. In 1942, President Roosevelt sent Johnson, still also a member of Congress, as part of a three-man survey team to the South Pacific to report back on military conditions there. One day the trio was part of a mission to observe the bombing of a Japanese island air base. Johnson's aircraft turned back with generator trouble before it came under enemy fire. General Douglas MacArthur awarded Johnson the Silver Star. He was the only one aboard the plane to receive it. Critics pointed out that he had not really been in combat.

Meanwhile, Johnson and the team found that conditions were poor, equipment was substandard, and greater coordination was needed. This caused a sensation in Congress and, as a result, he was named to head an important subcommittee on naval affairs. His investigations led to controversial legislation, which was blocked, but his South Pacific mission itself led to an overall upgrade in importance of that theater of the war.

WINNING A SENATE SEAT

In 1948, Johnson again ran for the Senate, this time against two other candidates, one a former Texas governor. His campaign helicopter was dubbed "the Johnson Windmill." He led in the primary, but was short of the required majority. In the final round, Johnson was certified to have won by eighty-seven votes. There were charges of irregularity, including one that in a single precinct 202 people voted in alphabetical order at the end of the voter list—and all were dead! Nevertheless, a state Democratic convention upheld Johnson's victory. His opponent, Coke Stevenson, went to court, but to no avail.

Johnson was named to the Senate Armed Services Committee and quickly gained a reputation for efficiency with the deft way he handled investigations and publicized them. His careful cultivation of senior senators (mostly from the South) further strengthened his hand. In 1951, he became majority whip, the number-two position in the Senate.

After the Republicans took the Senate in 1952, Johnson was elected minority leader. In 1954, when the Democrats again took control, he was elected majority leader. In this position he perfected two things: an already excellent intelligence-gathering system and what became known as "the Johnson Treatment." Columnists Evans and Novak described the latter this way: "The Treatment could last 10 minutes or four hours. It came, enveloping its target, at the Johnson Ranch swimming pool, in one of Johnson's offices, in the Senate cloakroom, on the floor of the Senate itself—wherever Johnson might find a fellow Senator within his reach. Its tone could be supplication, accusation, cajolery, exuberance, scorn, tears, complaint and the hint of threat. It was all of these together. It ran the gamut of human emotions. Its velocity was breathtaking, and it was all in one direction. . . . He moved in close, his face a scant millimeter from his target. . . . From his pockets poured clippings, memos, statistics. Mimicry, humor and the genius of analogy made The Treatment an almost hypnotic experience and rendered the target stunned and helpless."

VICE PRESIDENT

His success resulted in his being a "favorite son" candidate of Texas at the 1956 Democratic National Convention. In 1960 he was part of a "stop Kennedy" coalition. There was, however, only one ballot and John F. Kennedy won it.

Kennedy needed strong support from the South and thus turned to Johnson to be his running mate. There are several versions of how this came about. What is important is that the strategy succeeded, and upon Kennedy's victory over Richard Nixon, Lyndon Johnson became vice president.

Johnson experienced some frustration in the new job but made the most of it. He spoke out for the expansion of civil rights and is generally credited with pushing Kennedy faster on the issue than he had planned to move. When Kennedy asked him to find a "scientific bonanza" with which to counter the Soviet Union's first man-in-space flight, Johnson pushed the idea of landing a man on the moon.

THE TEXAS BARBECUE THAT NEVER WAS

On November 22, 1963, the Kennedys landed in Dallas. After meetings and a parade, they were to go on to the LBJ Ranch for an overnight stay preceded by a Texas-style barbecue for about five hundred guests. Walter Jetton, renowned in the area as the Barbecue King of Fort Worth, was deep in preparation. Baking and cooking went on for days. The Secret Service and White House communications technicians swarmed the property in preparation for the event. The party was canceled. The president had been assassinated in his open sedan in Dallas by a lone gunman shooting from the Texas School Book Depository Building.

There is a famous photo of Lyndon Johnson on Air Force One being sworn in as the thirty-sixth president by federal judge Sarah T. Hughes, who administers the oath of office as a dazed Jacqueline Kennedy stands at Johnson's side.

LBJ AS PRESIDENT

Johnson soon appointed a commission, headed by Chief Justice Earl Warren, to investigate the Kennedy assassination. Its report concluded that Lee Harvey Oswald, the shooter, had acted alone. Skeptics challenged this, but the conclusion has never been definitively disproved.

Johnson promised to continue the Kennedy program and drew upon the nation's grief for support. The civil rights bill proposed by Kennedy in 1963 became a special project of Johnson's. In fall 1963 he got the needed support for House passage. In 1964 in the Senate he had Republican support but faced a filibuster by Southern Democrats. He managed to break the filibuster and signed the bill into law on July 2 that year.

THE 1964 ELECTION

Johnson's campaign managed to characterize his Republican challenger, Senator Barry Goldwater of Arizona, as "extreme." They were inadvertently abetted by a Goldwater remark at the Republican National Convention in San Francisco that summer ("extremism in the defense of liberty is no vice"). The most telling item was a television spot showing a little girl picking petals from a flower, counting. She gets to "nine" and the screen changes to show a nuclear bomb explosion. A male voice intones, "These are the stakes—to make a world in which all of God's children can live, or to go into the dark. We must either love each other or we must die." The screen goes black except for the line "Vote for President Johnson on November 3." The voice then says, "The stakes are too high for you to stay home." Not surprisingly, the Goldwater campaign was outraged. While the spot ran only once, it was picked up by the media and repeated many times and was the subject of much discussion.

It had an effect on voters.

On election day, Johnson, along with his running mate, Senator Hubert Humphrey of Minnesota, won 61 percent of the popular vote and the electoral vote 486–52. Johnson carried forty-four states; Goldwater, six. Johnson's coattails led to large Democratic majorities in both houses.

THE "GREAT SOCIETY"

In 1965, Johnson lost no time getting passage of a second civil rights bill, the Voting Rights Act—making it possible for many southern blacks to vote. It outlawed discrimination in voting and required several southern states to get federal pre-election clearance of voting procedures.

Next came the "Great Society" program, in which he declared a "war on poverty." The program created Medicare and Medicaid, federal funding for education, Head Start, and the National Endowments for the Arts and Humanities.

Despite this expansion of government, Johnson was a thrifty conservationist when it came to lightbulbs. He kept after White House staff and the LBJ Ranch staff to turn off unused lights.

The press joked that "LBJ" stood for "Light Bulb Johnson."

A series of urban riots rocked U.S. cities, beginning with the Watts riots in Los Angeles in 1965 and reaching a peak in 1968 following the assassination of Martin Luther King. There were riots in several dozen cities. Hardest hit were Newark, New Jersey, and Detroit. Johnson's political capital, eroding as the Vietnam War ground on, diminished even more.

With the breathtaking Great Society legislation largely behind him, Johnson shifted ever more attention to the Vietnam War, just as antiwar demonstrations were spreading on college campuses across the nation. More and more troops—largely draftees—were being sent to war without a declaration from the White House that the U.S. aim was to win.

By 1968, there were more than a half million U.S. troops in Vietnam and they were dying at the rate of a thousand a month. Johnson believed strongly in the "Domino Theory." That is, the loss of South Vietnam to the Communists would lead to neighboring countries falling into their sphere of control as well. He began to involve himself in targeting decisions and other details of the war. At one point he told former president Eisenhower that he was trying to win the war, although he never made a public statement to that effect. One result was that members of Congress of both parties who would otherwise have been inclined to support the war strongly were hesitant to do so.

Meanwhile, in the 1966 Congressional election, the Republicans made sufficient gains to block any more Great Society legislation.

In June 1967, Israel, in the Six-Day War, captured Egypt's Sinai Peninsula and Syria's Golan Heights. There were tense moments between the United States and the USSR over this.

By early 1968, the Democratic party was fracturing. Liberal antiwar senator Eugene McCarthy challenged Johnson in the New Hampshire primary. While Johnson won 49 percent to 42 percent, the media saw it as a victory for McCarthy. Within days, Robert Kennedy, by then a senator from New York, said he would run. Johnson's private polling showed that he would lose in the next primary, in Wisconsin.

On March 31, he announced he would not be a candidate for reelection. He did stage-manage a nomination for Humphrey at the tumultuous and demonstration-besieged Democratic National Convention in Chicago that summer.

THE WHITE HOUSE GOES TO THE RANCH

All the while, and throughout his Senate years and his time as vice president, Johnson was a frequent sojourner at his LBJ Ranch. He was very proud of it and loved showing it off to colleagues, friends, and famous visitors. During his presidency, he visited the ranch seventy-four times—for a total of five hundred days. When he went there, he in effect took the White House with him.

Bess Abell, who was the White House social secretary during the Johnson years, said of a typical guest arrival, "Mrs. Johnson would pick you up in a golf cart and you'd come in past the washing machine, the ice machine, the keg of beer and the ironing boards. There was a doormat with the words, 'All the World Is Welcome Here.'"

The Texas White House, as it came to be called by the press, is white with a three-hundred-year-old oak tree in the front lawn, facing the river. The swimming pool is there, too. Off to one side is the wing in which Johnson had his office. It is a single room with a portable screen dividing it. There are desks for two secretaries and armchairs before a fireplace. One has an embroidered pillow inscribed, "This is my ranch and I do as I damn please."

The house is comfortably furnished in cheerful colors, but is unpretentious. The dining room table can go from a circular one for four to a long rectangle seating fourteen. Outside the window is a large magnolia tree, planted by Mrs. Johnson from a seedling of the Jackson Magnolia at the White House.

Several rooms each have three television sets side by side, recalling the days when viewers had only ABC, CBS, and NBC to choose from. Johnson chose all three, more or less simultaneously.

Thirty-seven days after Kennedy's death, West German chancellor Ludwig Erhard was scheduled to come to the United States on a state visit. Johnson invited him to the ranch instead of Washington. The social highlight was a barbecue dinner held in the freshly decorated Stonewall, Texas, school gym, across the river. Famed pianist Van Cliburn played concert pieces for the guests. Johnson had every member of Erhard's party fitted for a Stetson hat before the dinner.

At a dinner for the members of the Organization of American States, who had been meeting in Atlanta, he brought in the Texas Fandango, a troupe that enacted a pageant based on Texas history, complete with horses and riders, pioneer wagons, and cattle.

After smaller dinners in the main house, LBJ would often take his guests on a walk by the river, about one-quarter of a mile to the family burial ground. He would show them the spot where he wanted to be buried, next to his mother and the spot he had saved for his wife.

GETTING DOWN TO BUSINESS

Lyndon Johnson worked continuously at the ranch. One notable meeting—about the escalating war in Vietnam—took place under the big oak tree in front of the house on December 22, 1964, with the president, the Joint Chiefs of Staff, and the defense and national security team members all sitting around a portable table.

As public opinion turned against the war, even the peaceful country setting of the ranch wasn't immune. At Easter time in 1967, antiwar protesters with signs paraded up and down the opposite side of the river, no more than two hundred feet from the ranch house.

AROUND THE WORLD IN FOUR DAYS

Jim Cross was an air force major when he became then–vice president Johnson's pilot. He took him to the ranch and elsewhere on the JetStar. Cross graduated to become the pilot of Air Force One when Johnson became president. Johnson promoted him to lieutenant colonel,

colonel, and finally brigadier general. Cross chuckles when he relates this story, saying, "He always liked to call me 'Major,' just to remind me of what I would have been had I not run into him."

A few days before Christmas 1967, bulletins carried the news that the prime minister of Australia, Harold Holt, had drowned in the ocean. Johnson alerted Cross that he wanted to go to Australia to attend the funeral. Johnson also mentioned there might be other stops, but he did not describe them. Cross and the crew scrambled to get Air Force One ready.

After the funeral in Australia on December 22, they flew to Khorat, Thailand, to visit U.S. military personnel; then to Cam Ranh Bay, Vietnam, on the twenty-third to visit more troops. There was some talk of also going to Korea, but that did not materialize. Instead, Johnson said he wanted to go to Karachi, Pakistan, which they did on the same day. There LBJ met with President Ayub Khan. Then, heading west (and gaining time zones in the process), they headed for Rome to see Pope Paul VI. Johnson's helicopter landed in the pope's Vatican City flower garden late that night, in time for him to make an impassioned plea for the pontiff's help with his peace plan.

Then, on the final leg home on Christmas Eve, Johnson came into the cockpit and sat in the jump seat right behind Cross. He said, "What time are we going to get to Andrews?" referring to the air force base near Washington, D.C. Cross replied that first they had to refuel at Lages Airport in the Azores. "Do we have a base down there?" Johnson asked. Cross said the United States did. "Do they have a PX?" "Yes, sir," said Cross. "Well," said, Johnson, "call the commander and tell him to open the PX because the president hasn't done his Christmas shopping. Have you done your Christmas shopping yet?" Cross said he had not. "Well, you're welcome to come." And shopping they went.

Air Force One returned to Washington 112.5 hours (4.7 days) after it had departed, with a satisfied president and plenty of Christmas presents.

AFTER THE PRESIDENCY

Johnson retired to the ranch, where he worked on his presidential memoirs, *The Vantage Point*, published in 1971. That year, the Lyndon Baines Johnson Library and Museum opened at the University of Texas in Austin.

In his will LBJ provided for the ranch to become part of a Lyndon Johnson National Historic Park. He wanted it to remain a working ranch.

Johnson died in his bedroom at the ranch on January 22, 1973, eight months shy of his sixty-fifth birthday. The cause was a heart attack, his third. He is buried in the family plot on the ranch, as he wished.

———·•·———

The Lyndon B. Johnson National Historical Park is approximately fifty miles west of Austin. It is in two sections. One is in Johnson City and includes President Johnson's boyhood home, his grandparents' log cabin settlement, and the National Park Visitor Center. The other is located on the north shore of the Pedernales River, approximately fourteen miles west of Johnson City, and comprises the land and buildings of the LBJ Ranch, including a replica of the late president's birthplace home (where the original stood), the Texas White House, the president's first school, and the family cemetery.

The park is operated by the National Park Service. It is open every day (except Thanksgiving, Christmas, and New Year's Day), 8:45 a.m.–5 p.m. Guided tours of the Texas White House (the ranch house) are available 10 a.m.–4:30 p.m. Guided tours are also available of the LBJ boyhood home in Johnson City. Hours are 9 a.m.–4:30 p.m. (closed noon–12:30 p.m.).

Directly across the river from the LBJ Ranch is the Lyndon B. Johnson State Park and Historic Site. In order to see the LBJ Ranch, visitors must first obtain a permit from the state park's visitor center. It is open 8 a.m.–5 p.m.

Lyndon Johnson National Historical Park: 100 Ladybird Lane, P.O. Box 329, Johnson City, TX 78636. Telephone: 830-868-7128. Website: www.nps.gov/lyjo/index/hm.

The Lyndon Baines Johnson Library and Museum, on the campus of the University of Texas in Austin, is open daily, 9 a.m.–5 p.m. (closed on Christmas Day). Address: 2313 Red River Street, Austin, TX 78705. Telephone: 512-721-0200. Website: www.lbjlibrary.org. Administered by the National Archives and Records Administration, the LBJ Library contains all of the papers from President Johnson's long public career.

Chapter Thirty-six

RICHARD NIXON

THE 37TH PRESIDENT

January 20, 1969 — August 8, 1974

A s a Californian who had spent most of his career in the East, Richard Nixon, on becoming president, decided to have two retreats: one in Florida, the other in Southern California. Thus he acquired comfortable homes in Key Biscayne and San Clemente, respectively.

HARDSHIP

Richard Milhous Nixon (his middle name was his mother's maiden name) was born January 9, 1913, in Yorba Linda, Orange County, California, to Francis (Frank) and Hannah Nixon, a devout Quaker. The austere customs of the Quakers prevailed in the Nixon home.

Richard had four brothers, two of whom died young: Harold, at age twenty-four, Arthur, at age seven. Frank's lemon ranch failed in 1922 and he moved the family to Whittier, where many Quakers lived.

There he opened a small grocery story. Frank had a reputation as a bully with a hot temper. Hannah devoted much of her time to tending her sick sons. There was not much time or warmth left for Richard.

The family was poor by any measure. These circumstances built in Richard a fierce ambition to succeed in life. But in the meantime he lacked emotional security and kept to himself much of the time.

He graduated second in his class at Whittier High School. In his senior year he lost an election for student body president. It wounded his pride that a more popular student beat him. His ego was boosted by the offer of a scholarship to Harvard, but he could not accept, for his parents could not afford the travel or the living funds involved. Instead, he received a scholarship at nearby Whittier College, a Quaker school. There he became a skilled debater, a good actor in student dramatic productions, student body president, and member of the baseball, football, and track teams. He graduated second in his class.

During his college years he lived at home and worked part-time at the grocery store. In 1933 he became engaged to the local police chief's daughter, but it did not last and they broke up two years later.

Nixon then received a full scholarship at Duke University's new School of Law. Duke was intent on attracting top students, so awarded such scholarships to academic standouts from various colleges. They also recruited to the faculty well-known legal scholars by offering high salaries. Nixon was elected president of the Duke Bar Association and graduated in 1937, third in his class.

A CAREER IN LAW

He returned to California and passed the state bar examination in 1937. He joined a local firm, Wingert & Bewley, working on commercial litigation, other business law matters, and wills.

Though practicing law did not excite him, he saw it as important background if he were to go into politics one day. In 1938 he opened a branch of the firm in the town of La Habra and later became a partner. For recreation he became interested in amateur dramatics. In January that year he was in the Whittier Community Playhouse's staging of *The Dark Tower*. Playing opposite him was Thelma "Pat" Ryan, a high school teacher. He was smitten and courted her steadily. He called on her many times at her home, often without advance notice. He took her on Sunday drives and also to the East Whittier Friends Church, where he taught Sunday school (he was a lifetime member of that church). It took several marriage proposals by him before she agreed. They were married on June 21, 1940. They honeymooned in Mexico, then took an apartment in East Whittier. In January 1942 they moved to Washington, D.C., where he had landed a job at the wartime Office of Price Administration (OPA).

The Nixons had two daughters: Patricia, who later married lawyer Edward Cox, and Julie, who married David Eisenhower, grandson of the thirty-fourth president.

WAR SERVICE

Although both his religion and his OPA status gave him exemptions from military service, he did not exercise them and received a navy commission in August 1942. After training he was assigned to Ottumwa Naval Air Station, in Iowa. After seven months he was assigned to be the naval passenger control officer for the South Pacific Combat Air Transport Command, a logistics job. He requested something more challenging, but this only resulted in his being given the command of cargo handling units.

He returned to the United States not having seen combat, but with two service stars and a commendation citation. He was named administrative officer at the Alameda Naval Air Station, in California.

In January 1945 he was transferred to Philadelphia and the Bureau of Aeronautics to negotiate the termination of various war contracts. There he received a letter of commendation from Secretary of the Navy James Forrestal and a promotion to lieutenant commander. He left active service on January 1, 1946.

INTO POLITICS

Back home in Whittier, Nixon was approached by several local businessmen about challenging five-term congressman Jerry Voorhis, whom they considered very liberal. Nixon, being a veteran and conservative, seemed to them ideal. He agreed to run in the 1946 election and won. He served in the House for four years. In 1948 he drew national attention when an investigation he led for the House Un-American Activities

Committee caused a break in the Alger Hiss spy case. Hiss was a senior State Department official. Whittaker Chambers, a former magazine editor and onetime communist, alleged that Hiss was a secret agent for the Soviet Union. Hiss's friends and defenders dismissed Chambers's allegations; however, Nixon was convinced he was telling the truth, for Chambers had microfilmed several incriminating documents and hidden them where only Hiss would have had access. Chambers also said the documents would prove they were typed on Hiss's typewriter.

In 1950 Hiss was convicted of perjury. As a result, Nixon earned the undying hatred of the American left in general and Hiss's friends in particular. Years later, after the fall of the Soviet Union, when previously classified documents were released in Russia, it became clear that Hiss had indeed been one of their spies.

In 1950 Nixon ran for the U.S. Senate against Democratic representative Helen Gahagan Douglas. It was a bitterly fought contest. Douglas, a former actress, was quite liberal, but Nixon said she was an apologist for far-left causes. She in turn called him "Tricky Dick," an epithet adversaries used for years afterward.

Nixon won the election in November. After taking his seat in the Senate in January 1951, Nixon gave many speeches opposing the spread of communism. He was also critical of then-president Truman's conduct of the Korean War. On domestic matters he voted for legislation supporting civil rights for minorities and for statehood for Alaska and Hawaii.

VICE PRESIDENT, 1953–61

Both his relative youth (he was thirty-nine) and his strong anticommunist rhetoric commended Nixon to the Republican Party's presidential nominee, Dwight Eisenhower, at the party's convention in July 1952.

That September, however, a *New York Post* article claimed that various friends had been contributing to a secret fund for Nixon's personal expenses with the expectation they would curry favor on policy matters. Some of Eisenhower's advisers urged him to drop Nixon from the ticket. Instead he told Nixon to make his case to the public, which he did. On national television on September 23, with Pat by his side, he said the fund was not secret, was used only for political purposes, and was audited by an independent review group. He said that his wife wore not mink, but "a respectable Republican cloth coat." He went on to "confess" that they had been given Checkers, a cocker spaniel, by a contributor and that they wouldn't give the dog back because his daughters would be beside themselves if he did. The performance was something of a tearjerker, but it worked well. It solidified the Republican base and gained him support from many other voters. It became known as the Checkers Speech.

The Eisenhower-Nixon ticket defeated Illinois governor Adlai Stevenson and his running mate, Alabama senator John Sparkman.

Nixon took his new duties seriously. Whenever Eisenhower was away he chaired meetings of the National Security Council. As president of the Senate he ruled on procedural matters that opened the way for passage of Eisenhower's 1957 civil rights bill. He and his wife also took several goodwill trips. On one, ending in Caracas, Venezuela, a mob of anti-American protesters attacked his motorcade, surrounding it and throwing rocks. Nixon remained cool under pressure and ordered the driver to move ahead slowly and deliberately. He received high praise on his return.

In 1959 he was in Moscow for the opening of the American National Exhibition. Among other things it featured an up-to-the-minute kitchen with all the latest appliances an American housewife might have or expect to get. On July 24, he and Soviet general secretary Nikita Khrushchev, touring the exhibit, stopped at the kitchen, where the Russian engaged in bluff and bluster and Nixon rebutted him in what became known as the Kitchen Debate. Outside of Soviet media, Nixon was seen as having gotten the better of Khrushchev.

RUNNING FOR PRESIDENT, 1960

Nixon faced little opposition in seeking the Republican nomination for president. Republicans tend to follow an unwritten policy that might be called "it's his turn." For his running mate he chose former senator Henry Cabot Lodge, Jr. His opponent, John F. Kennedy, emphasized what he called the missile gap between the United States and the Soviet Union (it was largely a fiction) and called on voters to "get the country moving again," since there was a brief recession late in Eisenhower's second term.

Nixon had unwisely promised to campaign personally in all fifty states. This required a physically taxing schedule. He was very tired from a campaign trip when he and Kennedy appeared for the nation's first televised presidential debate. Looking tired and sallow (with no makeup), Nixon came off to television audiences as the loser to Kennedy, although radio listeners thought he had had won it.

Kennedy won the election very narrowly, by a 120,000-vote margin. Republican officials were convinced there had been voter fraud in Illinois and Texas. A number of investigations, recounts, and court challenges were undertaken, but Nixon decided against a full-scale national issue and called off the effort. Not long afterward, Kennedy met with him (they were personal friends from Congressional days) at an ocean-front villa of the Hotel Key Biscayne in Florida. It was said that Kennedy offered Nixon a job in the new administration, but he declined. He decided instead to return to California.

STARTING OVER IN CALIFORNIA

The Nixons did move and he practiced law and wrote his book *Six Crises*. It made the bestseller lists. California's Democratic governor Edmund G. "Pat" Brown was up for reelection in 1962 and Republican leaders urged Nixon to challenge him. After much urging he agreed to run.

He had an ultraconservative challenger in the primary. In the general election, his lack of enthusiasm for the campaign was noticed by many, and some suspected that he wanted to use the governorship to launch another presidential bid. He lost the election to Brown by almost three hundred thousand votes. The next day at a news conference, an embittered Nixon declared, "You won't have Nixon to kick around anymore because, gentlemen, this is my last press conference." Neither that nor journalists' political obituaries about him turned out to be true.

THE NEW NIXON

Nixon had a keen analytical mind, which served him well later when dealing with foreign policy.

His current need was to develop a strategy to make himself relevant nationally again and to show the statesman side of his personality. The first step was an extensive trip with the family to Europe in 1963. He had no trouble arranging meetings with leaders in the countries they visited and he wasn't shy about holding news conferences. In these he would demonstrate his mastery of complicated international issues.

After their return, the Nixons moved to New York City and he became a senior partner in a major law firm, renamed Nixon, Mudge, Rose, Guthrie & Alexander. They bought an apartment on Fifth Avenue, in the same building as Nelson Rockefeller's.

In spring 1964 he traveled to Vietnam and Japan. In several media appearances Nixon called on President Johnson to escalate the fight against communism in Southeast Asia, even suggesting that consideration be given to invading North Vietnam and Laos. He then wrote an article titled "Asia After Vietnam," which appeared in *Foreign Affairs*. In it he floated the idea of a new U.S. relationship with China.

In the 1966 Congressional campaign he appeared on behalf of a number of Republican candidates. In addition, he gave talks to many state and county Republican groups at their annual fund-raising dinners that year and the next. He was steadily and quietly gathering political IOUs around the country. On February 1, 1968, he announced he would seek the Republican presidential nomination.

THE 1968 ELECTION

The first half of 1968 was tumultuous nationally. Nixon won the Republican primary in New Hampshire, causing Nelson Rockefeller to drop out. Then the Reverend Dr. Martin Luther King was assassinated and riots broke out in several cities. Lyndon Johnson surprised the nation by saying he would not be a candidate for his party's nomination. In June Robert Kennedy was assassinated.

Then, in Chicago, the Democratic National Convention nominated Vice President Hubert Humphrey to succeed Johnson while rioters took over the streets around the convention hall and gave television viewers across the nation the impression that the Democrats represented chaos.

Nixon benefited from all this. At the Republican convention in Miami Beach, the popular new governor of California, Ronald Reagan, reluctantly let his name be put in nomination. He had gone to the convention only as a "favorite son" candidate and believed it was too early in his own political career to be a serious candidate. Rockefeller, back in the running, then tried to switch his supporters to George Romney, the governor of Michigan. Nixon came out the winner.

The party united behind him. He presented himself as a picture of stability, appealing to the large number of voters nervous over the disruptive events domestically and the escalating war in Vietnam. He campaigned under the slogan "Nixon's the One!" (One large poster in the window of a Times Square shop had a facetious take on this, showing a good-looking pregnant young black woman, patting her tummy over the caption "Nixon's the One!") On November 5, Nixon won by half a million votes.

THE PRESIDENCY

As president, Nixon had an ambitious agenda. A major objective was to get the Vietnam War under control. He also wanted to develop a relationship with China, in large part to checkmate the expansion of the Soviet Union's influence. He wanted also to pursue arms agreements with the USSR, move ahead on a Middle East peace process, and, at home, curb inflation, get tougher on crime, reform welfare, and step up desegregation.

VIETNAM, CHINA, AND THE SOVIET UNION

In March 1969 Nixon approved bombing North Vietnamese positions in Cambodia, after which he proposed reaching an agreement whereby U.S. and North Vietnamese troops would withdraw from South Vietnam. In June, he brought 25,000 soldiers home. In July he went to South Vietnam to implement a policy of "Vietnamization," by which South Vietnamese troops would steadily replace U.S. troops, with the United States continuing to supply the country with aid and military equipment. The withdrawal began, but he also authorized armed incursions into Laos to cut supply lines of the North Vietnamese. Skeptics in the press saw this as contradicting his campaign promise to bring the war to a conclusion and claimed there was a "credibility gap."

Many college students, riled by fears of being drafted, leftist harangues on campus, and the press's take on Nixon's Laos actions, launched strikes on several hundred campuses.

Nixon created a commission to study the draft issue. It reported that a professional volunteer army could take the place of a conscripted one. He ordered the draft to end in 1973.

In December 1972 he approved aerial bombing of North Vietnamese military and industrial targets. This led to peace talks and the Paris Peace Accords of 1973. It was silent as to the 145, 000 North Vietnamese troops in the highlands of South Vietnam. Soon steady American military withdrawals began, and by late 1973, all of our troops had come home. Although the United States was to continue to provide aid to the government of South Vietnam, the Democratic-controlled Congress refused. With a good-sized enemy army on South Vietnamese territory and no aid forthcoming, it was only a matter of time before the north would complete its conquest of the south. This occurred in April 1975, when Nixon was no longer in office.

Relations between Moscow and Beijing had soured by 1969–70 and there was tension along their shared border. Nixon decided to take advantage of this. He sent indirect messages to the Beijing authorities through third countries Romania and Pakistan. In response, the Chinese table tennis team invited an American team to a demonstration competition in China. This had been approved by Mao Zedong himself and was the first time an American group had been welcomed on the China mainland in more than twenty years.

Premier Chou En-lai then sent an indirect message to Nixon indicating that Nixon or a special envoy would be welcomed in China. Nixon sent Henry Kissinger, then his national security adviser, to China in 1971. The visit was kept secret. Its purpose was to plan a Nixon visit. Nixon then surprised the nation with the announcement that he would visit Communist China in 1972.

Once that was done, he sent California governor Ronald Reagan on a mission to Taiwan to assure the Nationalist leader Chiang Kai-shek that the U.S. diplomatic relationship with his Republic of China was secure. (In asking Reagan to do this Nixon was disingenuous, for his intention was ultimate normalization of relations with Beijing, which would require severing U.S. relations with Taiwan.)

The Nixons landed in Beijing in February 1972. The meeting with Mao and Chou and others went well. The stage was set for the development of full relations.

As a result, the Soviet leaders in the Kremlin were worried about a U.S.-China alliance. Nixon used this opportunity to arrange a meeting in Moscow beginning May 22, 1972. Out of this came an agreement for increased trade and, more important, the Strategic Arms Limitation Treaty (SALT I) and an Anti-Ballistic Missile Treaty. Nixon and Soviet leader Leonid Brezhnev announced a new era of "peaceful coexistence."

In late June 1974, Nixon returned to Russia. He and Brezhnev met at Yalta, where they discussed a possible mutual defense pact, expansion of détente, and a comprehensive test-ban treaty, but none of these materialized, for Nixon was in serious trouble back home.

DOMESTIC ISSUES

Nixon did a number of bold things in both the economic and social fields. During his time in office "entitlements" such as Social Security and Medicare increased from 6.3 percent of gross domestic product (GDP) to 8.9 percent. Food aid and federal welfare went from $6.6 billion to $9.1 billion. Meanwhile, defense spending decreased from 9.1 percent of GDP to 5.8 percent.

In 1970, Congress passed legislation giving Nixon the ability to set wage and price controls. He did so on a ninety-day basis. The plan held so far as wages were concerned, but it did not stop inflation.

He then indexed Social Security's annual payment adjustments and created a new federal welfare program, Supplemental Security Income. He also took the nation entirely off the gold standard. This had the effect of dropping the value of the dollar and increasing inflation because of the higher prices for imported goods.

Major environmental legislation was signed by Nixon, including the Environmental Policy Act, Clean Air Act, and Federal Water Pollution Control Act amendments. He established the Environmental Protection Agency, the Occupational Safety and Health Administration, the Council on Environmental Quality, and the Consumer Product Safety Commission. He transformed the cabinet-level Post Office

Department into a government-owned corporation, the U.S. Postal Service.

On June 17, 1971, he declared the opening of the "war on drugs," a war that four decades later has not yet been won.

CIVIL RIGHTS

Nixon, with his Quaker background, considered racism to be a moral shortcoming. He was determined to follow the courts in integrating schools. On the other hand, he did not favor forced busing of schoolchildren to achieve this. By fall 1970, two million southern black children had enrolled in newly integrated school districts for the first time. When he came to office 70 percent of them were still attending all-black schools. A year and a half later the number was down to 18 percent. Scholar Dean J. Kotlowski said of his action, "In this sense, Nixon was the greatest school desegregator in American history."

Kennedy's dream of putting a man on the moon came true during Nixon's first term. In 1969, the United States launched three manned lunar missions. In the third mission, Apollo XI, astronaut Neil Armstrong took his "giant step for mankind." In 1972 Nixon approved the development of the Space Shuttle program by NASA and also a cooperative program with the USSR that ultimately led to the development of the International Space Station.

NIXON IN THE AIR

During his five-and-a-half-year presidency, Richard Nixon made thirteen foreign trips. The first came barely a month after his inauguration. Between February 23 and March 2, 1969, he attended the meeting of the North Atlantic Council in Brussels and met with King Baudouin I of Belgium; met with British prime minister Harold Wilson and Queen Elizabeth II; addressed the Bundestag in Bonn, West Germany, and gave speeches in West Berlin; met with Italy's president and prime minister in Rome; met with President de Gaulle in Paris; and had an audience with Pope Paul VI.

From July 26 to August 3, 1969, he was in the Philippines, Indonesia, Thailand, South Vietnam, India, Pakistan, Romania, and the United

Kingdom again. He met with heads of state or heads of government at all stops.

He was in Mexico twice: in September 1969 for the dedication of a dam and in August the next year for an official visit with President Gustavo Diaz Ordaz.

From September 27 through October 5, 1970, he was in Italy, Vatican City, Yugoslavia, Spain, the United Kingdom, and Ireland. On November 12 he flew to Paris to attend the memorial services for Charles de Gaulle.

In 1971, he made a two-day trip, December 13 and 14, to an island in the Azores to meet with Portuguese prime minister Marcelo Caetano and French president Georges Pompidou to discuss international monetary problems. A week later he was in Bermuda for a meeting with British prime minister Edward Heath.

In February 1972, Mr. and Mrs. Nixon made the historic seven-day trip to China.

From April 15 to 17 that year he made a state visit to Ottawa, Canada. From May 20 to June 1 he was in Austria, the USSR (to sign the SALT I and ABM treaties), Iran (to meet with the shah), and Poland. Again, meetings were with heads of state or government.

In 1973, with the Watergate issue taking more of his time, he left Washington for two days of meetings (May 31 and June 1) in Reykjavík, Iceland, with French president Pompidou. He also met with Iceland's president and prime minister.

From April 5 to 7, 1974, he was in Paris for memorial services for President Pompidou, with informal side meetings with several heads of government.

In June and July 1974 he was on the road for nearly a month. It was to be his last trip as president. From June 10 to 12 he was in Vienna meeting with Austria's chancellor Bruno Kreisky. Then he went to Cairo to meet with President Anwar Sadat; then to Jedda, Saudi Arabia, for a session with King Faisal; then to meetings in Damascus with Syrian president Hafez al-Assad, followed by stops in Tel Aviv and Jerusalem and meetings with Prime Minister Yitzhak Rabin. In Jordan he was on a state visit to King Hussein. Next was a stop in the Azores to meet with President Antonio de Spinola of Portugal; then to a meeting of the Atlantic Council in Brussels, and, finally to

Moscow and Yalta, June 27–July 3, for meetings with Brezhnev and Premier Alexei Kosygin.

NIXON AT EASE

Ease is not a word usually associated with a person as serious and intense as Nixon was; however, like all his predecessors, he sought times and places to put both physical and mental distance between himself and the stresses of high office.

When Nixon was a member of the House of Representatives, a fellow congressman, George Smathers of Florida, recommended Key Biscayne as a vacation destination. Nixon took his advice in December 1951. During that visit Smathers arranged for his friend Charles "Bebe" Rebozo to take Nixon deep-sea fishing. Afterward, Rebozo told Smathers that Nixon "doesn't know how to talk, doesn't drink, doesn't smoke, doesn't chase women, doesn't know how to play golf, doesn't know how to play tennis . . . he can't even fish." Nevertheless, he and Nixon became friends. Ultimately, in fact, Rebozo could be described as his best friend.

Rebozo was the first child of Cuban immigrants. Born in 1912, he was close to Nixon in age. He ran a series of successful small businesses in Florida and in 1964 founded the Key Biscayne Bank & Trust Company. Nixon spent several more vacations in Key Biscayne, often visiting with Rebozo and his friend Robert Abplanalp, inventor of the aerosol valve. In 1969, Nixon purchased a house at 500 Bay Lane. It was soon dubbed the Florida White House by the traveling press. Both Rebozo and Abplanalp were neighbors.

Rebozo became a frequent guest at the White House and raised money for Nixon campaigns. He was married twice, to Claire Gunn, then to his lawyer's secretary, Jane Lucke, who said, "Bebe's favorites are Richard Nixon, his cat—and then me."

Rebozo was eventually investigated in connection with Watergate. Investigators learned that a hundred-thousand-dollar donation intended for the Republican Party was found in Rebozo's safe deposit box.

He was not prosecuted. Rebozo died in 1988.

During his presidency, Nixon visited his Key Biscayne retreat fifty-nine times, for a total of 198 days. Typically his visits were for three days, sometimes two. There were slightly longer ones for some Thanksgiving and Christmas holidays.

His first retreat was February 7–10, 1969. Leaving Andrews Air Force Base in Maryland, Air Force One's manifest included, in addition to the president, thirty-one passengers. Included were Secretary of State William P. Rogers, National Security Adviser Henry Kissinger, several presidential staff members, Nixon's valet, the White House physician, several members of the Military Liaison office, a press pool, and Secret Service agents.

On his first day at Key Biscayne, Nixon did as he often would do in years to come: he took a ride on Rebozo's houseboat, *Coco Lobo*. He dined that night at the Key Biscayne Hotel with Rogers, Kissinger, and Rebozo. The next day he attended services at the Community Congregational Church and had an afternoon meeting with Rogers and Kissinger. He also talked with his wife in Washington. He dined at home with Chief of Staff H. R. Haldeman, White House physician Dr. Walter Tkasch, and Rebozo. On his third day, the tenth, he worked alone until 2:29 p.m., then departed for Washington, arriving at the White House at 6:40.

His only foreign visitor at Key Biscayne was West German chancellor Willy Brandt, who arrived on December 28, 1971.

Nixon's last visit to Key Biscayne was on July 3, 1974. What a day it was! It began in Moscow with a signing ceremony with USSR leader Brezhnev of the protocol for the ABM Treaty and a treaty limiting underground nuclear weapons tests. After the ceremony, the Nixons flew to Loring Air Force Base in Maine, where the president delivered a brief televised report to the nation. They proceeded to Key Biscayne, arriving at their home at 11:50 p.m. The manifest to Florida showed thirty-five passengers in addition to the Nixons. One was Alexander Haig, then White House chief of staff. Another was Diane Sawyer, then a staff assistant. Only seven of these (plus the Secret Service detail) accompanied the first couple to their compound.

The next day, July 4, was devoted mostly to rest and relaxation, though the president did take a forty-nine-minute ride on the *Coco Lobo*. On the fifth he talked with Kissinger, who was in Rome, then with former Treasury secretary John Connally. Then he took a boat ride for a little over an hour.

On July 6 he talked with Vice President Gerald Ford in Washington, then he went for a drive around the general area for more than two hours.

At 6:49 that evening he and the First Lady arrived at the Key Biscayne Restaurant for dinner with Rebozo and Jane Lucke. After dinner the president was in a light mood and danced to "Thank Heaven for Little Girls" with ten-year-old Lisa Berry of Fort Lauderdale. He then went around the restaurant greeting the other patrons. At 10:56 the Nixons left for home.

The next morning, July 7, the president flew to Palm Beach to inspect Mar-a-Lago, the estate of Marjorie Merriweather Post, who had bequeathed the property to the nation. Nixon and Rebozo looked it over to ascertain if it would be suitable as a place for distinguished foreign guests to be entertained by U.S. presidents. After lunch back at home, he took a brief boat ride on *Coco Lobo*. At 7:38 p.m. the Nixons left by helicopter for Homestead Air Force Base near Miami and the trip back to Washington on Air Force One.

Soon after he was inaugurated in 1969, Nixon asked an aide to scout out possible retreats for him and his family on the coast of Southern California. They settled on La Casa Pacifica, located on the ocean in San Clemente, Orange County. A large home modeled after a Spanish country mansion, it is set in three and a half acres of landscaped grounds. Its original owner was H. H. Cotton, a prominent Democratic Party backer who had once entertained Franklin Roosevelt there. The Nixons purchased the estate from his widow. For security and privacy, the estate was enclosed by a wall. During his presidency, Nixon entertained there such guests as Japanese prime minister Eisaku Sato (January 6–7, 1972), South Vietnam's president Nguyen Van Thieu (April 2–3, 1972), USSR general secretary Brezhnev (June 23–24, 1973), and Mexican president Ordaz. Both Rebozo and Kissinger also visited several times.

THE LAST CAMPAIGN

When the 1972 reelection campaign began, Nixon thought Senator Ted Kennedy would be his opponent. However, things unfolded differently. Senator Edmund Muskie won the New Hampshire Democratic primary, then lost in Florida. Senator George McGovern emerged as the nominee. The Nixon-Agnew ticket swept to a landslide victory, carrying every state but Massachusetts and the District of Columbia. The electoral vote was 521–17. There were few Congressional coattails, however, for the Democrats retained control.

On June 17, burglars broke into the Democratic National Committee's headquarters offices in the Watergate hotel and apartment complex. The purpose was to eavesdrop on party secrets, which had hardly seemed worthwhile, given Nixon's huge lead in the polls.

THE SECOND TERM

An investigation began. Within a week of the break-in the president had been fully briefed on it. Though he apparently had no prior knowledge about a "Plumbers Group" of operatives and their plan to mount a break-in, he had no hesitation in covering up the genesis of the event (as later revealed in the secretly made White House tapes).

In June 1973, Nixon reimposed price controls. They were unpopular and were allowed to lapse in spring 1974. In October 1973, Egypt and Syria attacked Israel in what became known as the Yom Kippur War. The Nixon administration cut through red tape to airlift arms to Israel, which won the war. Members of the OPEC oil-producing countries were unhappy about this, along with the deflating effect on oil prices of Nixon's decision to go off the gold standard. They cut production and announced an embargo against the United States and the Netherlands (the one European country that joined the United States in supporting Israel). The resulting "oil crisis" caused many weeks of long lines at gasoline stations.

On January 2, 1974, Nixon signed legislation to set a national speed limit of 55 miles per hour in order to conserve gasoline (it was not repealed until 1995).

On October 10, 1973, Vice President Spiro Agnew resigned. He was charged with bribery, tax evasion, and money laundering, stemming from his years as governor of Maryland. Nixon chose Representative Gerald R. Ford of Michigan, the Republican minority leader, to replace Agnew.

The Watergate investigation continued. In time, several Nixon staff members and campaign operatives were implicated. Some went to prison; others resigned. Nixon began to spend more and more time at Camp David, thinking and planning various ways out of the problem. On April 29, 1973, he had his key aides, chief of staff H. R. "Bob" Haldeman and domestic policy adviser John Ehrlichman, come to the camp for separate meetings. Each one was told he had to resign.

In July 1973, aide Alexander Butterfield's Congressional testimony revealed that there was an Oval Office system to tape all conversations. A prolonged tug-of-war ensued between the White House and Congress over the release of the tapes. In April 1974, Nixon announced that the White House would release 1,200 pages of transcripts of taped conversations. Not satisfied, the Democrat-controlled House Judiciary Committee opened impeachment hearings. These resulted in bipartisan votes for Articles of Impeachment. The Supreme Court then ruled unanimously that the tapes must be released. One of these, released on August 5, revealed that Nixon was aware of the cover-up from its beginning and even proposed that the administration attempt to stop the FBI investigation. This tape became known as "the smoking gun."

In a televised message on August 8, Nixon announced his resignation, effective the next day.

AFTER THE PRESIDENCY

The Nixons returned to Casa Pacifica, initially to a life of seclusion. On September 8, 1974, a little over a month after Nixon's resignation, President Ford issued him a "full, free and absolute" pardon. Nixon expressed contrition for any mistakes he had made.

That evening he had abdominal pains and his left leg was greatly swollen. It was diagnosed as a recurrence of phlebitis, a circulatory ailment. He was rushed to Long Beach Memorial Hospital and put on an anticoagulant intravenous machine.

During Nixon's hospitalization, Watergate special prosecutor Leon Jaworski issued a subpoena for Nixon to testify in Washington. Nixon's physician, Dr. John Lungren, warned that his patient's condition made it impossible to sit for hours on an airplane. After being released from the hospital on October 4, Nixon had his lawyers file a motion requesting the judge to revoke the subpoena. This was rejected. On

October 23, Nixon was back in the hospital with vascular blockages and possible gangrene. A large blood clot was found in an artery leading to his heart. His life was in danger and he underwent surgery. He later required four blood transfusions and suffered internal bleeding. He was finally allowed to return home on November 14. The Watergate judge sent three doctors to evaluate Nixon's condition. They concluded that he was unable to testify. The judge ruled that his testimony would not be needed.

BACK ON THE WORLD STAGE

By spring 1975 Nixon's health was returning. He worked daily in an office in a Coast Guard station a short walk from his home. He wrote his memoirs, *RN: The Memoirs of Richard Nixon* and later on *The Real War* (altogether, he was the author of ten books).

In 1976, at the invitation of Mao Zedong, he visited China. In 1980, when the shah of Iran died in Egypt, Nixon attended the funeral, ignoring the State Department's request that he stay home. In February that year the Nixons moved to New York City and the following year to Saddle River, New Jersey. He regularly held small dinners for Washington journalists and policy scholars. Throughout the decade he traveled widely and gave interviews. His views on international affairs were sought by his successors and other policy leaders.

In January 1991 Nixon opened the Nixon Center, a Washington, D.C., think tank and conference center.

Pat Nixon died on June 22, 1993, from lung cancer and emphysema. Funeral services were held at the Nixon Library and Museum in Yorba Linda, California. The former president was deeply distraught at the time but composed himself to deliver a tribute to her at the service. Former presidents Ford and Reagan attended with their wives.

Less than a year later, Richard Nixon died on April 22, 1994, as the result of a severe stroke suffered four days earlier. He is buried alongside his wife on the grounds of the library.

The Richard Nixon Presidential Library and Museum opened in 1990 as a private institution, built and operated by the Richard Nixon

Foundation. It is located on nine acres of landscaped grounds that include Nixon's birthplace and boyhood home. On July 11, 2007, it became part of the National Archives and Records Administration's presidential library system.

In the museum, permanent exhibits include many artifacts and interactive displays covering the thirty-seventh president's life and times. Special galleries hold traveling exhibits. There is a full-size replica of the White House East Room, one of the Nixon post-presidential office at his New Jersey home, and another of the White House Lincoln sitting room as it was decorated in the Nixon years.

The library contains all the presidential papers, 500,000 photos, 700 hours of film, 4,469 hours of audio recordings, and 2,377 hours of taped Oval Office conversations.

Hours: Museum, Monday through Saturday, 10 a.m.–5 p.m.; Sunday, 11 a.m.–5 p.m. Closed on Thanksgiving, Christmas, and New Year's Days. The Library's Research Rooms: Monday through Friday, 9:30 a.m.–5 p.m. Location: 18001 Yorba Linda Boulevard, Yorba Linda, CA 92886. Telephone: 714-983-9120. Email: nixon@nara.gov. Website: www.nixonlibrary.org.

Chapter Thirty-seven

GERALD R. FORD

THE 38TH PRESIDENT

August 9, 1974—January 20, 1977

For Gerald and Betty Ford, summer vacations and winter ski trips to Vail, Colorado, had been a tradition since his days as minority leader of the U.S. House of Representatives. When he became president upon Richard Nixon's resignation on August 9, 1974, they skipped that year's summer trip.

FROM MICHIGAN TO PENNSYLVANIA AVENUE

He was born Leslie King, Jr., in Omaha, Nebraska, on July 14, 1913, to Leslie, Sr., and Dorothy Gardner.

His father apparently had a violent streak and his parents separated and divorced shortly after he was born. In 1916, his mother married Gerald Rudolf Ford, who was on the sales force at a family-owned paint company in Grand Rapids, Michigan. They called her son Gerald R. Ford, Jr. He was never formally adopted by his stepfather; however, he legally changed his name in 1935, when he was twenty-two. He grew up in Grand Rapids with three half brothers by his mother's marriage to Ford, Sr.: Thomas, Richard, and James. His biological father married a second time and had two daughters and a son, of whom Gerald Ford, Jr., was unaware until he was seventeen and was told King was his father. That same year he met his biological father by accident. He was waiting tables as a student when King came into the restaurant. Thereafter he had occasional contacts with King.

Of the parents with whom he spent his childhood and youth, Ford said, "My stepfather was a magnificent person and my mother equally wonderful, so I couldn't have written a better prescription for a superb family upbringing."

HIGH SCHOOL AND COLLEGE

At Grand Rapids South High School, Ford was an outstanding athlete. He was captain of the football team. In addition, he was an Eagle Scout.

At the University of Michigan he played both center and linebacker for the football team on its undefeated and national championship teams in 1932 and 1933. In 1934, he was chosen to be on the East team for the annual Shriners' East-West game in San Francisco (a benefit game for crippled children). In 1935 he played on the 1935 Collegiate All-Star football team.

The year he graduated from the university (1935) he received—and declined—contract offers from two professional football teams, the Green Bay Packers and Detroit Lions. Instead he took a football and boxing coaching position at Yale and applied to its law school. His first application was denied because he was coaching full-time. He then took summer courses at the University of Michigan Law School in 1937 and reapplied to Yale Law School. He was accepted in 1938.

He graduated in the top one-quarter of his class.

Ford also became an enthusiastic and very good golfer. For example, in 1977 he hit a hole-in-one during a Pro-Am tournament. He graduated in 1941 and passed the bar examination shortly thereafter. He opened a law office in Grand Rapids with his friend Philip Buchen (later White House counsel during Ford's presidency). The Japanese attack on Pearl Harbor changed his plans: He signed up for service in the U.S. Navy.

On April 13, 1942, Ford was commissioned as an ensign in the U.S. Naval Reserve and a week later reported for duty at the V-5 Instructor

School at Annapolis, Maryland. After receiving training there he was assigned to the Navy Preflight School at Chapel Hill, North Carolina, where he was an instructor. He was also the sports coach at the base, including football, boxing, and swimming. In June he was promoted to lieutenant junior grade and the following year to lieutenant.

He was then assigned to a new aircraft carrier, the USS *Monterey*. For a year and a half he was its assistant navigator, athletics director, and antiaircraft battery officer. The carrier saw extensive action in the South Pacific.

The ship sustained damage and a fire in a typhoon in December 1944, during which Ford was nearly pitched overboard by its sharp listing. He managed to get to a catwalk and then led a fire brigade to put out the fire. The damaged ship was sent back to Bremerton, Washington, for repairs.

Ford was detached from the ship and sent to Navy Preflight School at St. Mary's College in California. For his several months there he was assigned to the athletic department and coached football. In 1946 he reported to the Great Lakes Separation Center for his release from active service as a lieutenant commander. He received service medals for his years in South Pacific combat.

POSTWAR LIFE

Ford married Elizabeth Bloomer Warren, a onetime fashion model and dancer (she studied under Martha Graham and was part of her New York City troupe for a time). They were married on October 15, 1948, in Grand Rapids. Her previous marriage had ended in divorce. By the time they became engaged, he was running for a seat in the U.S. House of Representatives. Their wedding was briefly delayed until shortly before the election. In a 1974 *New York Times* profile by Jane Howard, Betty Ford was quoted as explaining, "Jerry was running for Congress and wasn't sure how voters might feel about his marrying a divorced ex-dancer." He won the election—the first of thirteen to the House.

They were to have four children: Michael, John, Steven, and Susan.

Ford had conducted a "shoe leather" campaign for the Congressional seat. The incumbent, a Republican, was an isolationist. Ford by then considered himself an internationalist and in tune with the times. He knocked on doors, met workers at factory gates, and milked cows.

During the twenty-five years he served in the House he developed a reputation as a mediator and conciliator, with conservative economic views and an internationalist approach to foreign policy. His style was one of moderation in dealing with his colleagues.

After President Lyndon Johnson's landslide sweep in 1964 and the loss of thirty-six House seats for the Republicans, several colleagues approached Ford to become minority leader. He agreed and was elected.

In the first year of the 89th Congress's term, Johnson, with heavy majorities in both houses, was able to pass 84 of 87 of his administration's "Great Society" bills. Criticism of the Vietnam War began to grow and Congressional Republicans complained that the United States was not doing what needed to be done to win the war. In 1966, Republicans gained forty-seven seats in the House. That was not quite enough to gain a majority, but it was enough to blunt more Johnson domestic legislation.

Ford also went public with his criticism that the Johnson administration had not publicly disclosed a plan to successfully conclude the Vietnam War. Stung, Johnson was defensive and famously declared that Ford had played "too much football without a helmet."

At about that time, Ford and Senator Everett Dirksen of Illinois began appearing together in a televised press conference series that attracted large audiences. They used the time to describe Republican alternatives to Johnson's initiatives. This, too, got under Johnson's skin and he was widely quoted in the press as saying, "Jerry Ford is so dumb he can't walk and chew gum at the same time."

When Richard Nixon became president, Ford's role shifted from criticism to support of administration policies. For example, he was instrumental in getting bipartisan support for a major revenue-sharing program for state and local governments.

THE VICE PRESIDENCY

In the ninth year of his leadership role in the House, Ford was chosen by Nixon as his vice president, replacing Spiro Agnew, who had pleaded "no contest" to criminal charges of tax evasion and money laundering and resigned on October 10, 1973. Canvassing Congressional leaders, Nixon learned that they all thought Ford was the natural choice.

This was the first time the Twenty-fifth Amendment's provision covering a vice presidential vacancy had come into play. On November 27, the Senate voted 92–3 to confirm Ford's appointment.

The next week the House confirmed him, 387–35.

An official vice presidential residence was being readied on the grounds of the U.S. Naval Observatory in Washington when, on August 1, 1974, Alexander Haig, President Nixon's chief of staff, contacted Ford to tell him that a newly found taped telephone conversation would be released indicating that Nixon had been involved in the cover-up of the break-in at the Democratic National Committee's headquarters at the Watergate complex.

ON BECOMING PRESIDENT

On August 9, Richard Nixon resigned the presidency and Gerald Ford took the oath of office in the East Room of the White House. He then spoke to the nation over television and radio, asking for the prayers of his fellow citizens. In his remarks he said that "our long national nightmare is over. Our Constitution works. Our great Republic is a government of laws and not of men. Here, the people rule, but there is a higher power, by whatever name we honor Him, who ordains not only righteousness but love, not only justice, but mercy . . . let us restore the golden rule to our political process and let brotherly love purge our hearts of suspicion and hate."

Eleven days later the new president nominated former New York governor Nelson Rockefeller to be his vice president. Despite conservative opposition, Rockefeller was confirmed by both houses of Congress.

Ford faced a formidable task: restore public confidence in government; cope with inflation jitters; and face the prospect of aggressive Soviet Union initiatives in several places. Added to these was the unpopularity of his September 8, 1974, issuance of an unconditional pardon for any crimes Nixon might have committed while president. Critics insisted it was the result of a quid pro quo between Ford and Nixon—that is, Nixon's resignation in exchange for a prompt pardon by Ford. Ford firmly stated that this was not the case, that he had pardoned the former president in the best interests of the nation.

In time, some original critics agreed. In presenting Ford with the John F. Kennedy Library Foundation's Profile in Courage Award in 2001, Senator Edward Kennedy said he had been an opponent of the Nixon pardon, but later concluded that history would prove that Ford had made the correct decision.

While Ford initially retained Nixon's cabinet, by fall 1975 all but Secretary of State Henry Kissinger and Secretary of the Treasury William Simon had been replaced. Former representative and ambassador Donald Rumsfeld became his chief of staff. When Rumsfeld became secretary of defense, Richard Cheney took his place at the White House.

The 1974 Congressional election was very bad for the Republicans, reflecting a national hangover from Watergate. The Democrats achieved a veto-proof majority of 291 in the House (to 144 Republicans) and a 61–39 majority in the Senate.

In October, the Ford White House launched a "Whip Inflation Now" campaign, urging Americans to spend and consume less. The slogan and speeches expanding on it were widely seen as public relations gimmicks without substance. Inflation was at 7 percent. Ford also proposed a one-year 5 percent income tax rate increase for corporations and rich individuals.

By January 1975 the unemployment rate had risen to 7.2 percent. Ford then changed course and proposed a one-year tax reduction to generate growth. He also proposed a reduction in federal spending. In March the Congress passed the Tax Reduction Act, without accompanying spending cuts.

This was not Ford's only change in position. When New York City was nearly bankrupt in October 1975, Ford declared he would veto any bill to bail it out. In November he made a policy U-turn and asked Congress to approve federal loans to the city.

FOREIGN AFFAIRS

During the twenty-nine-and-a-half months of his presidency, Ford made six overseas trips. On October 21, 1974, he went to Mexico.

From November 19 to 24 he was in Japan, Korea, and the USSR. From December 14 to 16 he was in Martinique, the French island in the Caribbean. The following spring from May 28 through June 3 his travels took him to Belgium, Spain, Austria, Italy, and the Vatican. From July 26 to August 4, 1975, he was in West Germany, Poland, Finland, Romania, and Yugoslavia. From November 15 to 17 he was in France. His last trip was December 1–7 to China, Indonesia, and the Philippines. Most of the stops were for face-to-face meetings with heads of state; two were for conferences, one at NATO, the other at the opening session of the Organization for Security and Co-operation in Europe.

In 1975, despite criticism from conservative circles, the Ford administration signed the Helsinki Accords, intended to monitor human rights internationally. Critics worried that the Soviet Union would subvert the accords to their own ends. The accords created Helsinki Watch, which ultimately became Human Rights Watch. Over time, the accords worked to turn a spotlight on abuses by the Soviet Union and others.

In August 1974 Turkey invaded the part of Cyprus heavily populated by ethnic Turks. Congress voted to suspend military aid to Turkey. Ford vetoed the bill. Nevertheless, relations with Turkey remained tense for nearly four years.

As for the Israeli-Arab "peace process," Kissinger's "shuttle diplomacy" was yielding little in the way of results. Efforts to get Israel to withdraw from the Sinai Peninsula were stuck. For six months in 1975, the U.S. government would not conclude a new arms agreement with Israel. In September that year the Sinai Interim Agreement was signed, and aid to Israel resumed.

The Paris Peace Accord in January 1973 resulted in U.S. withdrawal of troops from Vietnam. There was a cease-fire between north and south, release of American prisoners of war, and a guarantee of free elections in both parts of the country. Then-president Nixon promised South Vietnam that the United States would defend it in the event of a violation by North Vietnam.

It happened in December 1974. When North Vietnamese forces moved into South Vietnam, Ford asked Congress for an aid package for our allies. Congress, under pressure from antiwar activists and media commentators, voted down the request. Saigon fell in April 1975. As the Communists were closing in on the capital, U.S. military helicopters evacuated nearly seven thousand people, both American and South Vietnamese citizens.

Many conservative foreign policy analysts were critical of the Ford administration's embrace of Nixon's détente policy. Concerns were raised that Ford and Secretary of State Kissinger were mistakenly relying on trade expansion and cultural exchanges as means of getting the Soviet Union to modify its aggressive behavior. The criticism continued to grow in 1975 and 1976.

In addition to policy problems, Ford was the target of two assassination attempts, only seventeen days apart. On September 5, 1975, in Sacramento, California, Lynette "Squeaky" Fromme, a Charles Manson disciple, was in a crowd watching the president when she attempted to fire a Colt .45 at him. A Secret Service agent grabbed the gun, preventing it from firing. She was later convicted and sent to prison.

In San Francisco on September 22, Sara Jane Moore was in a crowd of onlookers and aimed a .38-caliber revolver at the president. At that instant a former marine knocked her arm, deflecting the shot, which hit a wall above Ford's head. She, too, was convicted and sent to prison.

The nation's bicentennial took place in 1976 and Ford presided over several important events celebrating it.

One vexation played up frequently by the news media and late-night television comedians was the notion that Ford was clumsy. Twice he had stumbled in public with cameras rolling. This was magnified, despite the fact he had been an outstanding athlete and was not clumsy.

IN THE AIR

Given the need to concentrate on domestic issues, President Ford made only seven trips outside the United States, and none after 1975. His first, to Mexico, was for a single day, October 21, 1974, to meet with President Luis Echeverria. Of his December 14–16 trip to the French Caribbean island of Martinique, it is said that he and the president of France, Valerie Giscard d'Estaing, had their best conversations about world affairs sitting by the swimming pool. He had three trips to Europe and two to Asia.

TIME-OUT

During Gerald Ford's Congressional years, he and his wife purchased a condominium in Vail, Colorado. That started what became a semi-annual tradition, a summer vacation in Vail and a winter skiing trip and family reunion at Christmastime. This continued during his presidency. For his first presidential Christmas they were at Vail from December 22, 1974, through January 2, 1975. The next summer, while Congress was on recess, they returned for two weeks, August 10–25. In December they were at Vail from the twenty-third to the thirtieth. In 1976, with the Republican National Convention behind them, they took a short vacation in the mountains, August 20–29. For his last Christmas season in office, they returned there for December 19, 1976, to January 2, 1977.

The Palm Springs, California, area became an alternative retreat location for them. From March 29 through April 7, 1975, they were guests at a home at Rancho Mirage, just east of Palm Springs. They returned for eight days in 1976, November 7–15, at the home of Ambassador Leonard Firestone. Firestone had been urging them to consider having a home in the Palm Springs area.

An avid and good golfer, Ford tried to get in a round even on what would otherwise be a working trip. For example, on July 11–13, 1975, after a full schedule of events in Chicago, he was in Michigan for a parade in Traverse City, a visit to the Interlochen Music Camp, and a speech he gave to a group of federal judges convening on Mackinac Island. While there, he did get in two rounds of golf.

THE 1976 ELECTION

When he assumed office, Ford indicated that he would not run in 1976 for a full term. In time, he changed his mind and by early 1975 was beginning to assemble a campaign team. Meanwhile, Ronald Reagan, whose second term as California governor ended in the early days of January 1975, was being urged by friends to run for the nomination the next year. Reagan was unsure, believing that fairness required that Ford be given a chance to do his job.

As the year wore on conservative unease over such things as Vietnam, Soviet adventuring, the Helsinki Accords, inflation, and unemployment led Reagan to allow preliminary campaign planning to go forward. He announced his candidacy in November.

Ford won the initial primaries, then Reagan made a comeback. The delegate count was virtually tied going into the July convention in Kansas City. Despite parliamentary maneuvers, Ford won by a close margin when the nomination vote was taken.

In the general election, Carter, playing up his "outsider" credentials, came out of the Democratic National Convention with a 33-point lead over Ford. Despite awkward statements to the effect that there was no Soviet domination over Eastern Europe or that Poland did not consider itself dominated by the USSR, Ford managed to narrow the gap. On election day, Carter won 50.1 percent of the popular vote to Ford's 48 percent. The electoral vote was 297–240.

POST-PRESIDENCY

In 1977 former president Ford became president (and later chairman) of the Eisenhower Fellowships, based in Philadelphia. He worked on his autobiography, *A Time to Heal,* which was published in 1979.

After his defeat in the 1976 election, the Fords decided to make the Palm Springs area their principal residence. They purchased a building site in Rancho Mirage and had a fifteen-room home designed and built for them along the thirteenth fairway of the Thunderbird Country Club. It was completed in 1977. Their new next-door neighbor was their friend Leonard Firestone (son of Harvey Firestone, founder of the tire company). Firestone was also a cofounder of the Betty Ford Center, on the campus of the Eisenhower Medical Center, in Rancho Mirage in 1982.

Gerald Ford and Jimmy Carter developed a friendship, beginning with their traveling together to the funeral of Egypt's Anwar el-Sadat in early 1981. In April that year Ford presided over the opening of the Gerald R. Ford Presidential Library in Ann Arbor, Michigan, on the campus of the University of Michigan. In September the Gerald R. Ford Museum opened in Grand Rapids. In October 2006 the Gerald R. Ford School of Public Policy was dedicated at the University of Michigan.

In 1999, President Clinton awarded the Presidential Medal of Freedom to President Ford.

When he died in his home at Rancho Mirage on December 26, 2006, of heart failure, Gerald Ford had the longest life span of any U.S. president, ninety-three years and 165 days. He is buried on the grounds of his presidential museum.

Betty Ford died on July 8, 2011, at age ninety-three. She was much admired for her courage in overcoming addiction to pills and alcohol. She founded the Betty Ford Center, which has treated many for alcohol and drug addiction, and was known for her candor as one of the first well-known women to openly discuss their breast cancer surgery.

The Gerald R. Ford Presidential Library and Museum. Although they are both part of the National Archives & Records Administration's presidential libraries system, the Ford Library and Museum are in two cities. The museum is in Grand Rapids, the library in Ann Arbor.

The museum's exhibits highlight the lives of President and Mrs. Ford. There are also temporary exhibits from the presidential libraries system, the Smithsonian Institution, and other sources. In addition, the museum has a number of events throughout the year. The library includes 25 million pages of memos, letters, reports, and other historical documents. It has the documents of President Ford from before, during, and after his presidency, as well as the papers of Betty Ford and personal papers of several other government officials. It also has 450,000 photographs, 3,500 hours of video, 3,000 hours of audio, and 797,000 feet of motion picture film.

Location: The Museum: In Gerald Ford's hometown of Grand Rapids, 130 miles west of Ann Arbor. Address: 303 Pearl Street N.W., Grand Rapids, MI 49504–5353. Telephone: 616-254-0400. Hours, 9 a.m.–5 p.m. daily (closed Thanksgiving, Christmas, and New Year's Day).

The Library: 1000 Beal Avenue, Ann Arbor, MI 48109. Telephone: 734-205-0555.

Hours: Monday–Friday, 8:45 am.–4:45 p.m. Closed on federal holidays.

Website (for both): www.fordlibrarymuseum.gov.

Chapter Thirty-eight

———•❖•———

JAMES EARL ("JIMMY") CARTER

THE 39TH PRESIDENT

January 20, 1977 — January 20, 1981

*F*ishing came as naturally to Jimmy Carter as breathing. He'd been a fisherman since childhood.

In time, his specialty was fly-fishing and he became an expert at it. Indeed, he devoted one of his books to the subject. As president, many of his home trips to Plains, Georgia, involved fishing and on thirty-one of his visits to Camp David he took side trips to fish in streams in Maryland and Pennsylvania.

GROWING UP IN GEORGIA

James Earl Carter, Jr., was born October 1, 1924, to James Earl, Sr., a local businessman, and (Bessie) Lillian Carter, a registered nurse. The family lived in Plains, a small town near Americus in southwestern Georgia. He had two sisters and one brother. The family's ancestors had come from England in the 1630s.

"Jimmy" was an early reader and bright student. A "born-again" Christian from a young age, Carter was a Sunday school teacher. At Plains High School he was a key member of the basketball team and active in Future Farmers of America. After graduation he enrolled at Georgia Southwestern College in Americus, then applied to the U.S. Naval Academy, to which he was admitted in 1943. He graduated fifty-ninth in a class of 820 midshipmen.

On active duty he was assigned to diesel-electric submarines in both the Atlantic and Pacific fleets. He then qualified to command such a submarine. This prompted him to apply for the navy's new nuclear submarine program, headed by Captain Hyman G. Rickover, well-known as a demanding boss. Carter saw nuclear power as the future of submarines and considered a career in the navy.

In 1952, while based in upstate New York for work on the nuclear propulsion system for the Seawolf class of submarines, Carter was chosen to be in charge of a team to go to Canada to help with the shutdown of a nuclear reactor at the Chalk River Laboratories. On December 12 that year, an accident had caused partial meltdown of a nuclear reactor. Carter developed a systematic plan to disassemble the reactor and seal it. Then he and the other team members put on protective gear and were lowered into the reactor to work for only a few seconds at a time, using tools to carry out the disassembly without being exposed to severe radiation.

Later, Carter said that this experience played a role in the development of his views about nuclear power and his decision to stop work on the neutron bomb.

His father died in July 1953. Carter then resigned his commission to go home to Plains to run the family business. Meanwhile, he had married Rosalynn Smith in 1946. They have four children: John William ("Jack"), James Earl III ("Chip"), Donnel Jeffrey ("Jeff"), and Amy Lynn.

PEANUT FARMING AND POLITICS

Carter took over management of the family peanut farming and warehouse business and successfully expanded it.

As his business prospered he began serving on local boards: hospitals, libraries, and schools.

In 1962 Carter ran for the state senate and was elected after contesting early returns as being fraudulent. In 1964 he was reelected.

By 1966 he had his eyes on the governor's office. He announced his candidacy but faced former governor Ellis Arnall and segregationist Lester Maddox in the Democratic primary. Carter ran third; the other two had a runoff, with Maddox winning the nomination. In the general election Maddox faced Republican Howard Callaway and Arnall was a write-in candidate. Maddox had come in second in a very tight race, but was chosen the winner by the George State Assembly. Carter, lacking statewide name recognition, had done well under the circumstances.

Carter returned to his business and over the next four years made nearly two thousand speeches around the state. In 1970 he ran again, but faced former governor Carl Sanders in the primary. Carter had refused to join the segregationist White Citizens' Council and found his peanut warehouse boycotted as a result. Also, the Carters and one other family in the Plains Baptist Church voted to admit blacks to its membership. This probably incurred the wrath of segregationists in the state but it was acceptable to the growing ranks of moderates in the state's voting population. He was elected over Republican Hal Suit.

GOVERNOR OF GEORGIA

Inaugurated on January 12, 1971, to a single term (the limit at that time), Carter in his inaugural address said that the time of racial segregation was over and that racial discrimination had no place in the future of the state. He was the first statewide public official in the Deep South to so declare. He then appointed a number of African Americans to statewide boards.

During his term Carter, to improve efficiency, condensed nearly three hundred state agencies and offices down to thirty.

In 1972 he called a news conference to state that Senator George McGovern would be unelectable as president if he were the Democratic Party's nominee. He said McGovern was too liberal on both foreign and domestic issues. In a triumph of ambition, however, Carter lobbied to become McGovern's vice presidential running mate when it became clear that McGovern would be the nominee for president. McGovern, however, chose otherwise.

In 1974, Carter chaired the Democratic National Committee's

congressional and gubernatorial campaigns, thus increasing his expo-
sure to party leaders leading up to the 1976 election.

RUNNING FOR PRESIDENT

By the time he announced his intention to run for president in 1976,
Carter in one national poll had 2 percent name recognition. Nevertheless, in the wake of Watergate, his "outside Washington" experience
proved to be an asset.

He had a national strategy, first appealing to conservative Christian
and rural voters in Iowa and southern states, then blitzing thirty-
seven states to build name recognition and support. He won the Iowa
caucuses and New Hampshire primary, then, with more than fifty
thousand political travel miles under his belt, went on to win the nomination. As Laurence Shoup wrote in his 1980 book, *The Carter Presidency and Beyond,* "What Carter had that his opponents did not was
the acceptance and support of elite sectors of the mass communications
media. It was their favorable coverage of Carter and his campaign that
gave him an edge. . . ."

In the general election he faced President Gerald Ford, who had
come to office upon the resignation of Richard Nixon in August 1974
and had prevailed for the 1976 Republican nomination after a close
battle with Ronald Reagan. Carter's early lead over Ford gradually
dwindled, and on election day Carter won a close race, 50.1 percent to
48 percent in the popular vote and 297–240 in the Electoral College.

THE CARTER PRESIDENCY

Inflation and high interest rates had begun before Carter took office
in January 1977. They were to become considerably worse during his
term. Some of his decisions proved successful; others were unpopular,
even drawing derision. On the plus side were the Camp David Accords, leading to peace treaties between Israel and its neighbors Egypt
and Jordan. The Panama Canal treaties, although actively contested at
the time, turned out to be another plus.

His calling for airline deregulation brought a number of positive
changes to that industry.

On the minus side were such things as his declaration of amnesty for Vietnam draft dodgers, and some purely symbolic energy conservation measures, including solar panels on the White House roof and the president wearing a cardigan sweater during a televised "Fireside Chat," urging Americans to turn down their thermostats.

His administration seemed to have no solution to "stagflation," the conflation of the inflation and interest rates that was well above 20 percent.

Other events during his term were the oil crisis of 1979; the nuclear accident that year at Three Mile Island in Pennsylvania; and the 1980 eruption of Mount St. Helens in Washington state.

The takeover of the U.S. Embassy in Tehran in 1979 by Islamist revolutionaries soon became a political albatross for Carter. His sending in a special military unit to rescue the American hostages ended as a complete failure, including the death of several U.S. soldiers. As a result, Carter was widely seen as inept.

In the summer of 1979 he told the nation that its "malaise" was, in effect, the fault of the American people themselves. This drew widespread criticism—even scorn—from many quarters. In 1980, in a symbolic punishment for the Soviet Union's invasion of Afghanistan in 1979, Carter canceled U.S. participation in the Summer Olympic Games. This angered the athletes, their supporters, and the international Olympic movement, and did not cause the USSR to withdraw from Afghanistan. Instead, the Soviets canceled U.S. wheat purchases and boycotted the 1984 Olympics in Los Angeles. It was not until 1989 that they withdrew from Afghanistan.

Famous for his attention to detail, Carter was frequently cited by critics as spending time scheduling the use of the White House tennis court. While the story may be apocryphal, it illustrates the growing frustration of the body politic.

TRAVELS AND RETREATS

During his presidency, Carter made fourteen trips overseas: five to Europe, three to Asia, two to the Middle East, and one each to South America, Central America, Africa, and Mexico. The G-6 nations' meetings (later G-7 and G-8) had been started by President Ford. There were four of them during Carter's term. His Middle Eastern trips were due to his efforts to act as a broker in peace negotiations. His two-day trip to Panama was to sign a protocol confirming documents that ratified the pair of Panama Canal treaties.

Most of the Carters' retreats were to their home in Plains. Since winters are not heavy in southern Georgia, they went at all times of the year. They spent three Christmases there with family members. Their longest retreat was sixteen days in July 1979 (although it was interrupted by a three-day trip to Detroit). Most Plains visits were short—three or four days. Their first home retreat in February 1977 was a little more than two days long.

The Plains retreats tended to be uneventful and quiet. A well-known correspondent for a major newspaper once told me that he had been assigned to "Plains duty" one summer and that "it was the longest two weeks I ever spent."

Some visits began in Plains but moved to homes at St. Simon's Island or Sapelo Island off the Georgia coast. There were also fishing side trips to a friend's campsite near Calhoun, Georgia. In May 1977, the president cruised to Georgia and Florida aboard the USS *Los Angeles*. In August 1978 the Carters vacationed at Jackson Hole, Wyoming. In May 1979 there was a four-day visit to Virginia Beach, Virginia, and from August 17 to 24 they cruised the Mississippi River on the *Delta Queen*.

When it came time to campaign for reelection in 1980, Carter faced the insurgency of Ted Kennedy, who was a darling of the liberal wing of the Democratic Party. Ultimately, Kennedy withdrew, but the insurgency caused a rift in party ranks that weakened Carter in the general election.

Carter had reintroduced draft registration for young men, thus angering many potential young supporters. Although he led Reagan for a time in the polls, that melted away. A turning point came in public perception of the candidates in their one debate. Carter entered the debate filled with facts and figures. All Reagan had to prove was that, if elected, he would not start a war. Carter's didactic presentation reached a climax when he ticked off a list of supposed Reagan liabilities. Reagan, composed and smiling, said, "There you go again." Reagan was widely declared the winner of the event.

By the time of the 1980 general election campaign, Carter's popularity had declined. In November, the Republican ticket of Reagan and
George H. W. Bush routed the Carter–Walter Mondale ticket, 525 electoral votes to 13. The Democratic ticket won only Minnesota (Mondale's home state) and the District of Columbia.

AFTER THE WHITE HOUSE

Jimmy Carter may be the most active former president the nation has
experienced. After Reagan's inauguration, the Carters returned to their
home in Plains and the peanut farm business. He had put the enterprise
in a blind trust during his presidency and, on returning, discovered
there had been mismanagement of this asset, creating a large debt for
him to resolve, which he did.

He soon drew widespread attention for doing carpentry work on
houses being built for low-income citizens as part of the nonprofit
Habitat for Humanity program. Meanwhile, in 1982 he established the
Carter Center at Emory University in Atlanta. The nonprofit center's
mission is to advance human rights and reduce dread diseases.

By the time he left office, Carter was widely seen as indecisive and
ineffectual. Yet after leaving office he became quite outspoken. He
and his center teams have monitored countless elections around the
world—including eighty-one elections in thirty-three countries since
1989—and have gained widespread respect for the objectivity of their
observations.

In the public health realm, the center's staff has worked with international health experts and public health officials in countries afflicted
with such diseases as river blindness, Guinea worm disease, and malaria. These debilitating diseases reduce human energy and productivity
and adversely affect several countries in the Americas and Africa. In the
case of the Guinea worm disease, the center's efforts have contributed
to a 99 percent decline in reported instances of the ailment, from 3.5
million in 1986 to barely three thousand in 2009.

By 1986, the Jimmy Carter Library and Museum opened in Atlanta.
It is part of the National Archives and Records Administration system
of presidential libraries.

As a former president, Jimmy Carter has become a prolific writer.

Twenty-one of his twenty-three books have been written since he left the White House. His wife, Rosalynn, cowrote one of them, and their daughter, Amy, illustrated a children's book he wrote.

In 2002, Carter was awarded the Nobel Peace Prize. He is the only former president to receive it. (Presidents Theodore Roosevelt, Wilson, and Obama received it while in office.)

Carter has been anything but indecisive on public policy matters since he left office. In 1994 he traveled to North Korea, ostensibly as a private citizen, but privately at the behest of then-president Clinton to see if a treaty could be developed that would result in that nation ending its nuclear program. This was worked out and Carter announced it on CNN without the Clinton administration's advance knowledge. His intention was to goad the administration into positive action. This was not appreciated by the Clinton White House. Later on the Clinton administration signed what was called the Agreed Framework. Under it, North Korea was to freeze and then dismantle its nuclear program. It made a show of razing one facility, but several years later it was learned the North Koreans had never stopped the development of nuclear weapons.

Over several years of the first decade of this century Carter met with various people active in terrorist or terrorist-sponsoring groups in the Middle East, including a leader of Hamas and Syrian president Bashar Assad. On one trip he laid a wreath at the grave of Yasser Arafat. A sharp critic of Israeli policy, on two public occasions he insisted that Israel had 150 nuclear weapons. Most of these efforts on Carter's part were considered to be strictly "freelance" and motivated, in his view, by his concern for human rights.

In 1994 he led a mission to Haiti to attempt to restore to power the democratically elected but corrupt president Jean-Bertrand Aristide.

Most former presidents are open to being consulted by their successors, but otherwise keep their opinions to themselves. Carter is an exception. He criticized President Clinton for pardoning the fugitive financier Marc Rich. He criticized President George W. Bush for the Iraq War and British prime minister Tony Blair for supporting it. His criticisms have tended to be pointed and harsh. Although he won the presidency with the support of many evangelical Christian voters, in 2006 on a BBC television program he criticized what he said was the growing influence of the "Religious Right" in U.S. politics.

Critics of the former president say his outspoken comments tend toward stridency and self-righteousness; however, it is unlikely such criticism will dampen his comments.

At home the Carters live comfortably in their one-story home on two acres of land at the edge of Plains, as they have for many years. Under an unusual arrangement the National Park Service maintains the exterior of the home and its grounds (at a cost to the taxpayers in 2010 of $67,841).

In exchange, the federal government has the right to add the property to a Jimmy Carter Historic Site when the Carters are deceased. They are not the first presidential couple to provide such a transfer of their property; however, this is apparently the first time the NPS has entered into an agreement to maintain the grounds at public expense before the death of the principals.

In his retirement, President Carter has other hobbies besides fly-fishing. A correspondent for Britain's *Financial Times* reported on March 4, 2006, that Carter "invites me home to see the workshop where he paints and makes furniture—skills learned at Plains High School in classes designed to equip boys to be farmers or craftsmen." He continues to teach Sunday school and is a deacon of the Maranatha Baptist Church in Plains.

———————

The Jimmy Carter Library and Museum and adjacent Carter Center are situated on thirty-seven acres of parkland. The library contains the papers of Mr. Carter's public career and the museum has exhibits depicting the events of his life. The museum is open Monday through Saturday, 9 a.m.–4:45 p.m., and Sunday, noon–4:45 p.m. The library is open Monday through Friday, 8:30 a.m.–4:30 p.m.

Location: 441 Freedom Parkway, Atlanta, GA 30307–1498. Telephone: 404-865-7100. Website: www.jimmycarterlibrary.gov.

The Carter Center is a separate entity from the Library and Museum. It is operated in partnership with Emory University. Its mission statement lists five elements: "1) The Center emphasizes action and results. Based on careful research and analysis, it is prepared to take timely action on important and pressing issues; 2) The Center does not duplicate the effective efforts of others; 3) The Center addresses difficult

*problems and recognizes the possibility of failure as an acceptable risk;
4) The Center is nonpartisan and acts as a neutral in dispute-resolution
activities; 5) The Center believes that people can improve their lives
when provided with the necessary skills, knowledge and access to resources." Monitoring elections, mediating conflicts, supporting defenders
of human rights worldwide, and helping eliminate disease are its main
activities.*

*Location: One Copenhill, 453 Freedom Parkway, Atlanta, GA
30307. Telephone: 404-420-5100, 800-550-3560. Email: carterweb@
emory.edu. Website: www.cartercenter.org.*

*The Carter residence in Plains, Georgia, is not open to the public as
it is the private residence of former president Carter and Mrs. Carter.*

———•◦•———

Chapter Thirty-nine

RONALD REAGAN

THE 40TH PRESIDENT

January 20, 1981 — January 20, 1989

"If this isn't actually heaven, it's in the same Zip code."

That's how Ronald Reagan described for a friend his ranch, nestled in a saddle of the Santa Ynez Mountains twenty-seven miles north of Santa Barbara, California. For Reagan, this 688-acre mixture of open fields, chaparral shrubs, and oak and Madrone forests embodied everything he savored of the outdoor life.

A LONG WAY FROM TAMPICO

Ronald Wilson Reagan was born February 6, 1911, the second son of John (Jack) and Nelle Reagan, in a flat above a bakery in the small northwestern Illinois town of Tampico. They moved several times during his early years, as his father, a shoe salesman, pursued his never-quite-successful career.

Ronald and his brother, Neil, grew up in a household free of envy and prejudice, thanks to both his father's and mother's strong sense of egalitarianism. It has been said that Ronald Reagan got his determination to succeed from his mother and his sense of humor from his father.

When he was nine, the family settled in Dixon, a city of about eight thousand in the same part of Illinois. There Ronald's interest in the theater developed and both boys were active in sports. An excellent swimmer, Ronald spent seven summers as the lifeguard at the city's park on the Rock River. There he carved seventy-seven notches in a log to mark his rescues.

Reagan went on to Eureka College, a small liberal arts college twenty-five miles east of Peoria. The faculty, staff, and fellow students had a lasting influence on him. In his freshman year he gave what amounted to his first political speech, calling for a student strike over what were felt to be undue draconian cuts in programs.

He landed his first job three months after graduation, broadcasting football games on WOC Radio in Davenport, Iowa. From there he went to a large regional station, WHO in Des Moines. Accompanying the Chicago Cubs on their spring training trip to California in 1937, he managed to get a screen test at Warner Bros. This led to a contract and ultimately roles in more than fifty full-length feature films. His film career was interrupted by his service during World War II. His nearsightedness kept him from going overseas, so he was assigned to an Army Air Force film production unit in Southern California.

During his film career he served as president of the Screen Actors Guild, in which position he learned the art of negotiation, for he had to deal with the heads of the major film studios in working out contracts for his members.

He and film star Jane Wyman were married in 1940, but divorced in 1948. They had two children, Maureen and Michael. He and Nancy Davis were married in 1952 and had two children, Patricia and Ronald Prescott.

Reagan was host of television's *General Electric Theater* for most of the 1950s. His contract also called for him to give talks at GE factories around the country, meeting workers as they came off shift. From these sessions he honed his views on the issues facing the nation. After his GE tenure he was host of *Death Valley Days*.

After years of being a Democrat he became a registered Republican in 1962. In 1966 he ran for governor of California and beat the two-term incumbent, Edmund G. "Pat" Brown. He won a second term in

1970. In 1976 he campaigned for the Republican nomination for president, but lost in a close race to Gerald Ford at the party convention in Kansas City that summer. In 1980, as the Republican nominee, he defeated incumbent president Jimmy Carter. In 1984, he defeated former vice president Walter Mondale, winning all but one state and the District of Columbia.

OBJECTIVES ON TAKING OFFICE

When he entered the White House, Reagan had three objectives: Get the nation's economy back on track, limit the growth and reach of the government, and develop a strategy to bring the Cold War to a successful conclusion.

Less than two months into his presidency, Reagan was shot by a would-be assassin.

The bullet barely missed his heart. He soon recovered and addressed a joint session of Congress to promote his across-the-board tax cut legislation. It passed and he signed it at the ranch in August 1981. By the time it became fully effective in late 1982, the nation began one of the longest periods of economic growth in its history. The second objective was harder to achieve, although the welfare reform that passed a few years after he left office was inspired by reforms he had proposed.

The third objective was a major success. He devised a strategy (he dubbed it "Peace Through Strength") to put steady pressure on the Soviet Union to choose between an arms race, and thus risk bankruptcy, or negotiate an end to the Cold War. Three Soviet leaders died before he found one—Mikhail Gorbachev—who fully understood the consequences of the Reagan administration's strategic moves. At their second summit in Reykjavik, Iceland, in October 1986, Reagan refused to shelve his Strategic Defense Initiative in exchange for Gorbachev's signature on a wide-ranging nuclear weapons reduction treaty. The Russian leader realized then that he had no choice but to end the Cold War.

In retirement, Reagan traveled to Central and Eastern Europe, Russia, and Asia and gave several speeches to U.S. organizations. He wrote his memoirs and oversaw a collection of his speeches in book form. For several years he held regular office hours in the Century City section of Los Angeles. In November 1994, in an open letter to the American people, he announced that he had been diagnosed with Alzheimer's disease. His public appearances ceased. He died at his home in the Bel Air section of Los Angeles in June 2004.

SEEING THE RANCH FOR THE FIRST TIME

It was love at first sight for Reagan when his friend William Wilson took him and his wife, Nancy, to see what was then called Tip Top Ranch, one weekend in late 1973. Climbing up steep, twisting, narrow Refugio Canyon Road from the Pacific shore, Reagan, on seeing the property spread out before him, said to Wilson, "It's absolutely gorgeous here, I love it." Wilson replied, "Better not talk like that or the price will go up." The owner, Ray Cornelius, put them on horses for a tour of the property and, as Nancy Reagan put it in a 2002 interview for *Ronald Reagan and His Ranch,* "I think we decided right then that we wanted to buy it."

Reagan had learned to ride horses when he was in the army's Cavalry Reserve in the late 1930s, during his years as a radio broadcaster in Des Moines. He became an accomplished rider and often quoted the aphorism "There's nothing better for the insides of a man than the outside of a horse." In western films in which he starred he did his own riding rather than having stuntmen substitute for him.

His love of horses, combined with a desire for a complete change of scene between film assignments, led Reagan to buy a small ranch in the eastern end of Southern California's San Fernando Valley in the late 1940s. Then, in 1951 he purchased a 290-acre ranch in the mountains behind Malibu. He called it Yearling Row and planned to breed and raise jumpers and hunters. In the late 1960s a film studio that owned adjacent land it used for "location" scenes purchased the ranch from the Reagans. By 1973, when he was in his second term as governor of California, Reagan was itching to have another ranch. Tip Top Ranch was to fill the bill, although they renamed it Rancho del Cielo—Ranch in the Sky.

It took several months to complete the purchase. The Reagans took title to the property in November 1974, a few weeks before he was to complete his governorship. The ranch had a small adobe house at its center, estimated to have been built in 1871. The Reagans planned to expand it and to make a nearby seasonal pond into a year-round one.

HISTORY AT ITS FEET

Rancho del Cielo had been a silent witness to history on the coastal shelf more than two thousand feet below. In 1769, Alta California, as the territory was then called, was only nominally Spanish. The new visitador-general, on arriving in Mexico City, the Spanish Empire's North American capital, in 1765, was determined to colonize the territory. He commanded the governor of Baja California, Don Gaspar de Portola, to lead an expedition north to San Diego and on to Monterey.

Following the coastal plain, they camped at a spot that would later become the site of Santa Barbara. About twenty-five miles north of there, they passed a canyon they called "el Refugio"—the Refuge—the same canyon that today has a road that takes one up the mountain to the Reagan ranch.

Seventy-seven years later, in December 1846, John C. Frémont (to become, in 1856, the Republican Party's first nominee for president) led a contingent of sixty soldiers southward along the coastal plain that Portola had trod. Nicknamed "the Pathfinder," Fremont was on what he described as a scientific expedition; however, his real purpose was to aid the effort by American settlers to acquire California from Mexico. On this particular march, his immediate goal was to capture the garrison town of Santa Barbara to aid the "Bear Flag Revolt," which had been staged in Sonoma, in Northern California, by American settlers. Frémont took Santa Barbara two days after Christmas in a bloodless operation. Most of the town's residents were in church at the time.

After the war with Mexico in 1847, the United States acquired California in the Treaty of Guadalupe Hidalgo in 1848. At about that time, settlers began to clear brush in the more gently sloping and level areas in the Santa Ynez Mountains. It is likely that Jose and Juana Pico took up residence in 1870 on what was to become the Reagan ranch. There they grew vegetables and enough grapes to make nine hundred gallons of wine a year. They also raised horses, cattle, chickens, and hogs.

In August 1898, the Picos acquired title to 160 acres of the ranch from the U.S. government under the Homestead Act.

PLANNING CHANGES AT THE RANCH

A few days after his term as governor ended in early January 1975, Ronald Reagan held a scheduling meeting in his new office, which was inside the suite of Deaver & Hannaford, Inc., a new public relations/public affairs firm established by Michael Deaver and this author. Both of us had been assistants to the governor in Sacramento and he had approved a plan we submitted to coordinate his public program after leaving office. We had engaged several people from his Sacramento staff to do, in microcosm, what 105 people had been doing in the governor's office.

All of us were familiar with scheduling meetings. We would review details of upcoming events and discuss requests for his appearances thirty to sixty days ahead. In this meeting, one of the first things he said was, "Now remember, block time on my schedule for work days at the ranch."

For the next two and a half years Reagan devoted nearly every spare day he had to working at the ranch. Two aides, Willard "Barney" Barnett and Dennis LeBlanc, volunteered to help him.

Together, they worked on closing in a screened porch to make a new L-shaped living/dining room. They reroofed the house and lined the pond with heavy-duty plastic to prevent seasonal evaporation. They expanded the main bedroom. (A two-bedroom guesthouse was built after he became president.) Reagan himself laid the stone patio in front of the house, using stones found on the property. Mrs. Reagan joined them to do much of the painting and the laying of tile floors.

The result was a small, warm, but simple and comfortable home of 1,500 square feet. The dining room looks over Lake Lucky, the restored pond, and the ranch's main pasture, toward oak and madrone forests on the hillside beyond.

About one hundred feet behind and above the house is the Tack Barn, with a well-equipped tack room, workshop, and garage where Reagan's Jeep and small tractor are still parked. Modern presidents are not allowed to drive on public streets, so driving his Jeep about the ranch was a special pleasure for President Reagan. The horses were kept in another barn a few hundred feet above the Tack Barn.

DAILY RANCH ROUTINE

After the house remodeling was finished and all the fences built, Reagan developed a routine that continued nearly every day that he was at the ranch during his presidency. The Reagans' longest sojourns were in summer, when Congress was on vacation; however, they made a number of smaller trips throughout the year, especially when presidential business took him to the West.

At the ranch he rose early for a light breakfast; then signed documents for the daily courier to take to the temporary White House staff office at a Santa Barbara hotel; then had his daily national security briefing by his national security adviser (usually on a secure telephone line, occasionally in person). Then he would go to the Tack Barn and saddle and tack up his and his wife's horses. The Secret Service detail, headed by John Barletta, would meet him there and they would confer as to the route for the ride. He would then ring a railroad bell as a signal to his wife that they were ready to mount (the bell had belonged to her grandfather).

The routes would vary. Sometimes they would go to the highest point on the property, 2,587 feet, where they could look down on the Pacific Ocean to the west and the Santa Ynez Valley to the north and east. Sometimes they would pass Heart Rock, a large sandstone block where two trails intersected. There, in 1977, he had carved "RR + NR." Other family members added their initials later.

Another riding trail landmark was the Pet Cemetery. There, under the trees on a rise above the pasture, Ronald Reagan had created a final resting place for the faithful animals he considered part of the family. His favorite horse, Little Man, is there, as is Nancy Reagan's No Strings. Duke and Duchess, a bull and a cow, are there, as well as several dogs. Each has a memorial sandstone, carved by Ronald Reagan himself.

After lunch, the president devoted most of the afternoon to clearing brush and chopping wood (the house was heated only by two fireplaces). He often said he did some of his best thinking during these vigorous afternoons.

A few major events occurred when Reagan was at the ranch. In August 1981, he signed the tax-cut bill he had masterfully maneuvered toward passage by Congress that summer. It provided across-the-board rate cuts, which triggered an economic expansion that lasted well beyond his White House years. On a September day in 1983 he got word at the ranch that a Soviet missile had shot down a Korean airliner, killing all aboard, including a U.S. member of Congress. After working out initial plans for the U.S. reaction, he returned to Washington.

Although as president, Reagan attended to any official business that needed his attention and he was always available, he used Rancho del Cielo as a genuine retreat from the intense daily schedule of the White House. The staff left the Reagans alone as much as possible.

When one considers that both he and Nancy had been in the public eye for most of their adult lives, their desire for occasional breaks in which their privacy was paramount is readily understandable.

He had been a radio sportscaster, film star, three-time president of the Screen Actors Guild, television host, two-term governor of California, candidate for the presidential nomination in 1976, and the nominee in 1980. She had been a movie actress when they met, later First Lady of California, then a campaigner during his presidential bids.

FAMOUS VISITORS

They did have visitors for day visits. On February 1, 1983, one of the wettest California days in memory, Queen Elizabeth and Prince Philip arrived for what all had expected to be an afternoon of horseback riding. Reagan was reciprocating a ride that he and the queen had taken in Windsor Park the year before when he was in England to address Parliament. Riding was out of the question in the torrent, however, and the Secret Service soon recommended that the entire party head down the mountain in four-wheel-drive vehicles.

In August 1984, the papal nuncio, Archbishop Pio Laghi, came for a working lunch with Reagan to discuss the U.S. response to a Polish parliamentary decree calling for the release of political prisoners. National Security Adviser Robert McFarlane joined them. This was at a time when the Reagan administration and the Vatican were both working energetically to aid democratic movements behind the Iron Curtain, especially in Poland. Their cooperation came to be known in the White House as "the Holy Alliance."

In August 1985, Vice President George H. W. Bush and his wife, Barbara, spent an afternoon with the Reagans.

The Reagans entertained several other famous visitors after he left the White House: former British prime minister Margaret Thatcher in early 1991, Mikhail and Raisa Gorbachev in May 1992, and Canadian prime minister Brian Mulroney and his wife, Mila, in April 1993.

Throughout Reagan's presidency the couple continued a tradition begun several years before. Two good friends, Betty Wilson and Marion Jorgensen, organized for their circle of close social friends an annual party at the ranch at the time of Nancy Reagan's birthday, July 6. The two women and their husbands were occasional weekend visitors at the ranch, where they joined the Reagans on horseback rides.

Altogether, Ronald Reagan spent 347 days of his presidency at the ranch. Much of August was spent there each year, while Congress was on recess. They were there a few days every year at Thanksgiving. Other than that, the visits were occasional, whenever they could be planned.

Reagan also used Camp David, spending many of his Washington weekends there.

OUT IN THE WORLD

During his two terms, President Reagan went to Europe seven times, Asia three times, and South America once. Among these trips were three fateful summits with Soviet leader Mikhail Gorbachev: at Geneva, Switzerland in 1985; Reykjavík, Iceland, in 1986; and Moscow in 1988. On another trip, in June 1987, he gave a speech in front of the Brandenburg Gate in Berlin that had far-reaching consequences. He made the famous statement, "Mr. Gorbachev, open this gate! Mr. Gorbachev, tear down this wall!" The Wall went down in 1990 and the Soviet Union was gone a year later.

On a June 1982 trip to London he enunciated what became known as the Reagan Doctrine in a speech to Parliament. He also enjoyed that horseback ride with Queen Elizabeth II in Windsor Park. In June 1984, commemorating the fortieth anniversary of the D-Day landings in Normandy, he stood before a group of veterans of that day and recounted the bravery of them and their comrades with the summation, "These are the boys of Pointe Du Hoc."

His first two trips outside the United States were to Mexico and Canada, respectively. His second pair of trips was later that year, in reverse order. During his presidency, he made three more to Mexico (including one international conference in Cancún) and three to Canada.

All his travels were on Boeing 707s, the longtime Air Force One planes. He ordered new 747s, which would mean greatly expanded facilities and cargo capacity and a much greater range of travel without refueling. His successor, George H. W. Bush, was the first president to use the new plane.

MOVING TO PRIVACY

In November 1994, when he wrote his open letter about the Alzheimer's disease diagnosis, his public appearances ended. He visited the ranch for the last time in the late summer the next year, 1995.

In April 1998, the Reagans sold the ranch to the Young America's Foundation. The foundation conducts Student Leadership Conferences several times a year at its Santa Barbara offices, a remodeled hotel building in the city's downtown. There students hear from speakers in public life, media personalities, and others about the nature of public affairs and government. The foundation takes the students in small groups to experience a day at Rancho del Cielo.

Ronald Reagan died on June 5, 2004. A seven-day state funeral was declared. On June 7, his casket was taken to the Ronald Reagan Presidential Foundation and Library in Simi Valley, California, then flown to Washington, D.C., on June 9 for public viewing in the Rotunda of the U.S. Capitol.

President George W. Bush declared a national day of mourning on June 11, the day of the Reagan state funeral at the Washington National Cathedral. Later that day, the casket was returned to California for a late afternoon memorial service and interment at the library.

———•◦•———

Rancho del Cielo is not open to the public; however, the foundation has Reagan Ranch Exhibit Galleries at its downtown Santa Barbara ranch headquarters, 217 State Street, Santa Barbara, CA 93101. Telephone: 805-957-1980 or (toll-free) 888-USA-1776. Website: www.reaganranch .org.

The Ronald Reagan Presidential Library and Museum is at 40 Presidential Drive, Simi Valley, CA 93065–0600. Telephone: 805-577-4000; (toll-free) 800-410-8354. Email: reagan.library@nara.gov. Website: http://www.reaganfoundation.org/library-and-museum-overview .aspx. The remodeled museum was reopened in February 2011. The library and museum are operated by the National Archives and Records Administration. Also housed at the site is the Ronald Reagan Presidential Foundation, which conducts many lectures and other programs. Museum: 10 a.m.–5 p.m. year-round except Thanksgiving, Christmas, and New Year's Day. Research Room: Mondays–Fridays, 9 a.m.–5 p.m. Closed on federal holidays.

Reagan considered Dixon, Illinois, his hometown and lived there from age nine to twenty-one. The Ronald Reagan Boyhood Home & Visitor Center is at 816 South Hennepin Avenue, P.O. Box 816, Dixon, IL 61021. Telephone: 815-288-5176. Email: connie@reaganhome.org. Website: www.reaganhome.org. Open April 1–November 15, Mondays through Saturdays, 10 a.m.–4 p.m., Sundays, 1–4 p.m.

The Reagan Birthplace & Museum is at 111–113 South Main Street, Tampico, IL 61283. Telephone: 815-622-8705. Open April–October, Monday–Saturday, 10 a.m.–4 p.m.; Sundays 1–4 p.m. Email: reagan birthplace@wisp.net. Website: www.tampicohistoricalsociety.com.

Eureka College, Reagan's alma mater, has a Ronald Reagan Museum, open to the public. During the school year, hours are Monday–Friday, 8 a.m.–9 p.m., Saturdays, 10 a.m.–6 p.m., Sundays, noon–9 p.m. During summer, Monday–Friday, 8 a.m.–4 p.m., Saturdays, 10 a.m.–2 p.m. Closed Sundays and holidays. The museum is on the campus at 300 East College Avenue, Eureka, IL 61530–1500. Telephone: 309-467-6407. Website: http://reagan.eureka.edu.

Chapter Forty

GEORGE H. W. BUSH

THE 41ST PRESIDENT

January 20, 1989 — January 20, 1993

$\mathcal{T}$here was no question where George Herbert Walker Bush would spend his summer retreats when he became president. They would be spent where he had been spending them since childhood, at the family's compound on Walker's Point, close to the town of Kennebunkport in southern Maine.

His grandfather, George H. Walker, a St. Louis banker, had purchased the property near the end of the nineteenth century. In 1903 he built the large gray-shingled main house. The compound later passed on to his daughter, Dorothy Walker Bush, whose husband, Prescott, was to become a U.S. senator from Connecticut.

George and his sister Nancy spent many happy summers and family gatherings at the seaside compound.

STARTING THE ROAD TO LEADERSHIP

George H. W. Bush was born in Milton, Massachusetts. Not long afterward, the family moved to Greenwich, Connecticut. His education began there at the Greenwich Country Day School. He went on to Phillips Academy in Andover, Massachusetts, where his leadership abilities were in full play: president of the senior class, student council member, editor of the school newspaper, and captain of the baseball and soccer teams.

He put plans for college on hold after the nation entered World War II in December 1941.

Upon graduation Bush signed up for a ten-month training course to become a U.S. Navy aviator. He received his commission as an ensign in the U.S. Naval Reserve on June 9, 1943. He was just a few days shy of his nineteenth birthday and therefore the youngest naval aviator at the time.

COURAGE AND DETERMINATION

Bush was assigned to Air Group 51 in the South Pacific, based on the aircraft carrier USS *San Jacinto*. In September 1944, with a crew of two, he piloted a Grumman TBM Avenger in an attack on Japanese installations on the Bonin Islands. Although his plane was hit by antiaircraft fire and the engine was on fire, he completed the bombing mission before giving the order to bail out. One man's parachute did not open. The fate of the other is not known. Bush managed to inflate a small rubber raft and waited in it for several hours (with U.S. aircraft circling overhead) until the submarine USS *Finback* picked him up.

Soon thereafter he was back flying missions—fifty-eight in all that year. He was awarded the Distinguished Flying Cross and three Air Medals. At the beginning of 1945 he was assigned to Norfolk Naval Base in Virginia to train new pilots. He was discharged in September, shortly after the Japanese surrender.

POSTWAR LIFE

In January 1945, after his return from the South Pacific, he married Barbara Pierce. They had six children, George Walker (later to become the forty-third president), Pauline (who died of leukemia at age four), John Ellis ("Jeb"), Neil, Marvin, and Dorothy ("Doro").

Prior to joining the navy, Bush had been accepted at Yale. He now enrolled in a special program that compressed a normally four-year course schedule into two and a half years. At Yale, he was captain of the baseball team and played in two College World Series. He graduated in 1948 with a B.A. degree in economics and was Phi Beta Kappa.

He decided there was opportunity in the oil business, so he moved his family to Midland, Texas. His father's business connections opened some doors for him, but he developed his own success and by 1951 started his own company, which drilled onshore. In 1954 he started another, which did offshore drilling. Having prospered, he left his companies in 1966 for a career in politics and public service.

POLITICS AND PUBLIC SERVICE

In 1964, George H. W. Bush became chairman of the Harris County (Houston) Republican Party. His eye was on elective politics and he won a Republican primary in order to challenge incumbent U.S. senator Ralph Yarborough. Bush lost, but ran two years later for a House of Representatives seat and won. He was reelected in 1970. Then President Richard Nixon prevailed upon him to run again for Yarborough's Senate seat. Former representative Lloyd Bentsen defeated Yarborough in the Democratic primary. He was more moderate than the liberal Yarborough and went on to defeat Bush.

Nixon then appointed Bush as U.S. ambassador to the United Nations, a position he held for two years, 1971–73. Then, with the Watergate issue at the fore in 1973, Nixon asked him to take the chairmanship of the Republican National Committee. He did so and defended the party and Nixon as the popularity of both declined sharply. In his position, he called for Nixon to resign, which Nixon did on August 9, 1974.

Gerald Ford, who thus became the thirty-eighth president, then named Bush to be chief of the U.S. Liaison Office in China (the United States had not yet established formal diplomatic relations with mainland China). Although he did not have the title of "ambassador," Bush performed the duties of one and is generally credited with having done a good job during his fourteen months there.

In 1976, President Ford called him back to Washington to become director of the Central Intelligence Agency. He served for a little over a year. He rebuilt morale at the CIA, which had been under sustained attack from a committee headed by liberal Democratic senator Frank Church. Late in his time on the job, Bush gave national security briefings to Jimmy Carter, both as a presidential candidate and president-elect.

RUNNING FOR PRESIDENT IN 1980

George Bush then turned his sights on the presidency. During 1979 he attended more than eight hundred political events and traveled a quarter of a million miles rounding up support. He was one of eight Republicans—including front-runner Ronald Reagan—who saw 1980 as a Republican year, given the vulnerability of Carter.

Bush concentrated his efforts on the Iowa caucuses (Reagan mostly stayed away from Iowa). He won and proclaimed he had "the big mo" (momentum) heading into the New Hampshire primary. Reagan, however, redoubled his efforts there and won, 50–23 percent over Bush. Bush continued campaigning but lost most of the primaries and dropped out of the race in May.

Then, at the Republican National Convention in Detroit in July, Bush was surprised when Reagan telephoned him to ask him to be his running mate. He agreed and they defeated the Carter-Mondale ticket.

VICE PRESIDENT, 1981–89

A frequent vice presidential duty is to attend state funerals, and Bush did. This gave him personal contact with many sitting heads of state, which proved helpful to Reagan and to him. Also, as president of the Senate and a former member of Congress, Bush maintained friendly contact with many on Capitol Hill, and this, too, proved helpful to the Reagan-Bush administration.

He carried out several special assignments for Reagan, including a personally risky trip in late 1983 to El Salvador to tell that Central American nation's military leader to put a stop to "death squads" and to hold free elections. He was also chairman of two task forces. The first coordinated efforts of various federal agencies to cut down the volume of drugs coming into the United States. The latter task force reviewed federal regulations and recommended many revisions intended to check the growth of the government.

In his second term, Bush became the first vice president to serve as acting president under the law. This occurred on July 13, 1985, when Reagan had surgery to removed polyps from his colon and only lasted for eight hours.

When news of what came to be called the Iran-Contra Affair broke in the fall of 1986, Bush insisted that he had been "out of the loop." Although polls showed the public to be skeptical, Reagan's public acceptance of full responsibility (though he, too, was not privy to the details of what was being done in his name) laid to rest most of the skepticism toward both men.

PRESIDENT, 1989–93

Bush began preparing for a 1988 presidential campaign three years beforehand. Senator Bob Dole, Representative Jack Kemp, former Delaware governor Pete DuPont, and televangelist Pat Robertson also entered the race. Concentrating on winning New Hampshire's primary, Bush began clearing the field. Reagan's tacit approval of his candidacy was an asset.

His nomination acceptance speech at the Republican National Convention in New Orleans included his pledge, "Read my lips: no new taxes."

Several missteps by the Democratic candidate, Massachusetts governor Mike Dukakis, worked to Bush's advantage. On election day, Bush and his running mate, Senator Dan Quayle of Indiana, won the popular vote with 53.4 percent to 45.6 for the ticket of Dukakis and running mate Senator Lloyd Bentsen of Texas. The Electoral College vote was 426–111. Many analysts considered Bush's victory to be, in effect, a vote for Reagan's "third term."

Bush presided during a time of great change. Early in his term the Berlin Wall came down. By 1991, the Soviet Union had disintegrated. He met with Mikhail Gorbachev on the island of Malta in early December 1989, shortly after the fall of the Berlin Wall. They met again in July 1991 to sign the Strategic Arms Reduction Treaty, calling for major cuts in nuclear weapons by both sides.

In May 1989 Panama elected a new president to succeed strongman Manuel Noriega, who annulled the election. Bush sent U.S. troops to Panama to conduct military exercises. Noriega thwarted an attempted October military coup and clamped down on large public demonstrations against him. He had already been indicted in the United States on drug trafficking and other charges.

In December, after a U.S. serviceman was shot by Panamanian military personnel, Bush ordered a full-scale invasion, Operation Just Cause. In short order, the U.S. forces were in control of the country. The elected president, Guillermo Endara, took charge of the government. Noriega was captured and sent to the United States, where he was tried, convicted, and sent to prison in April 1992.

In June, President Bush and First Lady Barbara Bush visited Panama to demonstrate U.S. support of the democratically elected government. U.S. troops left for home.

In 1989 and 1990 Bush worked to reduce the federal deficit. He also faced a recession in 1990. This prompted him to reach a compromise with the Democrats on a bill that would make spending cuts but also increase the marginal income tax rate and eliminate certain exemptions for high-income taxpayers. He gave in on efforts to get the capital gains tax rate reduced. He could not get support for this from the Congressional Republicans. He signed the bill in late 1990 and later regretted it, for the breaking of his "no new taxes" pledge later cost him the support of many Republicans in his 1992 reelection campaign.

During his presidency, Bush proposed an International Space Station. Work began on it long after he had left office, in 1998. In 1990 he signed the Americans with Disabilities Act. Bush, along with Canadian prime minister Brian Mulroney, led negotiations for the North American Free Trade Agreement. Despite much criticism from some Democrat circles, negotiations gradually moved ahead. It remained for President Bill Clinton to preside over its passage, in 1993.

After Saddam Hussein's Iraqi army invaded Kuwait on August 1, 1990, Bush led the successful effort to assemble an international coalition. He demanded that the Iraqis withdraw from Kuwait. Saudi King Fahd asked for military aid from the United States, whose forces were stationed in the kingdom for the duration of the action. On January 17, 1991, coalition forces launched a four-week air attack, followed by a blitzkrieg-like land invasion. It was over in one hundred hours, al-though Bush came under criticism for not having coalition troops push on to Baghdad and remove Saddam from power. Nevertheless, Bush's approval rating in polls went as high as 91 percent.

A humanitarian effort in Somalia the next year did not fare well. Responding to a UN request, the United States provided nearly two-thirds of the personnel for Operation Restore Hope. In June 1993, a local warlord, feeling threatened by the humanitarian campaign, at-tacked Pakistani troops and then American marines, killing nineteen. The United States withdrew soon afterward. On December 16, 1989, he had a visit with French president François Mitterrand on the island of St. Martin in the French West Indies.

SETTING THE TRAVEL PACE
FOR PRESIDENTS

Bush "41" set the fast pace that now marks international presidential travel. In his one term he went to Europe eleven times, Asia twice, and South America once. There were also several shorter trips, such as his first as president, to Ottawa, Canada, on February 10, 1989, to meet with Prime Minister Mulroney. He had three other such visits to Canada to meet Mulroney, one in 1990 and two in 1991. He had three summit meetings, two with leaders of the fading Soviet Union. The first, with then–Soviet chairman Gorbachev, was on the island of Malta in the Mediterranean, December 1–3, 1989; the second was in Helsinki, Finland, September 8–9, 1990 (by then, Gorbachev had a new title, president of the Soviet Union). The third was in Kiev, July 29–August 1, 1991, to sign the Strategic Arms Reduction Treaty. Bush also ad-dressed the Ukrainian parliament. This was just before the attempted coup to derail a Gorbachev-promoted referendum to convert the Soviet Union into a federation of independent states. The coup failed. For the third summit, Bush traveled on the Boeing 747 that was the new Air Force One. (It had been ordered late in the Reagan administration.)

TIME OFF AT KENNEBUNKPORT

Most of the Bushes' retreats to their compound at Walker's Point in Maine were made during warm months; however, they made three- and four-day visits in February in three of their four White House years, 1989, 1990, and 1991. There were two November visits. President Bush went there on November 3, 1991, to inspect hurricane damage in the area. In his final year, 1992, the Bushes went for a family gathering at Thanksgiving, November 25–29.

All told, there were twenty-five presidential trips to Walker's Point during the presidential years, covering 155 days in all. The longest visits were in August and September, when Congress was adjourned for its summer vacation. During these visits the president would often take his celebrated "cigarette" boat out for a spin. (This is the speedboat so slender it resembled a cigarette.)

He often went fishing in another open boat. On these trips, the Secret Service detail, always ready, was not far behind in an inflatable boat. One man was outfitted in scuba gear.

The president combined business with pleasure by inviting fifteen heads of state, heads of government, or ambassadors for seaside visits. These included Canadian prime minister Brian Mulroney (three times), British prime minister John Major (twice), Jordan's King Hussein, Danish prime minister Poul Schlüter, Prime Minister Toshiki Kaifu of Japan, Israeli prime minister Yitzhak Rabin, President Carlos Menem of Argentina, Czech president Vaclav Havel, Polish president Lech Walesa, Chinese ambassador Li Daoyu, Sheik Falah bin Zayed and Sheik Abdullah bin Zayed of the United Arab Emirates, Yousef el Otaiba, personal representative of the president of the UAE, and Ambassador Tiger Yang of Singapore.

THE 1992 CAMPAIGN AND BEYOND

Despite the great success of Operation Desert Storm to free Kuwait, President Bush's approval ratings dropped when a relatively brief recession hit in 1991. Even after it was technically over, people believed it was ongoing. Although he had been ahead of potential Democratic rivals in the early polls, by the time Arkansas governor Bill Clinton became the party's nominee he focused almost entirely on the economy, following the slogan put up on the wall in their Little Rock headquarters: "It's the economy, stupid." Increased unemployment and general unease about the economy were factors in Bush's defeat, as were the surprisingly strong showing of third-party candidate Ross Perot (19 percent of the vote) and alienation of some conservatives over Bush's breaking of his "no new taxes" pledge. Clinton won the popular vote by 43 to 38 percent and the electoral vote 370–68.

POST-PRESIDENCY

Formally, George H. W. Bush retired to his home in Houston and to Walker's Point, but "retire" has been a relative term. He holds an annual fishing tournament at Islamorada, a Florida Keys island; served for six years as chairman of the board of trustees for the Eisenhower Fellowships; celebrated his seventy-ninth and eightieth birthdays with parachute jumps; visited Kuwait in 1993 to commemorate the coalition's victory over Iraq (during which a plot to assassinate him was thwarted); and teamed with Bill Clinton to raise aid funds for victims of Hurricane Katrina. After the huge tsunami hit islands in the Indian Ocean in late 2004, the pair created the Bush-Clinton Tsunami Fund and raised large sums, with which 7,500 new homes were built for victims who had lost everything.

In 1993, Queen Elizabeth awarded an honorary knighthood to Bush. He is one of three U.S. presidents so honored (Eisenhower and Reagan are the other two).

In February 2011, President Obama awarded President Bush the Medal of Freedom, the highest civilian award in the nation.

The George Bush Presidential Library and Museum was opened to the public in late 1997. It is on ninety acres on the west campus of Texas A&M University, in College Station. It holds his presidential and vice presidential papers and the papers of his vice president, Dan Quayle. The museum's permanent exhibits span the president's life from childhood through his years of public service. Included are a Torpedo bomber similar to the one he piloted in the South Pacific, a slab from the Berlin

Wall, and replicas of his offices at Camp David and on Air Force One. There are also galleries with temporary traveling exhibits.

Hours: Monday–Saturday, 9:30 a.m.–5 p.m. Sunday, noon–5 p.m. Closed on Thanksgiving, Christmas, and New Year's Day. Address: George Bush Presidential Library and Museum, 1000 George Bush Drive West, College Station, TX 77845. Telephone: 979-691-4000. Website: http://bushlibrary.tamu.edu.

The Bush Compound at Walker's Point, in Kennebunkport, Maine, is not open to the public, since it is the Bush family's retreat and summer home.

Chapter Forty-one

---◆•◆---

WILLIAM J. CLINTON

THE 42ND PRESIDENT

January 20, 1993—January 20, 2001

*B*etween his first election as governor of Arkansas in 1978 and the beginning of his 1992 presidential campaign, Bill Clinton and his wife, Hillary, lived in the governor's mansion in Little Rock for all but two years. They did not own a home or a retreat, for there had seemed to be no need for either during those years. Yet, once he was president, they faced the question of where to go for a retreat— a real vacation—from the Oval Office. The eyes of the nation would be on them. For six of his eight White House years, the answer was Martha's Vineyard, the popular island off Massachusetts. There they lived as guests of generous friends.

After three years of this and with his reelection campaign coming up, Clinton wanted to learn what the American people thought about his vacation routine. He asked his political adviser, Dick Morris, to take a poll to see where people thought the president should rest from the cares of daily work. Not surprisingly, those polled said Martha's Vineyard was "elitist." They liked something simpler, more rustic. So the Clintons went to Jackson Hole, Wyoming, where, not surprisingly, the president was photographed riding a horse, while wearing blue jeans, a denim shirt, and Stetson hat. They vacationed there in 1996 and 1997.

THE BOY FROM HOPE

Bill Clinton was born August 19, 1946, in Hope, Arkansas, as William Jefferson Blythe III. His father, William Jefferson Blythe, Jr., died in an auto accident three months before his son's birth. Afterward, Bill's mother, Virginia, went to New Orleans to study nursing and left him in the care of his maternal grandparents, Eldridge and Edith Cassidy. Shortly after Virginia finished nursing school in 1950, she married Roger Clinton, who owned an auto dealership in Hot Springs. That year the family moved there.

Young Bill attended two elementary schools, one of them Catholic, then Hot Springs High School, where he became a student leader and a good musician. He won first chair in the state band's saxophone section. He considered a career in music, but two events in 1963 pulled him toward public affairs. The first was a trip to Washington, D.C., where he was a "senator" in Boys' Nation and met President Kennedy at the White House. The second was Martin Luther King's "I Have a Dream" speech.

COLLEGE AND LAW SCHOOL

Scholarships made it possible for him to enroll at Georgetown University in Washington, D.C., where he earned a bachelor of science degree in foreign service. During the summer before his senior year he was an intern in the office of Arkansas senator J. William Fulbright. Following graduation he won a Rhodes scholarship to study at Oxford University. There he studied philosophy, politics, and economy. He left early, before earning a degree, in order to enroll in Yale Law School.

Later, during his presidential campaigning he was sharply criticized for appearing to have circumvented the draft during the Vietnam War. In 1992, an army colonel offered a notarized statement to the effect that Clinton had obtained a letter from Senator Fulbright's office supporting his supposed desire to enroll in ROTC, thus exempting him from the draft. The colonel said it was a ruse to get a new draft classification, which Clinton obtained.

He then went to Yale, where he met Hillary Rodham, a fellow law student. They began dating and were married on October 11, 1975. They had one child, Chelsea, born on February 27, 1980.

Bill obtained his law degree in 1973; Hillary's preceded his.

During his Yale years he took a short-term job with the McGovern presidential campaign, working in Texas, where he met several future political colleagues and allies.

AN EYE FOR POLITICS

Hillary grew up in a suburb of Chicago but was ready to become an Arkansan with Bill after Yale Law School. Initially, he joined the faculty of the University of Arkansas's law school. A year later, in 1974, he ran for the U.S. House of Representatives and lost to incumbent John Paul Hammerschmidt. In 1976 Clinton ran for attorney general of Arkansas and was elected without opposition.

The future looked bright, so in 1978 he decided to run for governor. He defeated Republican Lynn Lowe and became, at thirty-two, the nation's youngest governor.

During that term he concentrated on educational reform and road improvements; however, two things worked against him. One was an unpopular motor vehicle tax; the other was the escape of Cuban refugees detained at Fort Chaffee. Republican Frank D. White defeated Clinton for reelection. Clinton quipped that he was now the youngest *ex*-governor in the state's history.

He wasn't out of the governor's office for long. Initially he joined his friend Bruce Lindsey's law firm. He spent a good deal of time working on plans to recapture the governor's seat and did so in 1982. He held the job for ten years, during which time his actions helped boost the state's economy and strengthen its educational system. He began to develop a national network of contacts through the new Democratic Leadership Council, a party group interested in more moderate policies than those sought by the party's liberal base. In 1986–87 he was chairman of the National Governor Association.

At the 1988 Democratic National Convention he gave the opening night address—an unusually long one—and endorsed Massachusetts governor Michael Dukakis for president. He began to describe himself as a New Democrat, a moderate. In 1990–91 he was chairman of the Democratic Leadership Council.

When he declared his candidacy for president in 1992 his name recognition in polls stood at 2 percent. He ran third in the Iowa caucuses. During the New Hampshire primary campaign stories surfaced that he had had an extramarital affair. (During his governorship it was widely believed in Arkansas political circles that he had affairs. One of his female aides in the governor's office later told an interviewer that her job had been to keep an eye out for "bimbo eruptions" and seek to control public relation damage.) Clinton was well behind former senator Paul Tsongas of Massachusetts in the New Hampshire race. He and Hillary went on CBS's *60 Minutes* to counter the charges. This was an all-or-nothing strategy and it worked. He finished second to Tsongas, but came within single digits of winning. The press began frequently quoting Clinton's self-description as "the Comeback Kid."

Clinton's victories in the Texas and Florida primaries built his delegate count for the convention, but he had yet to win an election outside the South. Meanwhile, California's Jerry Brown (dubbed "Governor Moonbeam" by critics) was winning primaries. Clinton staked everything on a victory in New York state. He won and erased his identity as being only a regional candidate.

As the nominee for president, he chose Senator Al Gore of Tennessee as his running mate. He went on to defeat incumbent president George H. W. Bush by 43 percent to 37.4 percent of the vote. He and his surrogate speakers and staff harped on the theme "It's the economy, stupid." Two things helped him. One was the independent candidacy of H. Ross Perot, who gained 18.9 percent of the vote by concentrating on economic issues. The other was the drop in support from Bush's base after he had broken his no-new-taxes pledge and agreed to certain tax increases as part of a compromise with the Democrat-controlled Congress.

TWO TERMS IN THE WHITE HOUSE

As president, Bill Clinton often called his approach the Third Way, which was a blend of centrist and liberal positions. Dick Morris advised

him to use "triangulation" to get his issues passed. This involved feint-
ing to the right, then to the left so that he would end up with legislation that appeared to be in the center, where most American voters saw
themselves.

Early in his first term, President Clinton proposed certain tax increases to cap the federal budget deficit. He sought to do away with the
military policy of not allowing openly gay men and women to serve.
There was considerable opposition and the "Don't Ask, Don't Tell"
policy was the result.

In 1993 he also signed the North American Free Trade Agreement
(NAFTA), which Clinton and his allies in the Democratic Leadership
Council supported. The opposition was composed largely of protectionist Democrats and Perot supporters. Nevertheless, it passed both
houses.

Late that year he signed the Brady Bill, which required a five-day
waiting period for handgun purchases in order to allow law enforce-
ment agencies to determine if the purchaser had a criminal or mental
illness record.

The administration was distracted from its priorities in September
1993 by an investigative report in the *American Spectator* alleging that
Arkansas state troopers had arranged liaisons for then-governor Clinton with various women. There was prolonged coverage, controversy,
and legal proceedings before the matter was concluded.

His administration also expanded the so-called Earned Income Tax
Credit, by which certain low-income workers with no tax liability received tax "refunds." Critics said it was disguised welfare.

During the Clinton years the administration pushed the govern-
ment-chartered mortgage guarantors, Fannie Mae and Freddie Mac, to
get lending institutions to broadening their home loan practices. It used
the Community Reinvestment Act as the rationale for this. The number of home loans to low-income borrowers increased greatly. Many
could not afford the payments. Air began to stream out of the bubble
by late 2006 and by September 2008 was causing severe disruptions in
the economy

Early in the administration, Hillary Clinton was given the job of
leading a task force to overhaul the nation's health-care system into
one that was federally managed. Much of its work was done in secret,

raising suspicions in some quarters, although it also had its supporters. Ultimately, the task force's work did not produce legislation and was thus a defeat for the administration.

The First Lady, working with Senator Ted Kennedy, succeeded with legislation to create the Children's Health Insurance Program (CHIP) to provide government-paid health insurance for children in low-income families.

In August 1993, President Clinton signed the Omnibus Budget Reconciliation Act, which cut income taxes for low-income families and many small businesses and raised them for the 1.2 percent of highest earners (already paying a high percentage of the nation's annual tax bill), and called for balanced budgets in coming years.

There were controversies over firings in the White House Travel Office and alleged improper access to security clearance files by the White House's Office of Personnel Security. These were added to the Whitewater controversy over possible Clinton holdings in an Arkansas vacation property development that had turned sour and was potentially illegal. Ultimately all three faded, but they sowed further doubts about Clinton's integrity.

In 1996 the Clinton-Gore ticket was reelected over the Republican ticket of Senator Bob Dole and former representative Jack Kemp by 49.2 percent to 40.7. The Electoral College vote was 379–159.

MILITARY AND FOREIGN POLICY

Somalia was a country without a government in 1993. A detachment of U.S. marines was sent as part of an international peacekeeping force. Two of their helicopters were shot down by a warlord's rockets. Eighteen marines were killed and their bodies dragged through the streets of Mogadishu, the capital. Clinton withdrew U.S. forces entirely.

In 1995, U.S. and other NATO aircraft attacked Bosnian Serb targets in Bosnia for the purpose of driving the Serbs to peace talks. Late that year, in accordance with the Dayton Accords, Clinton deployed U.S. peacekeeping troops in Bosnia.

In 1998, bombings planned by the terrorist group al-Qaeda killed many at U.S. embassies in Kenya and Tanzania. In retaliation Clinton ordered a cruise missile strike on an al-Qaeda training camp in

Afghanistan and a chemical weapons plant in Sudan. It turned out that the al-Qaeda camp had already been abandoned and the supposed chemical weapons plant was only a pharmaceuticals plant. Criticism of his actions was widespread.

In 1999, the United States joined with other NATO members to put a stop to Serbian ethnic cleansing in Kosovo. Strategic targets in Serbia were bombed. The bombing campaign ended successfully by mid-June. A UN resolution then put Kosovo, a province of Serbia, under its administration with an international peacekeeping force. In the future, Kosovo residents were to determine by plebiscite whether they would be independent or associated with Serbia.

In 1998, the administration called for "regime change" in Iraq. A "no-fly zone" had previously been declared there in reaction to Saddam Hussein's deadly attacks on groups of his own citizens. A four-day bombing attack was carried out by U.S. forces and continued intermittently for the remainder of Clinton's second term.

Clinton made a personal effort to obtain an agreement between the Palestinian Authority and Israel to move toward lasting peace. He invited Yasser Arafat and Israeli prime minister Ehud Barak to Camp David. The Israelis made a generous offer, which Arafat refused (as he had done before and would again later). Clinton later said Arafat "missed an opportunity" to create a "just and lasting peace."

HIGH FLYING

As president, Bill Clinton made fifty-four trips outside the United States, an average of nearly seven in each of his eight years in office. He took his first in April 1993 to Vancouver, Canada, for a summit meeting with Russian president Boris Yeltsin and Canadian prime minister Brian Mulroney. His last trip was a little over a month before his second term expired. It was December 12–14, 2000, when he met with Irish prime minister Bertie Ahern, leaders in Northern Ireland, British prime minister Tony Blair, and Queen Elizabeth II and gave a speech at the University of Warwick.

Between these two trips he had high-level meetings in Japan, South Korea, Belgium, the Czech Republic, Ukraine, Russia, Belarus, Switzerland, Italy, Vatican City, the United Kingdom, France, Latvia,

Poland, Germany, Canada, Egypt, Jordan, Israel, Kuwait, Saudi Arabia, Philippines, Indonesia, Hungary, Haiti, Ireland, Spain, Bosnia-Herzegovina, Croatia, Australia, Thailand, Finland, Mexico, Costa Rica, Barbados, Netherlands, Romania, Denmark, Venezuela, Brazil, Argentina, Ghana, Uganda, Rwanda, South Africa, Botswana, Senegal, Chile, China, the Palestinian Authority (West Bank), Nicaragua, El Salvador, Guatemala, Honduras, Slovenia, Macedonia, Morocco, New Zealand, Norway, Turkey, Greece, Bulgaria, India, Bangladesh, Pakistan, Oman, Portugal, Nigeria, Tanzania, Colombia, Brunei, and Vietnam.

A few of these were state visits; most were "working" visits. Some were organization conferences such as NATO, Asia-Pacific Economic Cooperation, the Commission on Security and Cooperation in Europe, European Union, Summit of the Peacemakers, G-7 Summit on Nuclear Safety, Summit of Presidents of the Central American Republics, and the US-EU Summit. Some included visits to U.S. military cemeteries overseas and World War II memorial events. One was for the signing of a peace treaty (Bosnia's). Two were for funerals (King Hussein of Jordan and Prime Minister Keizo Obuchi of Japan), another included a commemorative ceremony for a deceased prime minister (Yitzhak Rabin of Israel). He gave speeches in several countries. Finally, one involved an actual vacation. He and the First Lady vacationed on the island of Majorca with King Juan Carlos I and Queen Sofia of Spain from July 4 to July 10, 1997. They had three solid days of business after that, one day each in Poland, Romania, and Denmark, where he met with one queen, two presidents, a former president, and a prime minister.

TIME OFF BACK HOME

As noted, the Clintons had no regular retreat of their own for vacations, or a favored resort from previous years. An invitation came from friends to spend their first vacation on Martha's Vineyard, one of two Massachusetts islands (the other being Nantucket) popular with upscale summer sojourners.

On August 12, 1993, they flew to Denver to meet Pope John Paul II. The next day they flew to Vail, Colorado, where they spent the night at the home of friends. The following day was devoted to golf at the Country Club of the Rockies and to relaxation. In the early evening

they were accompanied to a performance of the Bolshoi Ballet by former president and Mrs. Gerald Ford (who also had a home in Vail). It
took place at the Gerald R. Ford Amphitheater. After that, the four
went to a gala and dance until the early hours of the next morning.

Sunday the fifteenth included another round of golf. Then, after a
stop in Arkansas they were back in the White House on Wednesday,
the eighteenth. The next day they left for Martha's Vineyard at 3:45
p.m. They were met at the airport by their friends Vernon and Anne
Jordan. Through the twenty-ninth, they vacationed (with no public
events scheduled) at the home of friends on the island.

Their August vacations in 1994, 1995, 1998, 1999, and 2000 followed this pattern. Only 1996 and 1997 differed, when they went to
Jackson Hole, Wyoming, at least partly to demonstrate through photos
and film footage that the president favored the rugged outdoor life.

Their 1998 sojourn was interrupted when Clinton hurriedly flew to
Washington to approve the air attacks on the al-Qaeda training camp in
Afghanistan and the supposed chemical weapons plant in Sudan. Then
he returned to Martha's Vineyard for the rest of their vacation.

David Gergen, who had also worked for Presidents Nixon, Ford,
and Reagan, was counselor to the president in the Clinton White
House and observed in his book *Eyewitness to Power* that "[g]oing on
vacation helped him re-charge his batteries when he went to Martha's
Vineyard in the tough first year, 1993, and particularly in August of
1998 when he was forced to admit the Lewinsky scandal."

THE LEWINSKY AFFAIR

On January 17, 1998, the *Drudge Report* website broke the story that
Clinton had had a sexual relationship in and near the Oval Office with
a young woman intern. Within four days it was all over the media and
stayed there for months.

In 1995, Monica Lewinsky had become an intern and caught the eye
of the president. This led to sexual relations, which she later alleged to
have taken place nine times between November 15 that year and March
29, 1997. In April 1996 her supervisors relocated her to a job in the Defense Department. Her allegations indicate she returned for two more
sessions with Clinton.

At the Defense Department she became friends with a coworker, Linda Tripp. She confided the Clinton relationship to Tripp, who later reported it to a literary agent, who in turn suggested Tripp begin recording her conversations with Lewinsky. She did and took them to the offices of Kenneth Starr, the independent counsel investigating the Whitewater and Paula Jones cases (Jones was a Little Rock woman who alleged Clinton had seduced her when he was governor).

In January 1998, Lewinsky was asked to submit an affidavit in the Jones case. In it she denied a physical relationship with Clinton. Now that Starr had Tripp's tapes, which included details by Lewinsky of her affair with Clinton, he broadened his investigation. On January 26, Clinton held a news conference, with Hillary by his side. Among other things he said, "I did not have sex with that woman, Miss Lewinsky." He took no questions.

Conjecture swirled from then until August 17, when Clinton testified before a grand jury and, that evening, admitted on television that he had had a relationship with Lewinsky that "was not appropriate."

After Starr submitted his report to the House, the Republican leadership (the party controlled both houses) called a "lame duck" session in December 1998. The House voted out two impeachment charges, one each for perjury and obstruction of justice. The Senate declined to take up the trial with so little time left in the current term of Congress. So it was held in early 1999 and concluded after twenty-one days, on February 12, with fifty-five senators voting for acquittal and forty-five for conviction.

In January 2001, Clinton was ordered by the Arkansas state bar to pay a fine of twenty-five thousand dollars and his state license was suspended for five years. This was the result of an agreement by which Whitewater prosecutors promised not to pursue federal perjury charges in that matter against Clinton. The U.S. Supreme Court in October 2001 suspended him. Facing disbarment, he resigned his Supreme Court license in November.

POST-PRESIDENCY

Over time, Clinton regained his popularity, especially for his humanitarian work. Early in his post-presidential years he gave many speeches for large sums, then created the William J. Clinton Foundation, which, through its Clinton Global Initiative, has worked to combat HIV/AIDS, improve public health in many countries, and alleviate poverty. The foundation in 2005 reached an agreement with several soft drink manufacturers to stop selling sugared drinks in schools.

Clinton's resilience, affability, and charm have much to do with what successes he achieved in office and since. He and former president George H. W. Bush established the Bush-Clinton Tsunami Fund after the 2004 Asian tsunami. They went on to create the Bush-Clinton Katrina Fund after the 2005 hurricane that devastated New Orleans and much of the Gulf Coast.

Clinton's autobiography, *My Life*, was published in 2004, the same year his presidential library was dedicated in Little Rock, Arkansas.

His health has been a concern several times. In September 2004 he received a quadruple-bypass heart operation. The following March, he had surgery for a partially collapsed lung. In 2010 two coronary stents were placed in his heart. For years he favored high-calorie "comfort" foods such as hamburgers. To counter this, he jogged nearly every morning in his White House years. Now it is said he has moved to a healthy diet, with the emphasis on vegetables and fruits.

The William J. Clinton Presidential Library tells the story of President Clinton's life through photos, videos, and interactive and interpretive panels. One exhibit features an illustrated timeline of his career. The Clinton archives at the library contain 70 million pages of official records, 29 million emails, 2 million photographs, and 12,500 videotapes of his life and career. The research staff has begun digitizing the archives to make them accessible online. Location: 1200 President Clinton Avenue, Little Rock, AR 72201. Telephone: 501-374-4242. Research email: clinton.library@nara.gov. Website: www.clintonlibrary.gov.

The President William Jefferson Clinton Birthplace Home National Historic Site is in Hope, Arkansas, 110 miles from Little Rock. This was the home of his maternal grandparents, where he lived for his first four years. The two-story frame house was built in 1917. It was added to the National Register of Historic Places in 1994. The Clinton Birthplace

Foundation then restored the home to the way it had been when President Clinton was a small boy. It was opened for public tours in 1997. On April 16, 2011, it was dedicated as a National Historic Site. Address: 117 South Hervey Street, Hope, AR 71801. For current operating hours call 870-777-4455. Website: www.nps.gov/wicl.

Chapter Forty-two

GEORGE W. BUSH

THE 43RD PRESIDENT

January 20, 2001 — January 20, 2009

t the moment on December 9, 2000, when the U.S. Supreme Court ruled on the November presidential election, George W. Bush acquired thousands of lifelong enemies he had never met.

On election night the close results in Florida led to a recount. Bush won it. Then there was another one, with still some votes in doubt. The Florida Supreme Court ordered a third count, this time statewide and by hand. In *Bush v. Gore*, the U.S. Supreme Court reversed the Florida court, stopping the hand recount. It concluded that because different standards were used throughout the state's counties, a statewide hand count would violate the equal protection clause of the Fourteenth Amendment to the U.S. Constitution. It relied on the machine count, which showed Bush winning the state by 537 votes.

Al Gore made a gracious concession statement. This was not so with many of his supporters, who would not forgive Bush for winning. From then on a collection of angry leftists, antiwar and antiglobalization types, and left-leaning academics and intellectuals worked steadily to denigrate, discredit, and despise nearly everything the forty-third president did or said. (They were, however, silent for a while after the September 11, 2001, attacks.)

It is little wonder then, that under this constant barrage, with the opposition of Congressional Democrats and some in his own party, Bush relished more and more visits to his retreat, Prairie Chapel Ranch near Crawford, Texas. Over eight years he visited the ranch seventy-seven times, for a total of 490 days. He also had many weekend respites at Camp David.

THE ROAD TO THE WHITE HOUSE

George Walker Bush was born July 6, 1946, in New Haven, Connecticut, the son of George H. W. and Barbara Pierce Bush. He was followed by four siblings: Jeb, Neil, Marvin, and Dorothy. He attended public schools in Midland, Texas, then the Kincaid School, a Houston prep school (the family had moved to Houston). He completed his high school years at Phillips Academy in Andover, Massachusetts. He entered Yale University in 1964 and graduated four years later with a B.A. in history. He was his fraternity's president and played rugby. He then attended Harvard Business School, where he earned a master of business administration degree (he is the only U.S. president to have earned one).

In May 1968 he received a commission in the Texas Air National Guard (TANG). Two years of active-duty training were followed by assignment to Ellington Air Force Base, where he flew Convair F-102s with the 147 Fighter Interceptor Group. He was discharged from the TANG in October 1973 and transferred to inactive duty in the Air Force Reserve. He received an honorable discharge from it in November 1974.

At a barbecue in 1977 he met Laura Welch, a school librarian and teacher. After dating for three months he proposed marriage. She agreed and they were married on November 5. They settled in Midland. In 1981, their twin daughters, Barbara and Jenna, were born.

Prior to meeting Laura, George Bush had been stopped in his automobile in Maine for driving under the influence of alcohol. This was in 1976. With Laura's help he gave up alcohol entirely by 1986. He later said that she had put up with his "rough edges" and "has smoothed them off over time."

A START IN POLITICS

His career had begun in the oil business, but he decided to run for the U.S. House of Representatives in 1978. He lost by six thousand votes.

Back in business, he started several oil exploration companies. One of these he merged with Spectrum 7 in 1984 and became its chairman. It, in turn, was merged into Harken Energy, with Bush serving on its board of directors.

In 1988, he and his family moved to Washington, D.C., so he could work on his father's presidential campaign. Afterward, he returned to Texas and purchased part ownership in the Texas Rangers baseball team. For five years he was its managing general partner. The sale of his share in 1988 netted him a strong profit.

George became one of a small group of campaign advisers in his father's unsuccessful reelection campaign in 1992. He then returned to Texas. In 1994 he declared his candidacy for governor. His campaign emphasized welfare reform, reduction in crime, tort reform, and improved education.

Key advisers were Karl Rove and Karen Hughes, both of whom later held important positions in the Bush White House. His opponent was incumbent Democratic governor Ann Richards. He won, 53.5 percent to 45.9.

With a budget surplus in hand, he oversaw Texas-size tax cuts and added funding to organizations promoting education about the dangers of alcohol and drug abuse. He easily won reelection in 1998, with 69 percent of the vote. He was immediately touted by national party leaders as an ideal candidate for president in 2000.

In June 1999 he announced his candidacy for the presidency; however, this had been no secret to most Republican Party political insiders for several months. Until his active campaign there had been eleven well-known Republicans working toward the same goal of a Bush candidacy.

Although Bush won the Iowa caucus in early 2000, Senator John McCain of Arizona beat him in New Hampshire by a margin of 19 percent. Bush regained his footing in the following primary, in South Carolina, and defeated McCain, who considered it to have been a very negative campaign.

Bush asked Dick Cheney to vet several potential vice presidential running mates. When Cheney delivered his report, Bush said he wanted him to be the choice. Both were nominated at the party's convention.

The campaign against Democratic candidate Vice President Al Gore of Tennessee was hard-fought. On November 7, Bush won twenty-nine states (with Florida included in his column). Accusations of irregularities surfaced from both sides. The eyes of the nation were glued to television as rival monitoring teams stood next to the recounters in several counties. The state supreme court ordered a statewide hand count. The U.S. Supreme Court ruled against this. Thus Bush became the winner. Gore had a larger national popular vote total than Bush (not the first time this had occurred in U.S. history), but Bush had a five-point edge in the electoral vote.

In 2004, his support within his party was very wide and he easily won renomination. Senator John Kerry of Massachusetts was his rival in the general election. Several contradictory statements by Kerry about the Iraq War, combined with independent ad expenditures by an outside group that undercut Kerry's claims of combat heroism in Vietnam, helped Bush. The campaign was seen as a referendum on the Iraq War. Bush narrowly won an outright majority, 50.7 percent of the vote, to Kerry's 48.3 percent. He carried thirty-one states and 286 electoral votes to Kerry's 251.

THE PRESIDENCY, 2001–2009

Early in his first term, Bush projected a budget surplus of $5.6 trillion over the following ten years. Unforeseen circumstances changed this. He proposed tax cuts (some passed in 2002), the No Child Left Behind Act to raise students' proficiency in basic subjects, and opposed the Kyoto Protocol. The last, which came out of a UN conference on "climate change," would have imposed mandatory targets for reducing "greenhouse gas" emissions. The cost to the U.S. economy would have been several billion dollars a year. Later, in 2007, the Senate voted 95–0 in disapproval of the protocol.

SEPTEMBER 11, 2001

When al-Qaeda's plot to fly four hijacked U.S. airliners into buildings unfolded, the nation was stunned. The twin World Trade Center towers in New York City fell after being struck by two separate jets; another aircraft plowed into the Pentagon; a fourth jet, apparently intended for the White House or the U.S. Capitol, crashed into a field in Pennsylvania after heroic passengers rose up against the terrorists and stormed the cockpit.

More than three thousand people died as a result of this plot by Osama bin Laden and his radical Islamist followers.

The nation rallied as Bush addressed it from the Oval Office that evening. Three days later he visited the World Trade Center site, which came to be known as Ground Zero. Standing on a heap of rubble, Bush declared through a megaphone, "I can hear you. The rest of the world hears you. And the people who knocked these buildings down will hear all of us soon."

And they did. Within a few weeks, U.S. and allied forces had routed the Taliban regime in Afghanistan and had al-Qaeda retreating to mountain hideouts and then to Pakistan.

In his January 2002 State of the Union address, Bush said we would pursue a War on Terror and declared Iraq, Iran, and North Korea an "axis of evil."

THE WAR IN IRAQ

UN weapons inspections in Iraq were unproductive and disarmament mandates that had been set after the Persian Gulf War in 1991 were not being met by Saddam Hussein's government. Intelligence reports (also received by several allied countries) indicated that he had some weapons of mass destruction (nuclear, chemical, biological). In 2002, Bush made an effort to get the United Nations to enforce the disarmament mandates—to no avail.

On March 20, 2003, an invasion by a "coalition of the willing" (the United States and twenty other nations, most notably the United Kingdom) began. Baghdad fell on April 9. Although Bush soon declared an end of major combat, his administration had not fully calculated the potential trouble that sectarian guerrilla groups could cause, or the work of al-Qaeda affiliates to promote terror and killings.

Despite the insurgency, Iraq conducted its first free democratic elections in half a century in January 2005.

The killings continued, abetted by weapons sent in to Shi'a groups from Iran. The war's aftermath continued to go poorly until Bush in 2007 accepted the advice of his military commanders to engage in a major "surge," by which an infusion of additional U.S. troops would go neighborhood by neighborhood in Baghdad to clear out insurgents, al-Qaeda operatives, and snipers. The troops would stay encamped in the newly safe neighborhoods to ensure they would remain so. It worked, and within a few months even most of Bush's political opponents grudgingly acknowledged this.

After the successful invasion, no hard evidence was found of caches of weapons of mass destruction. Fomented by Bush-haters of various kinds, charges flew about that "Bush lied to us." Leftists chanted that Bush had conducted the war to get control of Iraq's oil (implying that a cabal of Bush and large oil companies was behind the invasion).

Not well articulated by Bush and his administration was the importance in their minds of breaking the lock of authoritarianism in the Middle East and the importance of ridding the region of the murderous Saddam Hussein.

Never stated but quite probably an underlying motive was the value of spiking al-Qaeda's largest dream, the launching of a worldwide Islamist state from a revived caliphate in Baghdad. The invasion did indeed succeed in slowing to a crawl Osama bin Laden's plan to move the world back to the seventh century.

OTHER DOMESTIC ISSUES

Not all of Bush's criticism came from the left, although hate-driven and irrational criticism did. Democrats in Congress based their arguments on philosophical or political disagreements with Bush initiatives. Criticism from the intelligentsia had largely put reason aside.

Republican opposition did arise, and over two initiatives in particular: the plan to create Medicare Part D, subsidized prescriptions for seniors (2003); and the 2006 proposal to let the approximately 12 million illegal aliens in the United States gain legal status through a "temporary guest worker" program. This would have allowed them—once they met certain requirements—to stay more or less permanently in the United States. Bush did not support amnesty for this group; however, critics on the right insisted that that was what it was. It was largely Republican opposition that killed the initiative in the Senate.

HURRICANE KATRINA

Bush and the federal government received widespread blame for much of what went wrong in the wake of Hurricane Katrina in 2005, through the musings of Louisiana officials, amplified in the news media.

Technically, the federal government cannot intercede in a disaster until asked to do so by the affected state. The governor was urged to do so, but did not. The mayor of New Orleans did not take charge of the local situation. The president, instead of going into the city at the earliest possible moment, flew over it, then gave a speech there a few days later. Blame should have been spread fairly evenly, but it was not. The event gave Bush-haters fresh fodder for months to come.

AROUND THE WORLD

Despite the many problems he faced, George Bush proved to be a record-setting president in terms of travel. He became the most-traveled president in U.S. history, beating the record of Bill Clinton, who had beaten the record of Bush's father, George H. W. Bush.

He was the fourth president to make an around-the-world trip (Lyndon Johnson, Nixon, and Clinton were the others).

His first trip was a one-day visit to San Cristobal, Mexico, with President Vicente Fox (the first of four trips he made there). The final one was a three-day trip to Lima, Peru, to attend the Asia-Pacific Economic Cooperation conference.

In between, he made forty-five trips abroad. Like the Mexico visits, his three trips to Canada were short ones. In addition, he had either bilateral meetings with leaders, conferences, or commemorative ceremonies in Spain, Belgium, Sweden, Slovenia, United Kingdom, Italy, Kosovo, China, Japan, South Korea, El Salvador, Germany, France,

Vatican City, Czech Republic, Russia, Lithuania, Romania, Portugal, Poland, Jordan, Qatar, Senegal, South Africa, Botswana, Uganda, Nigeria, Philippines, Thailand, Singapore, Indonesia, Australia, Iraq, Ireland, Turkey, Chile, Colombia, Slovakia, Latvia, Netherlands, Georgia, Argentina, Brazil, Panama, Mongolia, Afghanistan, India, Pakistan, Austria, Hungary, Vietnam, Estonia, Uruguay, Guatemala, Albania, Bulgaria, Israel, Palestinian Authority (Ramallah, on the West Bank), Kuwait, Bahrain, United Arab Emirates, Saudi Arabia, Egypt, Benin, Tanzania, Rwanda, Ghana, Liberia, Ukraine, and Croatia.

His three trips to Iraq were made on short notice and with no public notice, for security reasons. On November 27, six days after returning home from a state visit to the United Kingdom, he made a surprise Thanksgiving Day visit to Iraq, meeting with members of the Coalition Provisional Authority, the new Iraqi Governing Council, and U.S. troops.

On June 13, 2006, he met in Baghdad with Prime Minister Nouri al-Maliki and addressed U.S. troops. On September 3, 2007, at Al-Assad Air Force Base in Iraq, he met with General David Petraeus, Secretary of State Condoleezza Rice, Secretary of Defense Robert Gates, and Iraqi political leaders. Once again, he met with and addressed U.S. troops.

RETREATS FROM STRESS

In 1999, when he was governor, Bush purchased Prairie Chapel Ranch, six miles northwest of the village of Crawford, Texas (the nearest city is Waco). He purchased it from the heirs of nineteenth-century German immigrant Heinrich Engelbrecht. Engelbrecht and his family had raised hogs and turkeys.

The ranch is named after a nearby school. The original ranch house is now called Governor's House and is used when there are more guests than the main house and guesthouse can accommodate.

After they had bought the 1,583-acre ranch, the Bushes asked University of Texas architecture professor David Heymann to design a new house that would be highly energy-efficient. He did. The four-thousand-square-foot, four-bedroom house has a native limestone exterior and a white galvanized metal roof. It is a passive solar house, designed to capture winter sunlight. A central geothermal pump circulates water (usually at 67 degrees) through pipes three hundred feet belowground to keep the house warm in winter, cool in summer. This system uses no fossil fuels and consumes about 25 percent of the electricity that would be required by a conventional heating and cooling system.

Rainwater on the roof is collected in a twenty-five-thousand-gallon underground cistern. Wastewater from showers, sinks, and toilets is purified in underground tanks, then used to irrigate plantings surrounding the house—largely native shrubs and flowers.

The Bushes added a swimming pool, which is heated in winter by their geothermal system.

Overnight guests stayed in the main house, a nearby guesthouse, the Engelbrecht house, or a mobile home on the property.

During the Bush presidency, news conferences that didn't require his presence were held in the Crawford Middle School auditorium. Those in which he was involved were held in the helicopter hangar on the ranch ground. News reporters stayed in Waco hotels.

In 2002 the ranch was wired for videoconferencing so the president could receive secure briefings and hold long-distance meetings from the ranch house.

During those days and since, Bush has taken many visitors around the ranch in his pickup truck. This includes foreign dignitaries and reporters. He added an eleven-acre pond stocked with bass and baitfish. In addition, there are red-eared sunfish and bluegills. There are seven canyons on the property, which also has frontage on a creek and a small river.

George W. Bush was at his ranch seventy-seven times during his presidency, for a total of 490 days.

Senior White House staff members and cabinet officers met with him there for briefings and meetings.

He entertained many foreign dignitaries, providing a relaxed setting for him to discuss with them issues of mutual interest, but also to develop friendships. Among these guests were Russian president Vladimir Putin (November 2001), British prime minister Tony Blair (April 2002), Saudi Prince Bandar bin Sultan, former ambassador to the United States (August 2002), Chinese president Jiang Zemin (October 2002), Spanish prime minister Jose Maria Aznar (February 2003), Australian prime minister John Howard (May 2003), Japanese prime minister Junichiro Koizumi (the same month, but not the same days), Italian prime minister Silvio Berlusconi (July, 2003), Mexico's President Fox (March 2004 and 2005), Egyptian president Hosni Mubarak (April 2004), King Juan Carlos and Queen Sofia of Spain (November 2004), Canadian prime minister Paul Martin (March 2005), Israeli prime minister Ariel Sharon (April 2005), Colombian president Alvaro Uribe (August 2005), German chancellor Angela Merkel (November 2007), and Denmark's prime minister, Anders Fogh Rasmussen (February 2008).

Ranch guests were treated to southwestern cuisine and dress was casual. Bush mixed relaxation and exercise with business. He summed it up this way: "I think it is important for a president to spend some time away from Washington, in the heartland of America."

A lot of relaxation time for him meant hiking, jogging, fishing, bicycling (champion cyclist Lance Armstrong was a guest), bird hunting, and, like Reagan, clearing brush around the ranch.

ECONOMIC TROUBLE

Around the time of 9/11 Bush's approval ratings shot up to 90 percent, and they remained very high for several months. On average, his first-term approval rating was 50 percent or better. It began to slip in the second term as post-invasion problems in Iraq escalated. Political attacks from Congressional Democrats and constant hatred-inspired attacks from the far left fed the general unease over Iraq.

By late 2007 and early 2008 signs of economic trouble gathered. By mid-September 2008, when investment bank Lehman Brothers collapsed, it looked as if there might be a financial catastrophe at hand. Treasury secretary Henry Paulson and others recommended a government program to pump money into major banks to keep them solvent. The program was highly controversial on both the right and left. Many financial analysts now say it did its job (most of the funds have since been repaid). Nevertheless, Bush's approval ratings dropped sharply, below 30 percent. Republican candidates in that November's Congressional election scarcely ever mentioned his name. The country continued to move into a full-blown recession.

POST-PRESIDENCY

Following Barack Obama's inauguration, the Bushes flew to Texas and their ranch. They soon purchased a home in a Dallas neighborhood. Since then, he has had very little to say about policies and positions of his successor. At a private event in Calgary, Canada, in March 2009 he said he would not criticize his successor and that "President Obama deserves my silence."

He has appeared at events in the Dallas area. For example, in 2009 he conducted the coin toss at the Dallas Cowboys' first game in their new stadium and addressed brief remarks of appreciation to the audience at a Texas Rangers game. In 2010 he attended every home playoff game of the Rangers, and during the World Series he was accompanied by his father, "Bush 41," and threw out the first pitch in Game Four.

Following the Fort Hood shootings, the Bushes made a private, unpublicized visit to the survivors and families of victims. He worked on his memoir, *Decision Points,* which was published in fall 2010. It was well received, both in the marketplace and in reviews. Following the Haiti earthquake of January 2010, he and former president Clinton were asked by President Obama to establish a Clinton-Bush Fund to raise relief funds for victims.

————

The George W. Bush Presidential Library is temporarily located in Lewisville, Texas, while the permanent library is under construction on the campus of Southern Methodist University in Dallas. Ground was broken in November 2010 and the new Bush Center is expected to be dedicated in 2013.

The National Archives and Records Administration is in charge of this, the thirteenth library in the presidential group. When opened it will have a complete text record of President Bush's public years, many other archival materials, and several million electronic records. As with other modern-day presidential libraries, there will be extensive audiovisual and recorded holdings available to the public.

Meanwhile, the Bush Library had its first exhibit, held at SMU's Meadows Museum from October 23, 2010, to February 6, 2011. Titled "Breaking Ground: Presenting the George W. Bush Presidential

Center," it featured renderings and floor plans of the buildings, an architectural model, and information about the library and the Bush Institute, the nonprofit foundation that will organize public affairs programs at the library.

    Address: Office of George W. Bush, P.O. Box 259000, Dallas, TX 75225–9000. Website: www.georgewbushlibrary.gov.

Chapter Forty-three

BARACK OBAMA

THE 44TH PRESIDENT

January 20, 2009—

*W*ildly popular as a new president, Barack Obama had solid Democratic Party majorities in both houses of Congress behind him. He moved swiftly to deal with the economic recession by sharply increasing federal spending by $780 billion through a "stimulus" bill. Then he began the process of pushing for a sweeping revision of the nation's health care system. Given his initial popularity, he couldn't easily go home to Chicago for a vacation in 2009. Living in a city neighborhood, the Obamas would have had a stream of friends wanting to call and crowds of gawkers coming as close as the Secret Service would allow them.

On July 17 that year the White House announced that the Obamas would spend an eight-day vacation on Martha's Vineyard, an island about seven miles off the Massachusetts coast. They arrived August 23 at Blue Heron Farm, a 28.5-acre property on an arm of Tisbury Great Pond, a quiet, rural part of an island that is known for privacy and quiet pursuits.

Obama was not the first president to enjoy Martha's Vineyard. John Adams is said to have come there in his younger days in the 1760s.

Ulysses S. Grant visited in 1874. Franklin Roosevelt sailed the waters there. Richard Nixon visited and Bill Clinton vacationed on the island in all but one of his presidential years. The Clintons have returned since.

For nearly a century, Martha's Vineyard has been a haven for successful, rich, and liberal-minded people who seek to vacation in unostentatious ways. For more than a century it has attracted blacks as well as whites. It was early in desegregating everything, including its beaches. In the days of slavery, it was an important link in the Underground Railroad. Even earlier, Vineyard Haven attracted freed slaves who worked as laborers and sailors. By the late nineteenth century, middle-class blacks were buying land and summer homes.

Obama visited Martha's Vineyard before he was elected president. In August 2004, he interrupted his campaign for the U.S. Senate to attend a 50th anniversary forum about the Supreme Court's historic *Brown v. Board of Education* decision. In 2007, he returned for a fundraising event in anticipation of his 2008 presidential campaign. He called Martha's Vineyard "one of those magical places where people of all different walks of life come together; where they take each other at face value."

A summer regular since childhood has been Obama adviser Valerie Jarrett. She may have been the one to suggest it to him as an ideal vacation site.

Most of the Obamas' stay was uneventful; however, it was interrupted by news of the death of Massachusetts senator Edward M. Kennedy. The president left to attend the funeral. While he was on vacation, he also renominated Ben Bernanke as chairman of the Federal Reserve Bank.

Otherwise, their sojourn proceeded as they had planned. He played golf. The family went swimming, had picnics, read, and relaxed. Several times they browsed in stores and chatted some with people they met; however, the nature of the place is that they were not pestered by autograph-seekers, despite the fact that Martha's Vineyard's year-round population of sixteen thousand swells to well over one hundred thousand in summer.

During his first year in office, Obama spent twenty-six days, in whole or part, "on vacation." That is fewer than Presidents George

W. Bush or Ronald Reagan and more than Bill Clinton or Jimmy Carter.

Very early in February, the family spent a four-day weekend at home in Chicago. The president played basketball with friends and took First Lady Michelle Obama to dinner on Valentine's Day.

After the Vineyard vacation, he took the family on a business/pleasure trip to Montana, Wyoming, Colorado, and Arizona. He held several "town hall" meetings about his plan to pass health care legislation. In Wyoming he also went fly-fishing. The family visited both Yellowstone National Park and the Grand Canyon during the trip.

HAWAII

In December 2009, the family went to his home state, Hawaii, to celebrate the Christmas and New Year's holidays. This was the second of three holiday vacations in Hawaii. For all three the Obamas rented Paradise Point Plantation on the windward side of Oahu.

The White House website, to show empathy for ordinary Americans, gushed the next year, in December, "Given the current economic crisis, President Obama understands that a Hawaii vacation is out of reach for many Americans, which is why, in a spirit of openness and transparency, President Obama decided to share his vacation with the American People."

As a demonstration of his generosity, the site posted several photos of "The Winter White House," including one of a gate that the site described as a replica of a White House gate. The Secret Service had "thoughtfully" installed the replica, the website said.

When it came time to leave for Hawaii in 2010, the president had much to think about. His party had taken a drubbing at the polls in November. The Republicans had taken over the House of Representatives with sixty-five new members and enjoyed a solid majority. They elected more senators, trimming the Democrats' majority to 51–47 (plus two independents who usually voted with the Democrats).

The Obamas left Washington on December 23, as soon as the Congressional lame-duck session finished. The White House website described the trip this way: "The President's 2010 Hawaii vacation officially began the moment he stepped aboard Air Force One. He immediately headed back to his personal office, shed his 'President's clothes' and got into the Aloha Spirit. . . . On his flight to Hawaii he enjoyed several old episodes of the original 'Hawaii Five-O' (television show), while sipping a mai tai and munching spam musubi."

One thing Obama definitely did not want repeated was a communications problem that plagued his 2009 Hawaii vacation. On Christmas Day that year, the Nigerian "Underwear Bomber" had been apprehended before he could blow up a Northwest Airlines plane arriving in Detroit. Instead of the secure, state-of-the-art telecommunications system Obama had expected, he had to rely on operators to put him through to his counterterrorism adviser. One call was dropped in mid-conversation. This problem had been corrected by the time the Obamas arrived in 2010.

He made no public comment about the Underwear Bomber for several days. Meanwhile, the telephone lines were busy between the Winter White House and counterterrorism adviser John Brennan in Washington. Nevertheless, Obama found time on December 28 to have a telephone conversation with the owner of the Philadelphia Eagles, praising the restoration of quarterback Michael Vick to his old job after the star was released from prison for his role in a dog-fighting ring that killed pit bulls by hanging, drowning, and electrocution.

The Obamas had a quiet Christmas dinner, also attended by his half sister, Maya Soetoro-Ng. The next day they attended church. Two days after that they had the traveling press scurrying to write about their excursion to an ice cream shop where the president bought several flavors of Shave Ice (the Hawaii name for Sno-Cones).

On New Year's Eve, the Obamas went to a theater in a shopping mall to see the popular film *Avatar*—after the theater had been cleared of other people. A Democratic state senator, Clayton Hee, said of this, "[W]hen you close down shopping centers you're pushing the envelope of the patience that people might otherwise have."

Some in the media noted that both on Martha's Vineyard and on Oahu, there were many more "sightings" of the Obamas than there were interactions with local citizens. This prompted critics to emphasize what they described as Obama's "aloofness."

Other activities filled out the family's days, such as golf for the president, swimming, picnics and barbecues, basketball, and tennis.

A CHANGED PUBLIC MOOD—2010

When it came time for the Obamas to plan their 2010 summer vacation, there had been a sea change in Washington. Criticism by Republicans was growing, as was the Tea Party movement, and some commentators noted the administration's failure to bring down the stubborn 9 percent unemployment rate and to control federal spending. Public opinion polls showed growing opposition to "Obamacare," the sweeping health care legislation passed in late 2009 by a close vote. Also, the public wanted emphasis on creating jobs and reducing the federal deficit.

Because Obama did not seem to be listening, his "favorable" poll numbers were declining.

The honeymoon mood of 2009 had been replaced by widespread unease and skepticism in 2010. Nevertheless, the Obamas arranged to again rent Blue Heron Farm in the Chilmark section of the island. The Obamas themselves paid for the rental of the property. Local real estate agents told the press that the rental of such a place could be as high as forty thousand dollars a week. Given the stubborn negatives in the nation's economic situation, this news was catnip to Obama critics.

Their ten-day vacation began on Friday, August 20. That day, the president took their daughters to a bookstore, then played a round of golf. The next day, the family had a picnic lunch on Chilmark's private beach. Another day they swam at a beach on the south side of the island where former president Bill Clinton had summered.

The First Family were unfazed by a turn in the weather when a Nor'easter blew through for nearly three days. They stayed in, played Scrabble and other board games, and read.

When they were moving about, crowds clustered at intersections and by a farmers' market to wave, though the Obamas did not stop to converse. If the president had done more strolling and shopping he might have seen the poster in the window of one shop. It featured a large photo of his predecessor, George W. Bush, with the caption, "Miss me yet?"

TIME OUT FOR GOLF

As president, Barack Obama has played several dozen rounds of golf. When he is in Washington it is usually at the Andrews Air Force Base, just outside the capital, in Maryland. One notable game much noted in the news media before it took place, but with near silence afterward, was his foursome on Saturday, June 18, 2011. After several declarations that they would play together, President Obama and House Speaker John Boehner finally did. Joining them were Vice President Joe Biden and Ohio governor John Kasich (a former U.S. representative). Boehner and Biden were widely credited with being among Washington's best golfers; however, other than all four saying they had had a good time on the course, mum was the word as to the scores. Just before the game, Boehner had teasingly promised Obama he would credit his handicap one point for every trillion dollars Obama agreed to cut federal spending.

A PERIPATETIC PRESIDENT

Eager to make his mark on world affairs, President Obama made six trips to Europe during his first year in office, 2009. On the first of these, March 31–April 3, he and his wife, Michelle, dined with Queen Elizabeth II, carrying on the tradition of every U.S. president since Truman (except for Lyndon Johnson). Two of these European trips were very brief. One was a quixotic October 2 effort in Copenhagen, Denmark, to deliver a pitch to the International Olympic Committee to award the 2016 Olympic Games to Chicago; the other was December 9–11, to Oslo, Norway, to accept the Nobel Peace Prize.

Following another tradition of making the first presidential trip to one of our immediate neighbors, Obama flew to Ottawa, Canada, on February 19, 2009, to meet Prime Minister Stephen Harper and Governor General Michaëlle Jean. In April he went to Mexico City to meet with President Felipe Calderon. Through May 2011, President Obama had eighteen trips outside the United States.

2011 RETREATS

In the third year of his presidency, Barack Obama planned to take his family again to Martha's Vineyard in August and Hawaii in December. Both occurred, but he left for them in the midst of Congressional battles over budget and tax issues.

The Obamas once again rented Blue Heron Farm on Cobbs Hill Road in the wooded area of Chilmark. It has four dwellings, a swimming pool, basketball court, one-hole golf course, and access to a private beach.

While they themselves paid an estimated fifty thousand dollars to rent the property, the entourage that must accompany a traveling president cost U.S. taxpayers several million dollars. It involved Coast Guard ships on duty offshore, the presidential helicopter, armored SUVs, and aides housed nearby.

The Obamas had planned to stay for eleven days, from August 18 to 28, but in midweek the weather forecasts called for storms and a possible hurricane, so they cut their retreat short by a day. On Thursday, the twenty-fifth, the family spent the early afternoon at the beach, but cut the outing short as the skies darkened.

In December, the president had intended to go to Hawaii at the conclusion of the Asia-Pacific Economic Cooperation conference, but instead sent his family ahead while he dealt with a tussle between Congressional Democrats and Republicans over the extension of a payroll tax "holiday" that was scheduled to end on December 31.

In the previous three years they had rented Paradise Plantation Estate in the Kailua area of Oahu. However, according to the White House website, it was not available in 2011 because during the 2010 retreat, the president's dog, Bo, had created an "incident" on the carpet and, despite replacement of the damaged carpet, the house was no longer available. The one they did rent featured five bedrooms, a lagoon-style pool, a spa, and tropical waterfalls. The estimated monthly rental rate was $75,000, so the Obamas probably paid approximately $40,000 for a seventeen-day vacation. Much was made in the news media of the estimated taxpayer bill for the trip of about $4 million, compared with $1.5 million in 2010.

Michelle and their daughters, Malia and Sasha, arrived on Sunday evening, the eighteenth. The president joined them on Wednesday, the twenty-first. The Hawaii state Democratic chairman, Dante Carpenter, had inquired of the White House if the president would consider attending a simple Democratic Party event and had received no answer. Given the intensity of the Washington debate, he told a local reporter, "I think he's been up to his eyeballs in horse manure and gun smoke, not necessarily in that order. He may be looking for time with his family and that's about it. I can't blame him."

And that is the way the sojourn went. No public events, few "photo opportunities," and maximum private time.

———•◦•———

At this writing, President Obama has announced no plans for a presidential library. His Chicago home, on a quiet street in the Hyde Park section, is guarded by the Secret Service and access to the block is restricted.

Chapter Forty-four

CAMP DAVID

1942—

$\mathcal{C}$amp David began life inauspiciously in 1938—and it wasn't then Camp David. It was a project of the Works Progress Administration (WPA) of Franklin Roosevelt's New Deal. It was situated on 143 acres of government-owned land in the Catoctin Mountains of Maryland, about sixty miles northwest of Washington, D.C., close to the state line with Pennsylvania.

In 1935, WPA crews went to work constructing a cluster of very simple wooden cabins, intended to be used as a boys' camp, although it soon became a place for underprivileged urban families to use as a getaway from tough times. When it opened in 1938, it was called Camp Hi-Catoctin.

It was not until 1942 that its purpose would change dramatically,

President Franklin Roosevelt was looking for a wartime place for weekend retreats within driving distance of Washington. Shortly after his election in 1932 he visited 164-acre Camp Rapidan, which his predecessor, Herbert Hoover, had purchased in 1929. It is in the Shenandoah Valley where two creeks merge to become the Rapidan River. Hoover had a group of cabins built and used the camp often during his presidency. It presented problems for Roosevelt, however. It was necessary to walk in from the end of the road. The trail was rough and not suitable for Roosevelt's wheelchair. While there was a pleasant swimming hole in the river, the water was usually cold and Roosevelt, by then used to the restorative qualities of Warm Springs, Georgia, found it unusable. So, for the remainder of the 1930s, he contented himself with a series of fishing trips and a vacation in Hawaii.

In early 1942, he asked Newton B. Drury, director of the National Park Service, to find a site within a hundred-mile radius of Washington, D.C., for a presidential retreat. He wanted it at a high enough elevation to escape the heat and humidity of the capital. Drury proposed three sites: one in Virginia and two in Maryland. One of the Maryland sites was Camp Hi-Catoctin.

On April 22, 1942, Roosevelt left the White House without it being noted on his public schedule. He was driven the two-hour trip to Hi-Catoctin. When Roosevelt first saw the place he said, "This is Shangri-la." It had brought to mind the serene and peaceful place of perfect peace in the James Hilton book (and later film) *Lost Horizon.*

The air was clear and, at 1,800 feet elevation, it lacked the humidity of Washington. The natural beauty was just what Roosevelt wanted. During wartime, it was difficult to take time to go to Warm Springs often, and so this camp, with its swimming pool, six four-cot cabins, office, central shower room, and recreation hall, would do nicely in its place.

Drury's staff estimated the camp could be renovated for presidential use for less than twenty thousand dollars—well below what work on the other sites would cost.

A week later, Roosevelt was back with staff members to sketch the improvements he wanted.

He wanted a screened porch on the cabin he would use. He also called for four bedrooms, two baths, and an indoor kitchen. He called the finished cabin "The Bear's Den." (Today it is called Aspen Lodge and is still the president's own cabin.)

Because he did not have the use of his legs, Roosevelt was concerned about fire emergencies. The construction crew devised a hinged section of bedroom wall that could easily drop down as a ramp for Roosevelt to exit by wheelchair. The cabin was simply furnished, but comfortable.

More cabins were built to accommodate visitors and staff who would accompany the president. In all, there were twenty cabins. Most were spare, without heat or running water (residents used a long water trough outdoors).

It is not hyperbolic to say that Roosevelt loved Shangri-la. It provided him with just the relaxed atmosphere to renew his energy level and gave him ample time to think through many of the wartime issues with which he had to deal.

His routine was to sleep late, then, after breakfast, confer with staff members, go over dispatches, and make telephone calls. He set down the rule that suits and ties were out and open-collar shirts and slacks were in. It wasn't all work for the president. He set aside time for working on his excellent stamp collection, playing gin rummy with guests or staff members, and reading novels (he preferred mystery stories).

Given wartime security needs, the navy unit that operated the camp surrounded it with a high fence topped with barbed wire. An alarm system was installed to detect any break in the fence. Perimeter lights and sentries completed the on-the-ground security plan. In addition, the press corps tacitly agreed to keep mention of even the existence of Shangri-la out of the news, lest it become a target of saboteurs. As a result, there were few mentions in the media.

From its inception in spring 1942 through 1944, Roosevelt visited Shangri-la twenty times, but his wife, Eleanor, rarely accompanied him. Winston Churchill, however, did join him in May 1943 for both relaxation and deep discussions of war plans. They enjoyed each other's company, whether it was to sip a drink on the porch Roosevelt had built at his cabin or to go trout fishing.

THE TRUMANS HAVE A DIFFERENT VIEW

President Roosevelt's successor, Harry Truman, did not visit Shangri-la until May 1946, a year after he assumed office; however, the women in his life, wife Bess and daughter Margaret, did not like it. They visited it in October 1945. Bess said it was "dull," and Margaret described it as "damp and cold." Of course, they were there on a rainy day.

Truman himself only visited the camp nine times in the nearly eight years of his presidency. He spent a total of twenty-seven days there, preferring instead weekend retreats on the presidential yacht *Williamsburg*, where he would play poker, sip bourbon, and converse with his friends. Nevertheless, he had brush cleared from around the camp's cabins and had them winterized.

When he was there, he took walks in the woods and used the swimming pool. On the frequent weekends when he wasn't using the camp, he would let staff members and their families stay there.

A NEW NAME

Shortly after his inauguration in 1953, Eisenhower said he would close Shangri-la as part of his campaign promise to cut down on presidential perks. A friend prevailed on him to visit it, however, and once there, he changed his mind. The wooded mountain setting and pleasant air appealed to him, as they had to Roosevelt. He decided to keep it. Not only that, but he also renamed it Camp David, after his grandson.

Wife Mamie decided to rename all the cabins after trees. The Bear's Den became Aspen Lodge. The conference lodge became Laurel. The names have remained unchanged since then. To satisfy his frequent urge to play golf, Eisenhower asked famed golf course designer Robert Trent Jones to lay out an abbreviated course at the camp. A three-hole course was the result.

The Eisenhowers were frequent Camp David visitors. This increased when he was recovering from his September 1955 heart attack. Travel to and from the camp became easier when he began going by helicopter in July 1957.

In September 1960, Soviet leader Nikita Khrushchev was invited to join Ike at Camp David for informal talks. He had no idea what the camp was about, and his embassy's officials were of no help, either. He guessed it might be a place where the American government kept people who were suspected of being disloyal. He was in for a great surprise and later described his visit as "a great honor."

Their first session was relaxed and cordial. Eisenhower then showed two of his favorite western movies. Khrushchev liked them. They took long walks in the woods and discussed the status and future of Berlin.

Twice, however, Khrushchev exploded in anger. He was usually defensive any time he thought the Soviet Union was being compared unfavorably with the United States. After the second of these outbursts, Eisenhower took him on a helicopter trip to his Gettysburg farm, not far away. This cooled off his guest, and when they parted they agreed not to set a deadline for negotiations over Berlin.

THE KENNEDYS AND HORSES

John Kennedy said soon after taking office that he had little interest in going to Camp David. He and Jacqueline had already rented Glen-Ora, an elegant farm in Virginia's horse country, and planned to spend many weekends there. They did, for nearly two years.

His first weekend at Camp David didn't endear it to him—because of the circumstances. On April 17, 1961, the Bay of Pigs invasion of Cuba had failed. He asked former president Eisenhower to meet him at Camp David to discuss what he should do next. Ike flew by helicopter from his farm and Kennedy from the White House. They strolled the wooded paths and discussed the issue.

Kennedy visited only two other times before 1963. Early that year, he and his wife were building their own home, Wexford, near Middleburg, Virginia, and their lease on Glen-Ora had expired. As a result, he had horse trails installed at Camp David, along with a pony ring for daughter Caroline. The First Lady found herself liking the place. They visited the camp sixteen times that year. There the young president often slept late, played with his children, took walks, and watched movies.

LBJ'S WAR DEBATE

Lyndon Johnson was not a heavy user of Camp David, preferring the Texas White House, his LBJ Ranch. After his first visit in January 1964, more than a year passed before he returned to the camp. In July 1965 a long and passionate debate ensued between two of his guests, Secretary of Defense Robert McNamara and adviser Clark Clifford, over the Vietnam War. Clifford argued against a continued large buildup of

American forces. McNamara took the other side. This went well into the evening and was renewed the next morning. Several other aides were in Laurel Lodge with them.

After the debate, Johnson spent several hours by himself, walking and driving around the grounds. When he announced his decision back at the White House it was to go with McNamara's plan for escalation. As the saying goes, the rest is history.

NIXON'S SOLITUDE

Richard Nixon did not like socializing, and relaxation did not come easily to him, either. Thus he took his workaholic habits with him to Camp David. Over his nearly fifty-five months in office, he visited Camp David well over 150 times. After his inauguration he was soon going there three and four times a month.

He wore a suit and tie and expected his staff members and guests to do the same. He liked the solitude of the camp, for it gave him good opportunities to work on grand plans for his administration. For example, during the first summer he and chief aides Haldeman and Ehrlichman spent a long weekend working up a plan to reorganize the White House. The next month, his cabinet joined him to work on a re-vamped welfare system. Two years later, in August 1971, he summoned several key members of the administration to Camp David with orders not to discuss their destination with anyone. Once there, they were not permitted to make telephone calls. Instead they spent the entire week-end working on a plan to improve the nation's economy. Out of this came Nixon's announcement of wage-and-price controls and dropping the gold standard.

After his landslide reelection in November 1972 he holed up with several aides to plan punitive actions against various organizations he perceived to be enemies. He also wanted to develop a harsh strategy to-ward North Vietnam and he planned a dramatic shakeup of his cabinet and other major posts.

On other occasions he and the First Lady had important foreign guests, such as French president and Mme. Georges Pompidou and So-viet leader Leonid Brezhnev. Nixon had arranged with the Ford Motor Company to donate a Lincoln sedan to Brezhnev, which was given to him at Camp David. Brezhnev proceeded to take his host on a harrowing, high-speed drive around the grounds.

On Sunday, April 29, 1973, Nixon had Haldeman and Ehrlichman come to camp and told each separately that they would have to leave the administration. His farewell to them later in the day was an emotional event.

His final visit to the camp was on August 3, 1974, with his wife, daughters, sons-in-law, and Bebe Rebozo. They went swimming, then spent time on the terrace. He left office six days later.

FORD OPENS UP

Gerald Ford considered it imperative to have an open presidency, in contrast to Nixon's secretiveness and distance from the public. On October 26, a little over two months after he had taken the oath of office, he invited CBS's Harry Reasoner to stroll the grounds with him, then interview him in Laurel Lodge. This was unprecedented but served the purpose of demonstrating Ford's openness.

The Fords were not Camp David regulars. He visited it only eighteen times during his two and a half years in office.

CARTER'S MIDDLE EAST BREAKTHROUGH

Jimmy Carter had one of the high points of his presidency in September 1978 when he invited Egypt's President Anwar Sadat and Israeli prime minister Menachem Begin to Camp David, along with their negotiating teams. The purpose: to see if the peace process that the two principals had been discussing could reach a conclusion. During this sojourn there was little contact with the outside world—especially daily contact with the news media. Thus the conferees could concentrate on the subject at hand without distraction. After thirteen days they agreed on the Camp David Accords, which ultimately resulted in a peace treaty between Egypt and Israel in March 1979. Carter's determination to prevent the sometimes tense talks from faltering was an important ingredient in the successful conclusion.

Initially President Carter was skeptical about keeping Camp David. He asked for outside advice as well as a cost analysis from staff.

By the time he received all of this he and the First Lady had visited the camp and decided it was a perfect place to refresh themselves and relax.

During most of his eighty-one visits to Camp David, Carter enjoyed simple and relaxed activities such as fishing, reading, movies, and his hobby of carpentry. He and First Lady Rosalynn jogged on the camp's pathways, took moonlit walks, and, in winter, cross-country skied the grounds.

In June 1979 the economy was doing poorly. There were long gasoline station lines as a result of the oil crisis. Carter's energy legislation had been defeated in Congress. Polls showed public unhappiness with the nation's direction. He called policy and political allies and advisers to Camp David for their views. He worked on a speech that turned out to be definitive. On July 15 he delivered what came to be known as the "malaise" speech. It deepened the public's gloom.

Worries intensified when, in mid-September, Carter signed up to participate in the 6.2-mile Catoctin Mountain Race, outside Camp David. Not quite two-thirds of the way through, he nearly collapsed. He was given oxygen, put to bed, and recovered; however, newspaper photos and television footage of an exhausted and nearly fainting president created a visual image that stuck.

On March 22, 1980, Carter made the fateful decision at Camp David to send a military reconnaissance plane to determine if a spot in the Iran desert would work as a staging area for a rescue mission to free the U.S. embassy hostages being held in Tehran. That mission led to the larger one, which was a complete failure.

REAGAN SEEKS PRIVACY

Ronald Reagan took more trips to Camp David than any other president before or since. They numbered 186—usually weekends—and a total of 517 days. Typically, the Reagans left the White House Friday afternoon and returned on Sunday afternoon. Life at camp for them was much like it was at their ranch. They wore jeans, had few guests, and were accompanied only by the Secret Service, the White House physician, and a few necessary staff members. Occasionally close friends or the Reagans' sons or daughters would join them. Most of the time, they prized having some time away from the public eye. They rode horses, read, and watched movies.

It was at Camp David in July 1981 that he made the fateful decision to fire the striking air traffic controllers. Over his two terms, he also taped 150 of his weekly radio addresses to the nation from camp.

Nancy Reagan had much redecorating done in the cabins, but other than expansion of the riding trails, little was done to the physical layout of the camp. One famous visitor was British prime minister Margaret Thatcher, who discussed world affairs with the president as they strolled through the woods.

PLANNING DESERT STORM

Two days after Saddam Hussein's army invaded Kuwait in August 1990, President George H. W. Bush gathered senior advisers around the big conference table in Laurel Lodge to develop a plan to force Iraq out of its small neighbor country.

After organizing a multinational coalition and getting ground forces into staging areas, Bush summoned the Joint Chiefs of Staff to Camp David the next January to discuss action plans. He made his final decision about the launching of the war at camp.

On Friday, February 22, 1991, Bush left for what appeared to be a routine Camp David weekend. The next morning he returned by helicopter to the White House to announce that the ground phase of the Gulf War had begun.

Although their seaside estate in Maine was where they spent their vacations, the Bushes spent twenty-four weekends and each Christmas week at Camp David. Family members or friends often accompanied them. The president had a horseshoe pit installed and played often with guests, including Mikhail Gorbachev.

Although he enjoyed socializing with family and friends, Bush kept in close contact with his office at White House. He also liked to walk his dog in the woods, bowl at the camp's bowling alley, and jog on the trails.

One jog in May 1991 ended when he experienced shortness of breath. He was experiencing different rates in his heart chambers. He was taken to the Naval Medical Center in Bethesda, Maryland, where he was diagnosed with an illness that had weakened his heart. He adjusted his activities accordingly.

CLINTON CHANGES HIS MIND

Shortly after Bill Clinton was elected, he flew to Los Angeles to make a courtesy call on former president Ronald Reagan. Reagan said afterward that the only gratuitous advice he gave Clinton was to make regular use of Camp David. (When he was leaving the presidency in 1989 he had said, "Of all the things about the presidency, we will miss Camp David the most.")

Clinton had been thinking of Camp David as largely a place to hold conferences. Once in office, he scheduled a conference of aides and advisers at Camp David with a "facilitator" to get them to open up about themselves. They went on to discuss many ideas beloved by policy wonks. (Clinton considered himself one.)

As time went on, however—and especially after daughter Chelsea had left for college—the Clintons spent more and more weekends at the camp. Hillary particularly liked the bowling alley (where she almost always beat her husband's score). He liked reading, watching movies, and channel-surfing television. They often had weekend guests. He would take them to a nearby golf course for a round (the three-hole course at camp was too tame for him). Evening conversations with guests ranged over many topics and often lasted into the early morning hours.

Clinton had one of the most discouraging moments of his eight-year presidency when, in July 2000, he could not get Palestinian leader Yasser Arafat and Israeli prime minister Ehud Barak to reach agreement on a Middle East peace settlement. He kept them at it, even while he had to absent himself for a few days for an economic summit meeting in Okinawa. Clinton relied on his famous charm and persuasiveness to break down intransigence. He thought he was making progress, but despite cordiality between negotiators for the two sides, the principals could not reach agreement over the future of Jerusalem and the talks ended.

BUSH "43"—A CAMP DAVID VETERAN

As president, George W. Bush already knew Camp David. He had visited it several times during his father's presidency. As president, he and First Lady Laura went often for the weekend, taking staff members and their families with them. He enjoyed organizing bowling tournaments on the camp's lanes. A vigorous exerciser, he enjoyed swimming, bicycling, shooting baskets, and walking the trails. He had a rock-climbing wall installed, along with an indoor tennis court and a batting cage. Among less energetic pastimes, he liked to assemble jigsaw puzzles.

The day after he had made his dramatic visit to Ground Zero in New York City, September 14, 2001, he was at camp with several senior aides and advisers, including Vice President Dick Cheney, Secretary of State Colin Powell, and Secretary of Defense Donald Rumsfeld. The topic was "next steps" in dealing with al-Qaeda. That night after dinner, Condoleezza Rice sang while Attorney General John Ashcroft accompanied her on the piano. Many others joined in, but Bush was lost in thought. Monday, back at the White House, Bush told Rice he had decided to launch an all-out attack on Afghanistan's Taliban regime and to catch Osama bin Laden and his henchmen. Camp David had provided the setting for calm reflection over a period of time—something not readily possible in the Oval Office.

Camp David's videoconferencing capability became an important element in keeping key people up to date on progress and planning of the action that ensued. For example, when British prime minister Tony Blair visited the camp to work with Bush they held a videoconference with Rumsfeld at the Pentagon and various military commanders in the field.

In 2008, the Bushes spent the last of twelve Christmases at Camp David. They had spent the holiday there for all eight years of his tenure and the four of his father. This time their extended family was with them: both daughters (and Jenna's husband), siblings and their families, and his parents.

Christmas Eve dinner featured Tex-Mex cuisine, but Christmas dinner itself consisted of roast turkey, cornbread dressing, green beans, sweet potatoes, mashed potatoes with giblet gravy, cranberry sauce, rolls, spinach salad, and, for dessert, pumpkin and pecan pie.

On Christmas Eve Bush spent the morning telephoning U.S. troops stationed around the world.

OBAMA VISITS

During his first year as president, Barack Obama made eleven trips to Camp David, for a total of twenty-seven days.

NAVY AHOY!

From the beginning Camp David has been a U.S. Navy installation staffed by sailors and marines. A navy commander is the senior officer. The camp's formal name is Naval Support Facility, Thurmont, Maryland. Personnel selected for duty there are given unusually rigorous security screening. Tours of duty at the camp are typically for eighteen to twenty-four months. Specialists on staff include carpenters, electricians, groundskeepers, corpsmen, and cooks.

The guarding of the camp is the responsibility of an elite Marine Corps unit, Marine Security Company, Camp David (MSC-CD). Each member has gone through specialized security training at the Marine Corps Security Forces School in Chesapeake, Virginia. Once they are officially candidates for Camp David, these marines first guard the barracks at the Marine Barracks in Washington, D.C., as well as the commandant of the Marine Corps and the chief of naval operations. If they succeed in this preliminary assignment phase, they undergo the very thorough "Yankee White" background check. By the time they are assigned to Camp David they have been trained in advanced security protocol, weapons, small-unit tactics, and various other procedures. The result is that Camp David may be one of the most secure facilities in the nation, if not the entire world.

The staff complement at Camp David has ranged from one hundred during World War II, down to twenty-nine in Truman's years. Camp David is not open to the public.

BIBLIOGRAPHY

Bragdon, Henry W. *Woodrow Wilson: The Academic Years.* Cambridge, MA: Belknap Press, 1967.

Burstein, Andrew. *The Passions of Andrew Jackson.* New York: Knopf, 2003.

Bush, George W. *Decision Points.* New York: Crown, 2010.

Cahalan, Sally Smith. *James Buchanan and His Family at Wheatland.* Lancaster, PA: James Buchanan Foundation, 1988.

Cannon, Carl M. *The Pursuit of Happiness in Times of War.* Lanham, MD: Rowman & Littlefield, 2003.

Caroli, Betty Boyd. *First Ladies.* New York: Oxford University Press, 1987.

Chidsey, Donald Barr. *And Tyler Too.* Nashville, TN: Thomas Nelson, 1978.

Clodworthy, William G. *Homes and Libraries of the Presidents.* 2nd ed. Blacksburg, VA: McDonald & Woodward, 2003.

Cole, Donald B. *Martin Van Buren and the American Political System.* Princeton, NJ: Princeton University Press, 2004.

Coolidge, Calvin. *The Autobiography of Calvin Coolidge.* New York: Cosmopolitan, 1929.

Ferling, John. *John Adams: A Life.* Knoxville: University of Tennessee Press, 1992.

Fuess, Claude M. *Calvin Coolidge: The Man from Vermont.* Boston: Little, Brown, 1940.

Gara, Larry. *The Presidency of Franklin Pierce.* Lawrence: University Press of Kansas, 1991.

Gergen, David. *Eyewitness to Power.* New York: Simon & Schuster, 2000.

Hannaford, Peter. *Ronald Reagan and His Ranch: The Western White House, 1981–89*. Bennington, VT: Images from the Past, 2002.

Heckscher, August. *Woodrow Wilson: A Biography*. Newton, CT: American Political Biography Press, 1991.

Hoogenboom, Ari. *Rutherford B. Hayes: Warrior and President*. Lawrence: University Press of Kansas, 1995.

Horn, Joan L. *Thomas Jefferson's Poplar Forest: A Private Place*. Forest, VA: Corporation for Thomas Jefferson's Poplar Forest, 2002.

Hugins, Roland. *Grover Cleveland: A Study in Political Courage*. Washington, DC: Anchor-Lee, 1922.

Karabell, Zachary. *Chester Alan Arthur*. New York: Times Books, 2004.

Kochmann, Rachel M. *Presidents' Birthplaces, Homes and Burial Sites*. Self-published, 1976, 1990.

Leech, Margaret. *In the Days of McKinley*. New York: Harper & Brothers, 1959.

Logan, Mrs. John A. *Thirty Years in Washington*. Hartford, CT: A. D. Worthington, 1901.

McCabe, James D. *Our Martyred President: The Life and Public Services of Gen. James A. Garfield*. Philadelphia: National, 1880.

Nevins, Allan. *Grover Cleveland: A Study in Courage*. New York: Dodd, Mead, 1932.

Niven, John. *Martin Van Buren: The Romantic Age of American Politics*. Easton Press, 1983.

Pinsker, Matthew. *Lincoln's Sanctuary*. New York: Oxford University Press, 2003.

Polk, James K. *The Diary of James K. Polk During His Presidency, 1845–49*. Chicago: A. C. McClurg, 1910.

Reinfeld, Fred. *The Great Dissenters: The Guardians of Their Country's Laws and Liberties*. New York: Thomas Y. Crowell, 1959.

Roosevelt, Elliott, and James Brough. *The Roosevelts of Hyde Park: An Untold Story*. New York: G. P. Putnam's Sons, 1973.

Roseboom, Eugene H. *A History of Presidential Elections*. New York: Macmillan, 1958.

Russell, Francis. *The Shadow of Blooming Grove: Warren Harding in His Times*. New York: McGraw-Hill, 1968.

Seviers, Harry J. *Benjamin Harrison, Hoosier President: The White House and After, 1889–1901*. 2nd ed. New York: University Publishers, 1962.

Shaffer, Janet. *Thomas Jefferson: From Shadwell to Poplar Forest*. Alexander, NC: Alexander Books, 2004.

Smith, Elbert B. *The Presidencies of Zachary Taylor and Millard Fillmore*. Lawrence: University Press of Kansas, 1988.

Trefousse, Hans L. *Andrew Johnson: A Biography*. New York: Norton, 1989.

Wallner, Peter A. *Franklin Pierce: New Hampshire's Favorite Son*. Concord, NH: Plaidswede, 2004.

Walsh, Kenneth T. *From Mount Vernon to Crawford*. New York: Hyperion, 2005.

Wise, John Sargeant. *Recollections of Thirteen Presidents*. Freeport, NY: Books & Libraries Press, 1968.

ACKNOWLEDGMENTS

*M*en and women involved in preserving the historic sites, homes, retreats, and legacies of presidents have been uniformly helpful in providing facts, verifying dates, and sharing anecdotes and insights. My thanks go to Karl Ash, Librarian, the William McKinley Presidential Library and Museum; Megan Brett, Manager, Database Research, James Madison's Montpelier; Bill Brooks of the Calvin Coolidge Memorial Foundation; Nan Card, Director, Manuscripts Collection, the Rutherford B. Hayes Presidential Center; Claire Comer, Shenandoah National Park; Marilyn Fisher, Curator, the Reagan Ranch (owned by Young America's Foundation); Patrick Kelley, Archives Technician, Clinton Presidential Library; Caroline Keynath, Chief of Interpretation, Adams National Historical Park; Tammy Kelly, Archivist, the Harry S. Truman Presidential Library and Museum; Abigail Malangone, Archivist, the Richard Nixon Library and Museum; William McNitt, archivist, the Gerald R. Ford Presidential Library and Museum; Marsha Mullin, Curator and Vice President/Museum Services, The Hermitage; Stephen Plotkin, Reference Archivist, and Michael Demon, researcher, John F. Kennedy Presidential Library; Mary Thompson, Research Librarian, Mount Vernon; Russ Whitlock, Superintendent, and Liz Lindig, Program Assistant, the Lyndon B. Johnson National Historical Park; Craig Wright, Archivist, Herbert Hoover Presidential Library.

Special thanks for providing a memorable visit to the LBJ Ranch go to Bess Abell and Tyler Abell, Brigadier General USAF James Cross (Ret.), and Harry Middleton, director emeritus of the Lyndon B. Johnson Presidential Library.

Dick Snyder, the son of Eisenhower's White House physician, shared memories of the thirty-fourth president.

Robert Zapesochny provided invaluable research into several modern presidents. Two indispensable people have been Joy Amzitia, my literary agent, and Kathy Sagan, editor at Simon & Schuster, without whom there would not be a book. And, finally, my wife, Irene, who not only put up with the quirks of my writing schedule but also provided her usual excellent copyediting of the manuscript.

INDEX